PLANNING GUIDE

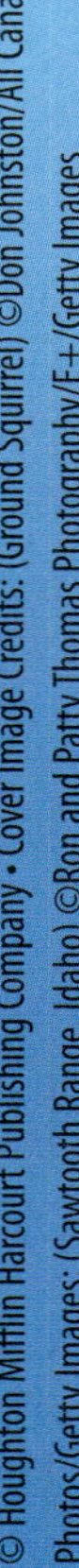

Printed in the U.S.A.

ISBN 978-0-544-29343-4

2 3 4 5 6 7 8 9 10 1678 22 21 20 19 18 17 16 15 14
4500490226 ^ B C D E F G

Table of Contents

PROGRAM OVERVIEW

About *GO Math!*

Planning Resources

END-OF-YEAR RESOURCES

Review Projects

Getting Ready for Grade 5

These lessons review prerequisite skills and prepare for next year's content.

Correlations

It's Common Core Math

GO Math! for Kindergarten-Grade 6 combines powerful teaching strategies with never before seen components, to offer everything needed to successfully teach and learn the Common Core State Standards.

Place Value and Operations with Whole Numbers

Critical Area

Critical Area Developing understanding and fluency with multi-digit multiplication, and developing understanding of dividing to find quotients involving multi-digit dividends

GO DIGITAL

Go online! Your math lessons are interactive. Use *i*Tools, Animated Math Models, the Multimedia eGlossary, and more.

Chapter 1 Overview

In this chapter, you will explore and discover answers to the following **Essential Questions**:

- How can you use place value to compare, add, subtract, and estimate with whole numbers?
- How do you compare and order whole numbers?
- What are some strategies you can use to round whole numbers?
- How is adding 5- and 6-digit numbers similar to adding 3-digit numbers?

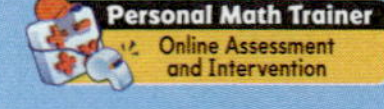

perfect for 21st century students.

GO Math! gets students engaged with learning, focused on working smarter, and ready for the future. The Interactive Student Edition offers the unique Personal Math Trainer powered by Knewton - a state of the art online, and adaptive, assessment and intervention system. In this tablet-based, mobile and online environment, students receive a completely personalized learning experience, focused on in-depth understanding, fluency and application of standards.

A way of thinking about learning,

GO Math! helps students engage with the Standards and Practices in new ways. Lessons begin with problem-based situations and then build to more abstract problems. All along the way students use multiple models, manipulatives, quick pictures, and symbols to build mathematical understandings. And, best of all, GO Math! is write-in at every grade level, so students are completely engaged.

that truly prepares students for the Common Core Assessments.

GO Math! works! Using manipulatives, multiple models, and rich, rigorous questions, students move through a carefully sequenced arc of learning where they develop deep conceptual understanding, and then practice, apply, and discuss what they know with skill and confidence.

PROBLEM SOLVING
Lesson 2.9

Name ____________

Problem Solving • Multistep Multiplication Problems

Essential Question When can you use the *draw a diagram* strategy to solve a multistep multiplication problem?

Common Core **Operations and Algebraic Thinking—4.OA.A.3** *Also 4.NBT.B.5*
MATHEMATICAL PRACTICES
MP1, MP4, MP8

Unlock the Problem Real World

At the sea park, one section in the stadium has 9 rows with 18 seats in each row. In the center of each of the first 6 rows, 8 seats are in the splash zone. How many seats are not in the splash zone?

Use the graphic organizer to help you solve the problem.

Read the Problem

What do I need to find?

I need to find the number of seats that ________ in the splash zone.

What information do I need to use?

There are 9 rows with ________ seats in each row of the section.

There are 6 rows with ________ seats in each row of the splash zone.

How will I use the information?

I can ________ to find both the number of seats in the section and the number of seats in the splash zone.

Solve the Problem

I drew a diagram of the section to show 9 rows of 18 seats. In the center, I outlined a section to show the 6 rows of 8 seats in the splash zone.

$$\begin{array}{r} 18 \\ \times\ 9 \\ \hline \end{array}$$ ← total number of seats in the section

$$\begin{array}{r} 8 \\ \times 6 \\ \hline \end{array}$$ ← seats in the splash zone

1. What else do you need to do to solve the problem?

Chapter 2

An online teacher tool offering the functionality of a planner...

GO Math! helps with the big jobs of teaching. Using the Teacher Dashboard and Smart Planner, teachers create lesson plans and access great resources that support the Common Core, but can be sequenced to align with district requirements, or classroom needs. There's more. The GO Math! technology and classroom instruction work together. Students alternate often between engaging with their teacher and classmates and focusing on online content personalized to their learning pace and progress.

Math on the Spot videos, available for every lesson in GO Math!, support teachers and students, within the classroom and at home.

Math on the Spot

3-Digit Number	1-Digit Number	Sum	Product
213	4	217	852
214	3	217	642
215	2	217	
216	1	217	

Access to all of these great resources is right at your finger tips–all organized by the Common Core State Standards to save you valuable planning and teaching time.

Create daily lesson plans with a single search.

Organize resources quickly.

Correlate to the Common Core State Standards at every step.

Grab-and-Go Resources,

GO Math! works for the busy teacher. Everything from Teacher Editions to activity centers to manipulatives are organized in a ready-made, grab-and-go way to save you time.

GO Math! Teacher Editions are color-coded by Critical Area and organized by chapters to help teachers quickly identify materials and flexibly organize their curriculum. And instruction is organized around the 5 Es - Engage, Explore, Explain, Elaborate, Evaluate. With this approach, GO Math! emphasizes in-depth understanding and communication within an engaging, inclusive classroom environment.

perfect for the busy teacher.

The Grab and Go Differentiated Centers Kits are ready-made differentiated math centers with activities, games, and literature. Resources for every lesson and special challenge materials make the Grab-and-Go Kits the perfect resource for independent practice.

Digital Resources

FOR LEARNING. . .

Interactive Student Edition

- Immerse students in an interactive, multi-sensory math environment
- Enhances learning with scaffolded, interactive instruction and just-in-time feedback
- Provides audio reinforcement for each lesson
- Makes learning a two-way experience, using a variety of interactive tools

FOR ASSESSMENT AND INTERVENTION. . .

Personal Math Trainer

- Creates a personalized learning path for each student
- Provides opportunities for practice, homework, and assessment
- Includes worked-out examples and helpful video support
- Offers targeted intervention and extra support to build proficiency and understanding

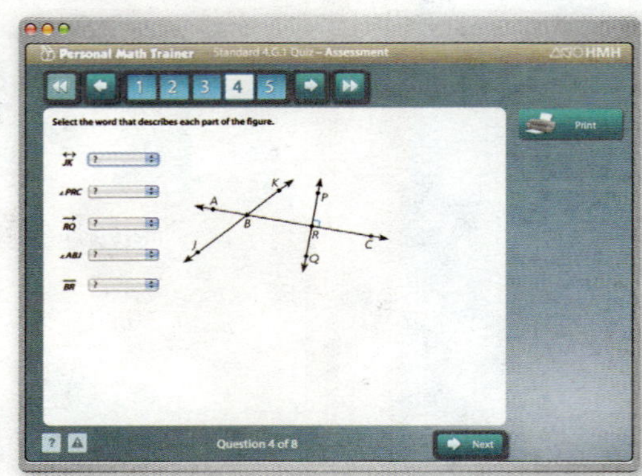

FOR DAILY MATH TUTORING. . .

Math on the Spot Videos

- Models good problem-solving thinking in every lesson
- Engages students through interesting animations and fun characters
- Builds student problem-solving proficiency and confidence
- Builds the skills needed for success on the Common Core assessments

FOR TEACHING. . .

Interactive Teacher Digital Management Center

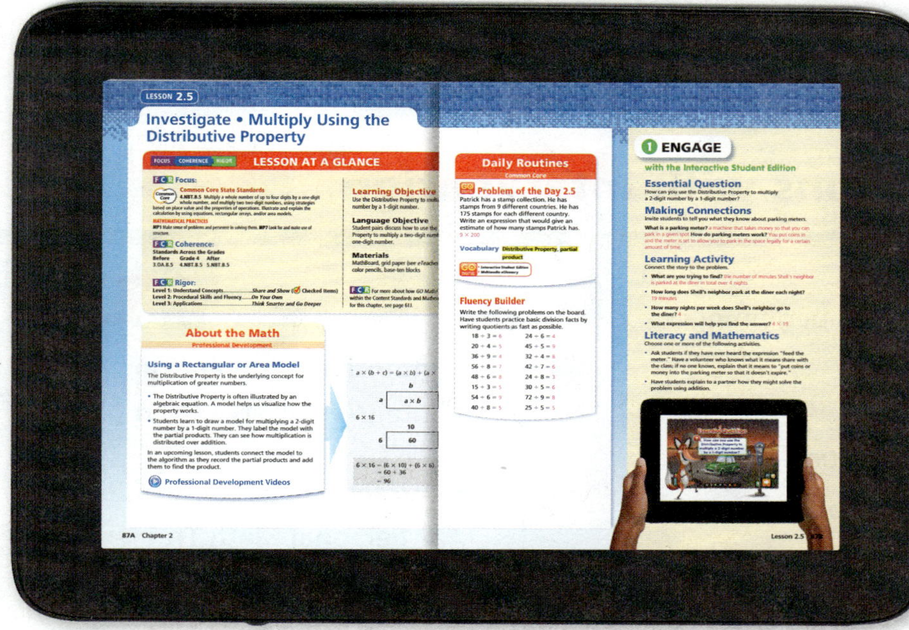

Teacher Edition

- Plan your lessons from the convenience of your classroom, at home, or on the go
- View student lessons 24/7
- Access *Math on the Spot* videos anytime, anywhere
- Offers Common Core-specific learning and instructional activities and suggestions

Professional Development Videos

- Learn more about the Common Core and Common Core content
- See first-hand the integration of the Mathematical Practices
- Watch students engaged in a productive struggle

DIGITAL RESOURCE. . .

Digital Management System

- Manage online all program content and components
- Search for and select resources based on Common Core standards
- Identify resources based on student ability and needs
- View and assign student lessons, practice, assessments, and more

Assessment → Diagnosis → Intervention

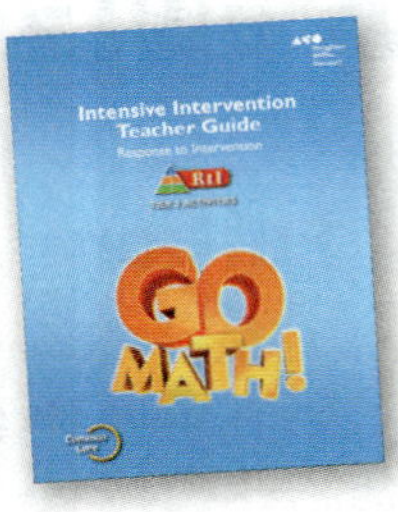

Data-Driven Decision Making

Go Math! allows for quick and accurate data-driven decision making so you can spend more instructional time tailored to students' needs.

Program Assessment Options with Intervention

Diagnostic

To allow students to be engaged from the beginning of the year

- **Prerequisite Skills Inventory** in *Chapter Resources*
- **Beginning-of-Year Test** in *Chapter Resources*
- **Show What You Know** in *Student Edition*

- **Intensive Intervention**
- **Intensive Intervention User Guide**
- **Strategic Intervention**
- **Personal Math Trainer**

Formative

To monitor students' understanding of lessons and to adjust instruction accordingly

- **Lesson Quick Check** in *Teacher Edition*
- **Lesson Practice** in *Student Edition*
- **Mid-Chapter Checkpoint** in *Student Edition*
- **Portfolio** in *Chapter Resources* and *Teacher Edition*
- **Middle-of-Year Test** in *Chapter Resources*

- **Reteach** with each lesson
- **RtI: Tier 1 and Tier 2 Activities** online
- **Personal Math Trainer**

Summative

To determine whether students have achieved the chapter objectives

- **Chapter Review/Test** in *Student Edition*
- **Chapter Test** in *Chapter Resources* (Common Core assessment format tests)
- **Performance Assessment Task** in *Chapter Resources*
- **End-of-Year Test** in *Chapter Resources*
- **Getting Ready for Grade 5 Test** in *Getting Ready Lessons and Resources*

- **Reteach** with each lesson
- **RtI: Tier 1 and Tier 2 Activities** online
-  **Personal Math Trainer**

Tracking Yearly Progress

Beginning of the Year

The Beginning-of-Year Test determines how many of this year's Common Core standards students already understand. Adjust lesson pacing for skills that need light coverage and allow more time for skills students find challenging.

During the Year

Chapter Tests, Performance Assessments, and the Middle-of-Year Test monitor students' progress throughout the year. Plan time to reinforce skills students have not mastered.

End of the Year

The End-of-Year Test assesses students' mastery of this year's Common Core standards. Reinforce skills that students find challenging in order to provide the greatest possible success.

Performance Assessment

Performance Assessment helps to reveal the thinking strategies students use to solve problems. The Performance Assessment Tasks in *GO Math!* can be used to complete the picture for how students reason about mathematics.

Go Math! has Performance Assessment for each Chapter and Critical Area. Each assessment has several tasks that target specific math concepts, skills, and strategies. These tasks can help assess students' ability to use what they have learned to solve everyday problems. Teachers can plan for students to complete one task at a time or use an extended amount of time to complete the entire assessment. Projects for each Critical Area also serve to assess students' problem solving strategies and understanding of mathematical concepts they learn in the Critical Area.

The Performance Assessment Tasks and Critical Area Projects offer the following features:

- They model good instruction.
- They are diagnostic.
- They encourage the thinking process.
- They are flexible.
- They use authentic instruction.
- They are scored holistically.

Go Math! Personal Math Trainer

- HTML5-based online homework, assessment, and intervention engine
- Pre-built online homework, tests, and intervention (with Personal Study Plans)
- Algorithmic, tech-enhanced items, with wrong answer feedback, and learning aids

Authors

Edward B. Burger, Ph.D.
President, Southwestern University
Georgetown, Texas

Juli K. Dixon, Ph.D.
Professor, Mathematics Education
University of Central Florida
Orlando, Florida

Matthew R. Larson, Ph.D.
K-12 Curriculum Specialist for Mathematics
Lincoln Public Schools
Lincoln, Nebraska

Martha E. Sandoval-Martinez
Math Instructor
El Camino College
Torrance, California

Steven J. Leinwand
Principal Research Analyst
American Institutes for Research (AIR)
Washington, D.C.

Contributor and Consultant

Rena Petrello
Professor, Mathematics
Moorpark College
Moorpark, CA

Elizabeth Jiménez
CEO, GEMAS Consulting
Professional Expert on English Learner Education
Bilingual Education and Dual Language
Pomona, California

Go Math! Reviewers and Field Test Teachers

Janine L. Ambrose
Instructional Coach
Grades Taught: K–7
Sunset Ridge Elementary
Pendergast Elementary School District
Phoenix, Arizona

Patricia R. Barbour
Teacher: Grade 2
Sara Lindemuth Primary School
Susquehanna Township School District
Harrisburg, Pennsylvania

Pamela Bauer
Speech/Language Pathologist, M.A., CCC/SLP
Special School District of St. Louis County
Kindergarten Interventionist
Arrowpoint Elementary
Hazelwood, Missouri

James Brohn
Principal
Morning Star Lutheran School
Jackson, Wisconsin

Earl S. Brown
Teacher: Middle School Math
Susquehanna Township Middle School
Susquehanna Township School District
Harrisburg, Pennsylvania

Rebecca Centerino
Teacher: Grade 1
Zitzman Elementary
Meramec Valley RIII School District
Pacific, Missouri

Jessica Z. Jacobs
Assistant Principal
Thomas Holtzman Junior Elementary School
Susquehanna Township School District
Harrisburg, Pennsylvania

Tonya Leonard
Teacher: Grade 3
Peine Ridge Elementary
Wentzville RIV School District
Wentzville, Missouri

Jennifer Love Frier
Teacher: Grade 1
Olathe School District
Olathe, Kansas

Michelle Mieger
Teacher: Grade 3
Cedar Springs Elementary
Northwest R-1
House Springs, Missouri

Jeanne K. Selissen
Teacher: Grade 4
Tewksbury School District
Tewksbury, Massachusetts

Jo Ellen Showers
Teacher: Grade K
Sara Lindemuth Primary School
Susquehanna Township School District
Harrisburg, Pennsylvania

Judith M. Stagoski
Grades Taught: 5–8
District: Archdiocese of St. Louis
St. Louis, Missouri

Pauline Von Hoffer
Grades Taught: 4–12
Curriculum Coordinator
Wentzville School District
Wentzville, Missouri

Content Standards

PROFESSIONAL DEVELOPMENT
by Matthew R. Larson, Ph.D.
K-12 Curriculum Specialist for Mathematics
Lincoln Public Schools
Lincoln, Nebraska

Why Common Core State Standards for Mathematics?

The Common Core State Standards Initiative was a state-led process initiated by the Council of Chief State School Officers (CCSSO) and The National Governors Association (NGA). The goal was to create a set of Career and College Readiness Standards in mathematics (and English/Language Arts) so that all students graduate from high school ready for college and/or work. The K–8 standards outline a grade-by-grade roadmap to prepare students for the Career and College Readiness Standards.

Two primary concerns motivated the Common Core State Standards Initiative. First, inconsistent curricular standards, assessments, and proficiency cut scores across the 50 states raised equity issues (Reed, 2009). These different systems often led to wide disparities between student scores on state assessments in reading and math compared to student performance on the National Assessment of Educational Progress (Schneider, 2007). Second, U.S. students are not leaving school with skills necessary for success in college or the workforce. Results of international assessments, including *PISA* (Baldi, Jin, Skemer, Green, & Herget, 2007) and *TIMSS* (Gonzales, Williams, Jocelyn, Roey, Kastberg, & Brenwald, 2008) indicate that U.S. students do not achieve in mathematics at the level of students in other countries. This raises concern about U.S. economic competitiveness in an environment where U.S. students compete with students all across the globe.

Organization of the Common Core State Standards for Mathematics

The *Common Core State Standards for Mathematics* are organized into content standards and standards for mathematical practice. The content standards are addressed in this article.

The content standards have three levels of organization. The standards define what students should understand and be able to do. These standards are organized into clusters of related standards to emphasize mathematical connections. Finally, domains represent larger groups of related standards. The development and grade placement of standards considered research-based learning progressions with respect to how students' mathematical knowledge develops over time. At the elementary (K–6) level, there are ten content domains. Each grade addresses four or five domains.

While the total number of standards in the *Common Core* is generally less than the number of standards in many current state standard documents (NCTM, 2005; Reys, Chval, Dingman, McNaught, Regis, & Togashi, 2007), the emphasis in the *Common Core* is not simply on a list with fewer standards, but on a list that is also more specific and clear.

Domain	Grade Level
Counting and Cardinality	K
Operations and Algebraic Thinking	K, 1, 2, 3, 4, 5
Number and Operations in Base Ten	K, 1, 2, 3, 4, 5
Measurement and Data	K, 1, 2, 3, 4, 5
Geometry	K, 1, 2, 3, 4, 5, 6
Number and Operations—Fractions	3, 4, 5
Ratios and Proportional Relationships	6
The Number System	6
Expressions and Equations	6
Statistics and Probability	6

Critical Areas

The *Common Core* also specifies critical areas for instructional emphasis at each grade level. These areas are shown below.

Grade	Critical Areas
K	• Representing, relating, and operating on whole numbers initially with sets of objects • Describing shapes and space
1	• Developing understanding of addition, subtraction, and strategies for addition and subtraction within 20 • Developing understanding of whole number relationships and place value, including grouping in tens and ones • Developing understanding of linear measurement and measuring lengths as iterating length units • Reasoning about attributes of, and composing and decomposing geometric shapes
2	• Extending understanding of base-ten notation • Building fluency with addition and subtraction • Using standard units of measure • Describing and analyzing shapes
3	• Developing understanding of multiplication and division and strategies for multiplication and division within 100 • Developing understanding of fractions, especially unit fractions • Developing understanding of the structure of rectangular arrays and of area • Describing and analyzing two-dimensional shapes
4	• Developing understanding and fluency with multi-digit multiplication, and developing understanding of dividing to find quotients involving multi-digit dividends • Developing an understanding of fraction equivalence, addition and subtraction of fractions with like denominators, and multiplication of fractions by whole numbers • Understanding that geometric figures can be analyzed and classified based on their properties, such as having parallel sides, perpendicular sides, particular angle measures, and symmetry
5	• Developing fluency with addition and subtraction of fractions, and developing understanding of the multiplication of fractions and of division of fractions in limited cases (unit fractions divided by whole numbers and whole numbers divided by unit fractions) • Extending division to 2-digit divisors, integrating decimal fractions into the place value system and developing understanding of operations with decimals to hundredths, and developing fluency with whole number and decimal operations • Developing understanding of volume.
6	• Connecting ratio and rate to whole number multiplication and division and using concepts of ratio and rate to solve problems • Completing understanding of division of fractions and extending the notion of number to the system of rational numbers, which includes negative numbers • Writing, interpreting, and using expressions and equations • Developing understanding of statistical thinking

This design permits instruction in each grade to focus on fewer concepts and skills in greater depth, while simultaneously building a foundation for the next grade. For example, in the *Common Core,* fractions are not a significant focus of the curriculum until third grade; although, students decompose two-dimensional figures in previous grades to develop a foundation for fractions in third grade. Similarly, probability is delayed until the middle grades in the *Common Core*.

The *Common Core* states that "mathematical understanding and procedural skill are equally important," but stresses conceptual understanding of key ideas and organizing principles, to structure essential big ideas. Similar to other recent recommendations (NCTM, 2000; NMAP, 2008), this emphasis on conceptual understanding and procedural skill, along with the standards for mathematical practice calls for a balanced approach to mathematics instruction and the curriculum.

Common Core State Standards for Mathematics and Go Math!

Nearly all content standards today, whether articulated by a state, NCTM, or the *Common Core,* share one thing in common: they call for a more focused and coherent curriculum that treats topics in a manner that will enable students to develop deep understanding of the content. *Go Math!* espouses this emphasis on a focused and coherent curriculum that teaches for depth of understanding to help students learn.

All standards documents share one additional feature: alone they are not enough to ensure that students achieve at higher levels (Fuhrman, Resnick, & Shepard, 2009). In *Go Math!,* the *Common Core State Standards* are merely the starting point. *Go Math!* represents a comprehensive system of mathematics instruction that provides teachers the tools they need to help students succeed with more focused and rigorous mathematics standards. Research-based *Go Math!* includes multiple instructional approaches, diagnostic assessments linked to differentiated instructional resources and tiered interventions, along with technology solutions to support and motivate students.

Standards for Mathematical Practice

PROFESSIONAL DEVELOPMENT
by Juli K. Dixon, Ph.D.
Professor, Mathematics Education
University of Central Florida
Orlando, Florida

Developing Processes and Proficiencies in Mathematics Learners

The *Common Core State Standards* include standards for mathematical practice as well as for content. "The Standards for Mathematical Practice describe varieties of expertise that mathematics educators at all levels should seek to develop in their students" (NGA Center/CCSSO, 2010, p. 6). What this means for elementary school students and how the mathematical practices apply to young learners are addressed in this article.

There are eight mathematical practices. They are based on the National Council of Teachers of Mathematics' (NCTM) Process Standards (NCTM, 2000) and the National Research Council's (NRC) Strands of Mathematical Proficiency (NRC, 2001).

It is likely that good teachers can find evidence of each of these standards for mathematical practice in their current teaching. Regardless, it is useful to examine them and think about how each contributes to the development of mathematically proficient students. What follows is a description of how they might look in an elementary school classroom. Each of these examples is reflective of experiences supported by *Go Math!*

Go Math! supports the Standards for Mathematical Practice through several specific features including:

- Lessons focused on depth of content knowledge,
- Unlock the Problem sections to begin lessons,
- Math Talk questions prompting students to use varied strategies and to explain their reasoning,
- Support for manipulative use and drawings directly on the student pages,
- Prompts that lead students to write their own problems or to determine if the reasoning of others is reasonable, and
- Real-world problems that encourage students to develop productive dispositions.

Practice 1: Make sense of problems and persevere in solving them.

This practice brings to mind developing a productive disposition as described in *Adding It Up* (NRC, 2001). In order for students to develop the diligence intended with this practice, they must be provided with problems for which a pathway toward a solution is not immediately evident. If students are asked to determine how much of a cookie each person would receive if 4 cookies were shared among 5 people, a solution pathway is evident if students understand fractions. The students could simply divide each cookie into five equal pieces and give each person one fifth of each cookie or $\frac{4}{5}$ of a cookie in all. Now, consider the same problem given the constraint that the first three cookies are each broken into two equal pieces to start and each person is given half of a cookie.

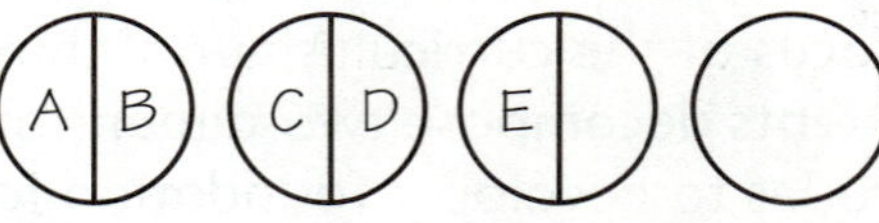

The problem is now more interesting and challenging. How will the remaining pieces of cookies be distributed among the five people? How will the students determine how much of a cookie each person has in all when all the cookies are shared? The students will likely refer back to the context of the problem to make sense of how to solve it, they will also very likely use pictures in their solution process. A solution is within reach but it will require diligence to persevere in reaching it.

Practice 2: Reason abstractly and quantitatively.

Story problems provide important opportunities for young learners to make sense of mathematics around them. Students often use strategies including acting out the problem to make sense of a solution path. Another important strategy is for students to make sense of the problem situation by determining a number sentence that could represent the problem and then solving it in a mathematically proficient way. Consider the following problem: *Jessica has 7 key chains in her collection. How many more does she need to have 15 key chains all together?*

A child is presented with this problem, but rather than focusing on key words, the child uses the story to make sense of a solution process. The child knows to start with 7 then add something to that to get 15. The child represents this story abstractly by writing $7 + \_\_\_ = 15$. Then the child reasons quantitatively by thinking $7 + 3 = 10$ and $10 + 5 = 15$ so $7 + 8$ must equal 15 (because 3 and 5 are 8). The child then returns to the problem to see if a solution of 8 key chains makes sense. In doing so, the child makes "sense of quantities and their relationships in problem situations" (NGA Center/CCSSO, 2010, p. 6).

Practice 3: Construct viable arguments and critique the reasoning of others.

Students need to explain and justify their solution strategies. They should also listen to the explanations of other students and try to make sense of them. They will then be able to incorporate the reasoning of others into their own strategies and improve upon their own solutions. An example of this follows.

A group of students explores formulas for areas of quadrilaterals. Students make sense of the formula for the area of a parallelogram as $b \times h$ by decomposing parallelograms and composing a rectangle with the same area. Following this exploration, a student conjectures that the formula for the area of the trapezoid is also $b \times h$. The student draws this picture and says that the trapezoid can be "turned into" a rectangle with the same base by "moving one triangle over to the other side."

This student has constructed a viable argument based on a special type of trapezoid. Another student agrees that this formula works for an isosceles trapezoid but asks if it will also work for a right trapezoid. This second student has made sense of the reasoning of the first student and asked a question to help improve the argument.

Practice 4: Model with mathematics.

Children need opportunities to use mathematics to solve real-world problems. As students learn more mathematics, the ways they model situations with mathematics should become more efficient. Consider the problem: *Riley has 4 blue erasers, Alex has 4 yellow erasers, and Paige has 4 purple erasers. How many erasers do they have in all?* A young child would likely model this problem with $4 + 4 + 4$. However, a mathematically proficient student in third grade should model the same situation with 3×4. This demonstrates how modeling will evolve through a child's experiences in mathematics and will change as their understanding grows.

A useful strategy for making sense of mathematics is for students to develop real-life contexts to correspond to mathematical expressions. This supports the reflexive relationship that if a student can write a word problem for a given expression, then the student can model a similar word problem with mathematics. Consider $\frac{4}{5} - \frac{1}{2}$. If a student is able to create a word problem to support this fraction subtraction, then, given a word problem, the student is more likely to be able to model the word problem with mathematics and solve it.

Practice 5: Use appropriate tools strategically.

At first glance, one might think that this practice refers to technological tools exclusively, however, tools also include paper and pencil, number lines and manipulatives (or concrete models). Mathematically proficient students are able to determine which tool to use for a given task. An example to illustrate this practice involves multiplying fractions. A student might choose to use a number line for one problem and paper and pencil procedures for another. If presented the problem $\frac{1}{3} \times \frac{3}{4}$, a mathematically proficient student might draw a number line and divide the distance from 0 to 1 into 4 equal parts drawing a darker line through the first three fourths. That student would see that $\frac{1}{3}$ of the $\frac{3}{4}$ is $\frac{1}{4}$ of the whole.

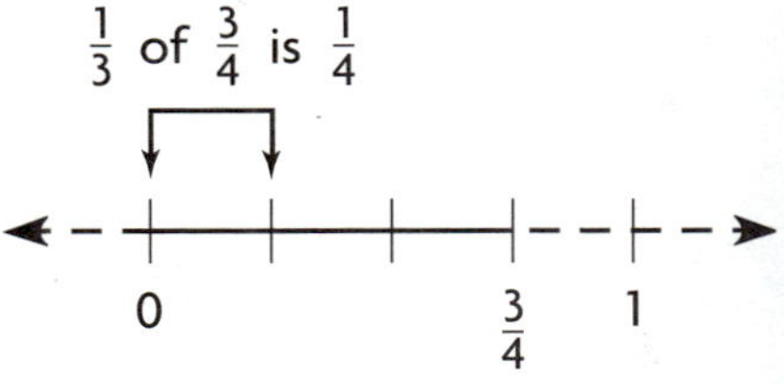

However, the same student presented with the problem $\frac{1}{3} \times \frac{4}{7}$ might not use a drawing at all but might find it more efficient to multiply the numerators and the denominators of the factors to get $\frac{4}{21}$ as the product. Both solution paths illustrate strategic use of tools for the given problems.

Practice 6: Attend to precision.

An important aspect of precision in mathematics is developed through the language used to describe it. This can be illustrated with definitions of geometric shapes. A kindergarten child is not expected to classify quadrilaterals. However, it is appropriate for a kindergarten child to name and describe shapes including squares and rectangles. Teachers seeking to support kindergarten children to attend to precision will include squares within sets of other rectangles so that these children will not use the language that all rectangles have two long sides and two short sides. These same students will be more likely to be able to correctly classify squares and rectangles in third grade because of this attention to precision when they are in kindergarten.

Practice 7: Look for and make use of structure.

Students who have made sense of strategies based on properties for finding products of single digit factors (basic facts) will be more likely to apply those properties when exploring multidigit multiplication. Consider the importance of the distributive property in looking for and making use of structure in this case. A student who has made sense of 6×7 by solving 6×5 and 6×2 has used a strategy based on the distributive property where 6×7 can be thought of as $6 \times (5 + 2)$ and then the 6 can be "distributed over" the 5 and 2. This same student can apply the distributive property to make sense of 12×24 by thinking of 24 as $20 + 4$ and solving $12 \times 20 + 12 \times 4$. A student who can make sense of multidigit multiplication in this way is on a good path to making sense of the structure of the standard algorithm for multidigit multiplication.

Practice 8: Look for and express regularity in repeated reasoning.

Whether performing simple calculations or solving complex problems, students should take advantage of the regularity of mathematics. If students who are exploring the volume of right rectangular prisms are given centimeter cubes and grid paper, they can build a prism with a given base and explore how the volume changes as the height of the prism increases. Students who look for ways to describe the change should see that the height of the prism is a factor of the volume of the prism and that if the area of the base is known, the volume of the prism is determined by multiplying the area of the base by the height of the prism. Identifying this pattern and repeated reasoning will help students build an understanding of the formula for the volume of right rectangular prisms.

As evidenced by the examples of mathematical practices in elementary school classrooms, "a lack of understanding effectively prevents a student from engaging in the mathematical practices" (NGA Center/CCSSO, 2010, p. 8). Teachers address this challenge by focusing on mathematical practices while developing an understanding of the content they support. In so doing, this process facilitates the development of mathematically proficient students.

Supporting Mathematical Practices Through Questioning

When you ask...	*Students...*
• What is the problem asking? • How will you use that information? • What other information do you need? • Why did you choose that operation? • What is another way to solve that problem? • What did you do first? Why? • What can you do if you don't know how to solve a problem? • Have you solved a problem similar to this one? • When did you realize your first method would not work for this problem? • How do you know your answer makes sense?	Make sense of problems and persevere in solving them.
• What is a situation that could be represented by this equation? • What operation did you use to represent the situation? • Why does that operation represent the situation? • What properties did you use to find the answer? • How do you know your answer is reasonable?	Reason abstractly and quantitatively.
• Will that method always work? • How do you know? • What do you think about what she said? • Who can tell us about a different method? • What do you think will happen if...? • When would that not be true? • Why do you agree/disagree with what he said? • What do you want to ask her about that method? • How does that drawing support your work?	Construct viable arguments and critique the reasoning of others.
• Why is that a good model for this problem? • How can you use a simpler problem to help you find the answer? • What conclusions can you make from your model? • How would you change your model if...?	Model with mathematics.
• What could you use to help you solve the problem? • What strategy could you use to make that calculation easier? • How would estimation help you solve that problem? • Why did you decide to use...?	Use appropriate tools strategically.
• How do you know your answer is reasonable? • How can you use math vocabulary in your explanation? • How do you know those answers are equivalent? • What does that mean?	Attend to precision.
• How did you discover that pattern? • What other patterns can you find? • What rule did you use to make this group? • Why can you use that property in this problem? • How is that like...?	Look for and make use of structure.
• What do you remember about...? • What happens when...? • What if you... instead of...? • What might be a shortcut for...?	Look for and express regularity in repeated reasoning.

Common Core

STANDARDS FOR MATHEMATICAL PRACTICES

Mathematical Practices in *Go Math!*

Mathematical Practices	Throughout *Go Math!* Look for...	Explanation
1. Make sense of problems and persevere in solving them. Mathematically proficient students start by explaining to themselves the meaning of a problem and looking for entry points to its solution. They analyze givens, constraints, relationships, and goals. They make conjectures about the form and meaning of the solution and plan a solution pathway rather than simply jumping into a solution attempt. They consider analogous problems, and try special cases and simpler forms of the original problem in order to gain insight into its solution. They monitor and evaluate their progress and change course if necessary. Older students might, depending on the context of the problem, transform algebraic expressions or change the viewing window on their graphing calculator to get the information they need. Mathematically proficient students can explain correspondences between equations, verbal descriptions, tables, and graphs or draw diagrams of important features and relationships, graph data, and search for regularity or trends. Younger students might rely on using concrete objects or pictures to help conceptualize and solve a problem. Mathematically proficient students check their answers to problems using a different method, and they continually ask themselves, "Does this make sense?" They can understand the approaches of others to solving complex problems and identify correspondences between different approaches.	**Some Examples:** **Problem Solving Lessons** Grade 3, Lesson 7.10 Grade 4, Lesson 13.5 Grade 5, Lesson 9.6 Grade 6, Lesson 6.5 **Unlock the Problem** Grade 3, Lesson 3.3 Grade 4, Lesson 6.5 Grade 5, Lesson 2.5 Grade 6, Lesson 7.4 **About the Math** Grade 3, Lesson 2.6 Grade 4, Lesson 13.5 Grade 5, Lesson 2.7 Grade 6, Lesson 9.3	**Students learn to:** • analyze a problem to determine relationships. • explain what information they need to find to solve the problem. • determine what information they need to use to solve the problem. • develop a plan for solving the problem. • use concrete objects to conceptualize a problem. • draw diagrams to help solve problems. • evaluate the solution for reasonableness.
	One Way/Another Way Grade 3, Lesson 1.9 Grade 4, Lesson 9.7 Grade 5, Lesson 6.3 Grade 6, Lesson 1.2 **Try Another Problem** Grade 3, Lesson 5.3 Grade 4, Lesson 5.3 Grade 5, Lesson 1.9 Grade 6, Lesson 4.4 **Share and Show** Grade 3, Lesson 4.10 Grade 4, Lesson 2.2 Grade 5, Lesson 2.9 Grade 6, Lesson 5.5	**Students learn to:** • use different approaches to solving a problem and identify how the approaches are alike and how they are different. • look at analogous problems and apply techniques used in the original problem to gain insight into the solution of a new problem.
	Check your answer. Is your answer reasonable? Estimate to check your answer. Grade 3, Lesson 1.3 Grade 4, Lesson 3.6 Grade 5, Lessons 2.1–2.2 Grade 6, Lesson 1.1	**Students learn to:** • develop different methods of checking their answers, such as using inverse operations or estimation using rounding. • use critical thinking to justify why an answer is reasonable and explain the solution process.

Teacher Edition Student Edition

Mathematical Practices	Throughout *Go Math!* Look for...	Explanation
2. Reason abstractly and quantitatively. Mathematically proficient students make sense of quantities and their relationships in problem situations. They bring two complementary abilities to bear on problems involving quantitative relationships: the ability to *decontextualize*—to abstract a given situation and represent it symbolically and manipulate the representing symbols as if they have a life of their own, without necessarily attending to their referents—and the ability to *contextualize*, to pause as needed during the manipulation process in order to probe into the referents for the symbols involved. Quantitative reasoning entails habits of creating a coherent representation of the problem at hand; considering the units involved; attending to the meaning of quantities, not just how to compute them; and knowing and flexibly using different properties of operations and objects.	**Some Examples:** **Unlock the Problem** Grade 3, Lesson 11.3 Grade 4, Lesson 2.2 Grade 5, Lesson 5.8 Grade 6, Lesson 8.2	**Students learn to:** • represent a real-world situation symbolically as an equation. • use a mathematical algorithm to solve a problem and then place the result back into the context of the original situation.
	Measurement and Geometry Lessons Grade 3, Lesson 11.6 Grade 4, Lesson 10.6 Grade 5, Lessons 11.6–11.10 Grade 6, Lessons 11.2	**Students learn to:** • construct and measure geometric figures by counting and then adding units in a systematic deconstruction of the figure that builds to a comprehensive understanding of a formula.
	Lessons on the properties of operations Grade 3, Lesson 4.9 Grade 4, Lesson 2.5 Grade 5, Lesson 6.10 Grade 6, Lesson 7.8 **Algebra Lessons** Grade 4, Lesson 7.9 Grade 5, Lesson 1.12 Grade 6, Lesson 7.3	**Students learn to:** • abstract a real-world situation and represent it symbolically as an expression or equation, using numbers, operations, and the grouping properties.
	Lessons on modeling with manipulatives and drawings Grade 3, Lesson 6.9 Grade 4, Lesson 2.1 Grade 5, Lesson 4.2 Grade 6, Lessons 2.5, 5.1	**Students learn to:** • represent real-world situations with concrete and pictorial models. • use the understanding that they have acquired to represent a situation abstractly with symbols and equations.

Teacher Edition   Student Edition

Mathematical Practices	Throughout *Go Math!* Look for…	Explanation
3. Construct viable arguments and critique the reasoning of others. Mathematically proficient students understand and use stated assumptions, definitions, and previously established results in constructing arguments. They make conjectures and build a logical progression of statements to explore the truth of their conjectures. They are able to analyze situations by breaking them into cases, and can recognize and use counterexamples. They justify their conclusions, communicate them to others, and respond to the arguments of others. They reason inductively about data, making plausible arguments that take into account the context from which the data arose. Mathematically proficient students are also able to compare the effectiveness of two plausible arguments, distinguish correct logic or reasoning from that which is flawed, and—if there is a flaw in an argument—explain what it is. Elementary students can construct arguments using concrete referents such as objects, drawings, diagrams, and actions. Such arguments can make sense and be correct, even though they are not generalized or made formal until later grades. Later, students learn to determine domains to which an argument applies. Students at all grades can listen or read the arguments of others, decide whether they make sense, and ask useful questions to clarify or improve the arguments.	**Some Examples:** **Math Talk** Grade 3, Lesson 4.8 Grade 4, Lesson 9.6 Grade 5, Lesson 11.9 Grade 6, Lesson 12.1	**Students learn to:** • use mathematical language to explain lesson concepts and construct arguments. • use deductive reasoning, definitions, and previously proven conclusions to explore the truth of conjectures.
	Vocabulary Builder Grade 3 Grade 4 Grade 5 Grade 6 **Vocabulary Builder** Grade 3 Grade 4 Grade 5 Grade 6 **Developing Math Language** Grade 3 Grade 4 Grade 5 Grade 6	**Students learn to:** • develop, build, and reinforce mathematics vocabulary. • discuss mathematical definitions. • strengthen their abilities to communicate mathematical ideas to others.
	Sense or Nonsense? Grade 3, Lesson 4.7 Grade 4, Lesson 4.9 Grade 5, Lesson 8.1 Grade 6, Lesson 2.6 **What's the Error?** Grade 3, Lesson 9.2 Grade 4, Lesson 4.2 Grade 5, Lesson 4.1 Grade 6, Lesson 11.2 **Think Smarter Problems** Grade 3, Lesson 8.1 Grade 4, Lesson 12.11 Grade 5, Lesson 6.3 Grade 6, Lesson 7.7 **Go Deeper** Grade 3, Lesson 8.8 Grade 4, Lesson 6.4 Grade 5, Lesson 1.9 Grade 6, Lesson 11.2	**Students learn to:** • use previously acquired skills, conclusions, and mathematical reasoning to establish whether a statement is true or false. • use modeling, drawings, equations, and written arguments to prove or disprove a given conjecture. • reason inductively about data. • reason about whether the arguments of others make sense.

Teacher Edition Student Edition

Mathematical Practices	Throughout *Go Math!* Look for…	Explanation
4. Model with mathematics. Mathematically proficient students can apply the mathematics they know to solve problems arising in everyday life, society, and the workplace. In early grades, this might be as simple as writing an addition equation to describe a situation. In middle grades, a student might apply proportional reasoning to plan a school event or analyze a problem in the community. By high school, a student might use geometry to solve a design problem or use a function to describe how one quantity of interest depends on another. Mathematically proficient students who can apply what they know are comfortable making assumptions and approximations to simplify a complicated situation, realizing that these may need revision later. They are able to identify important quantities in a practical situation and map their relationships using such tools as diagrams, two-way tables, graphs, flowcharts and formulas. They can analyze those relationships mathematically to draw conclusions. They routinely interpret their mathematical results in the context of the situation and reflect on whether the results make sense, possibly improving the model if it has not served its purpose.	**Some Examples:** **Unlock the Problem • Real World** Grade 3, Lesson 11.9 Grade 4, Lesson 2.12 Grade 5, Lesson 7.9 Grade 6, Lesson 12.4 **Investigate Lessons** Grade 3, Lesson 12.9 Grade 4, Lesson 1.5 Grade 5, Lesson 9.3 Grade 6, Lesson 13.3	**Students learn to:** • model in a 'hands-on' approach to analyze problems with: graphs, manipulatives, equations, and other mathematical tools.
	Project Grade 3 Grade 4 Grade 5 Grade 6 **Connect To... Cross-Curricular** Grade 3, Lesson 10.4 Grade 4, Lesson 13.4 Grade 5, Lesson 7.9 Grade 6, Lesson 9.2 **Literature** Grade 3, Lesson 1.8 Grade 4, Lesson 13.1 Grade 5, Lesson 4.2 Grade 6, Lesson 11.1	**Students learn to:** • model and solve real-world problems in Literature, Science, Social Studies, Art, and other disciplines. • appreciate how mathematics influences their lives in ways both large and small.

Teacher Edition **Student Edition**

Mathematical Practices	Throughout *Go Math!* Look for...	Explanation
5. Use appropriate tools strategically. Mathematically proficient students consider the available tools when solving a mathematical problem. These tools might include pencil and paper, concrete models, a ruler, a protractor, a calculator, a spreadsheet, a computer algebra system, a statistical package, or dynamic geometry software. Proficient students are sufficiently familiar with tools appropriate for their grade or course to make sound decisions about when each of these tools might be helpful, recognizing both the insight to be gained and their limitations. For example, mathematically proficient high school students analyze graphs of functions and solutions generated using a graphing calculator. They detect possible errors by strategically using estimation and other mathematical knowledge. When making mathematical models, they know that technology can enable them to visualize the results of varying assumptions, explore consequences, and compare predictions with data. Mathematically proficient students at various grade levels are able to identify relevant external mathematical resources, such as digital content located on a website, and use them to pose or solve problems. They are able to use technological tools to explore and deepen their understanding of concepts.	**Some Examples:** **Investigate Lessons with manipulatives** Grade 3, Lesson 6.6 Grade 4, Lesson 12.6 Grade 5, Lesson 5.5 Grade 6, Lesson 4.1	**Students learn to:** • use available tools to analyze problems through a concrete 'hands on' approach.
	Geometry and Measurement Lessons Grade 3, Lesson 10.7 Grade 4, Lesson 11.3 Grade 5, Lesson 11.6 Grade 6, Lesson 10.2	**Students learn to:** • use appropriate tools to enhance and deepen their understanding of measurement and geometry concepts.
	***i*Tools** **Animated Math Models** **HMH Mega Math** All student lessons	**Students learn to:** • use technological tools to enhance and deepen their understanding of concepts and explore consequences of varying the data given.
	Modeling feature Grade 3, Lesson 3.4 Grade 4, Lesson 5.4 Grade 5, Lesson 5.2 Grade 6, Lesson 11.3	**Students learn to:** • use concrete models to enable them to visualize problems.
6. Attend to precision. Mathematically proficient students try to communicate precisely to others. They try to use clear definitions in discussion with others and in their own reasoning. They state the meaning of the symbols they choose, including using the equal sign consistently and appropriately. They are careful about specifying units of measure, and labeling axes to clarify the correspondence with quantities in a problem. They calculate accurately and efficiently, express numerical answers with a degree of precision appropriate for the problem context. In the elementary grades, students give carefully formulated explanations to each other. By the time they reach high school they have learned to examine claims and make explicit use of definitions.	**Math Talk** Grade 3, Lesson 12.5 Grade 4, Lesson 5.5 Grade 5, Lesson 10.2 Grade 6, Lesson 3.2	**Students learn to:** • communicate precisely. • use mathematical vocabulary to communicate their ideas and explanations and to justify their thinking and solutions.
	Skill lessons on equations and comparisons ($<$, $>$, and $=$) Grade 3, Lesson 9.4 Grade 4, Lesson 6.7 Grade 5, Lesson 3.3 Grade 6, Lesson 8.9	**Students learn to:** • state the meaning of the symbols they use in mathematical expressions and sentences accurately. • use the equal sign appropriately • calculate accurately.
	Lessons with labeling (such as *x* and *y* axes tables, units such as inch or meter) Grade 3, Lesson 2.5 Grade 4, Lesson 12.2 Grade 5, Lesson 9.3 Grade 6, Lesson 9.4	**Students learn to:** • use correct measurement units to label solutions. • label axes correctly.
	Investigate Lessons with Bloom's Taxonomy questions Grade 3, Lesson 12.9 Grade 4, Lesson 3.3 Grade 5, Lesson 3.5 Grade 6, Lesson 13.3	**Students learn to:** • explain mathematical ideas to each other with correctly composed explanations. • discuss results of an activity and clarify misunderstanding if results are different.

Teacher Edition Student Edition

Mathematical Practices	Throughout *Go Math!* Look for…	Explanation
7. Look for and make use of structure. Mathematically proficient students look closely to discern a pattern or structure. Young students, for example, might notice that three and seven more is the same amount as seven and three more, or they may sort a collection of shapes according to how many sides the shapes have. Later, students will see 7×8 equals the well remembered $7 \times 5 + 7 \times 3$, in preparation for learning about the distributive property. In the expression $x^2 + 9x + 14$, older students can see the 14 as 2×7 and the 9 as $2 + 7$. They recognize the significance of an existing line in a geometric figure and can use the strategy of drawing an auxiliary line for solving problems. They also can step back for an overview and shift perspective. They can see complicated things, such as some algebraic expressions, as single objects or as being composed of several objects. For example, they can see $5 - 3(x - y)^2$ as 5 minus a positive number times a square and use that to realize that its value cannot be more than 5 for any real numbers x and y.	**Some Examples:** **Lessons with grouping** Grade 3, Lesson 1.5 Grade 4, Lesson 2.5 Grade 5, Lesson 1.9 Grade 6, Lesson 2.5 **Algebra Lessons** Grade 3, Lesson 4.4 Grade 4, Lesson 5.6 Grade 5, Lesson 1.3 Grade 6, Lesson 7.8 **Lessons with patterns and sequencing** Grade 3, Lesson 1.1 Grade 4, Lesson 2.3 Grade 5, Lesson 9.6 Grade 6, Lesson 1.7 **Modeling feature** Grade 3, Lesson 5.3 Grade 4, Lesson 8.3 Grade 5, Lesson 1.8 Grade 6, Lesson 7.7	**Students learn to:** • discern patterns as they use the distributive property to solve a problem. • use mathematical vocabulary to communicate their ideas and explanations and to justify their thinking and solutions. • analyze a problem to determine a rule to describe a number pattern.
8. Look for and express regularity in repeated reasoning. Mathematically proficient students notice if calculations are repeated, and look both for general methods and for shortcuts. Upper elementary students might notice when dividing 25 by 11 that they are repeating the same calculations over and over again, and conclude they have a repeating decimal. By paying attention to the calculation of slope as they repeatedly check whether points are on the line through (1, 2) with slope 3, middle school students might abstract the equation $(y - 2)/(x - 1) = 3$. Noticing the regularity in the way terms cancel when expanding $(x - 1)(x + 1)$, $(x - 1)(x^2 + x + 1)$, and $(x - 1)(x^3 + x^2 + x + 1)$ might lead them to the general formula for the sum of a geometric series. As they work to solve a problem, mathematically proficient students maintain oversight of the process, while attending to the details. They continually evaluate the reasonableness of their intermediate results.	**Computation Lessons** Grade 3, Lesson 6.7 Grade 4, Lesson 8.1 Grade 5, Lesson 4.1 Grade 6, Lesson 2.1 **Connect To…** Grade 3, Lesson 11.8 Grade 4, Lesson 4.11 Grade 5, Lesson 4.7 Grade 6, Lesson 2.1	**Students learn to:** • see the relationship between addition and subtraction and between multiplication and division. • recognize how structure and calculations are repeated as they build and write fractions as decimals and write decimals as fractions. • discover shortcuts for finding sums, differences, products, and quotients of both whole numbers, decimals, and fractions. • discover relationships between patterns on the multiplication charts and equivalent fractions or ratios.

Teacher Edition Student Edition

Critical Area

Common Core CRITICAL AREA

Developing understanding and fluency with multi-digit multiplication, and developing understanding of dividing to find quotients involving multi-digit dividends

Place Value and Operations with Whole Numbers

Personal Math Trainer

Look for this symbol for a gateway to your personalized learning path!

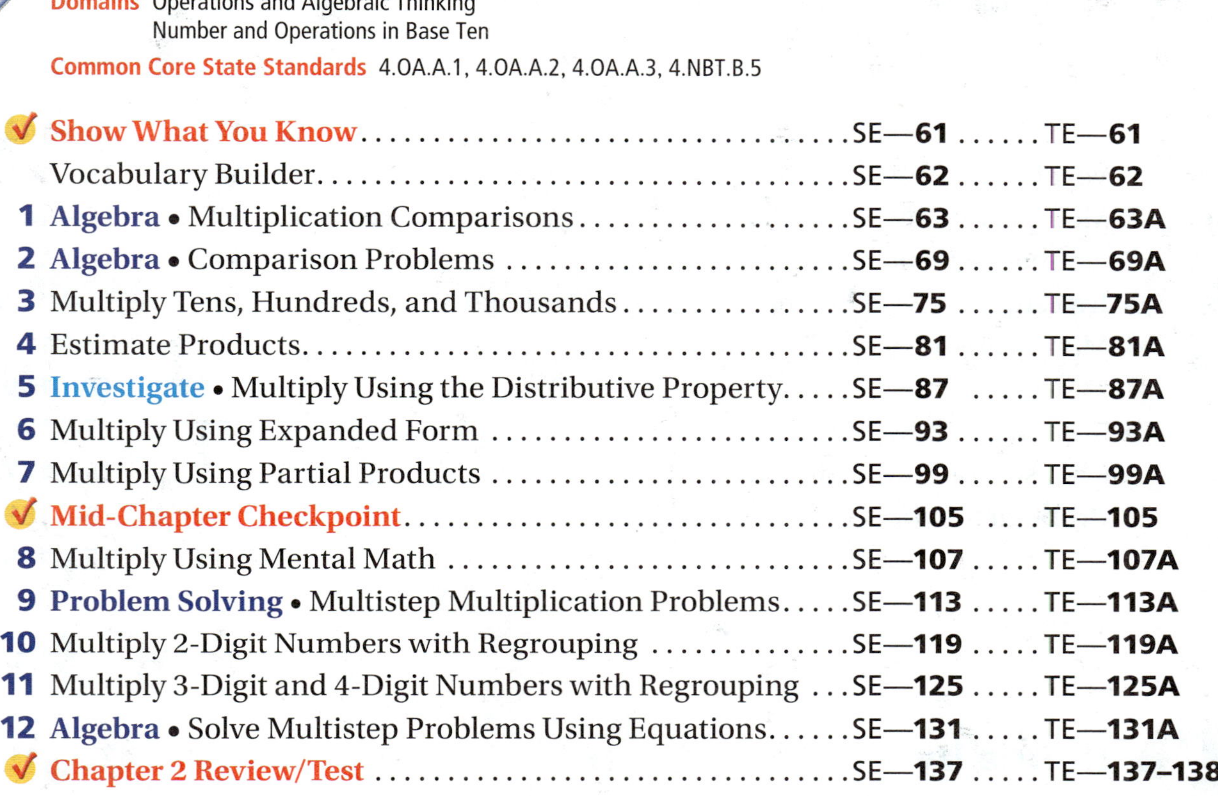

		STUDENT RESOURCES	TEACHER RESOURCES
2	**Multiply by 1-Digit Numbers**	SE—**61**	TE—**61**

Domains Operations and Algebraic Thinking
Number and Operations in Base Ten

Common Core State Standards 4.OA.A.1, 4.OA.A.2, 4.OA.A.3, 4.NBT.B.5

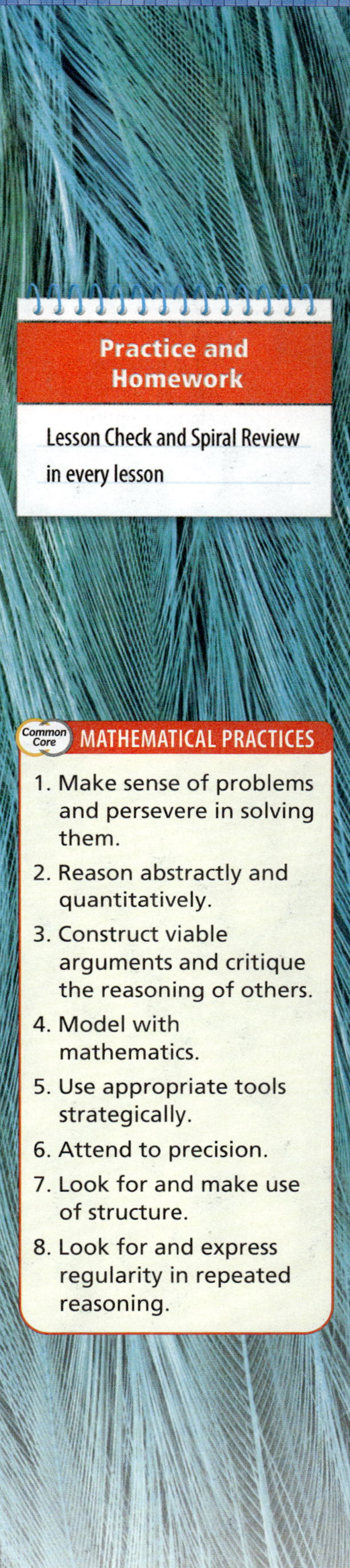

Key: SE—Student Edition; **TE**—Teacher Edition

Personal Math Trainer
Look for this symbol for a gateway to your personalized learning path!

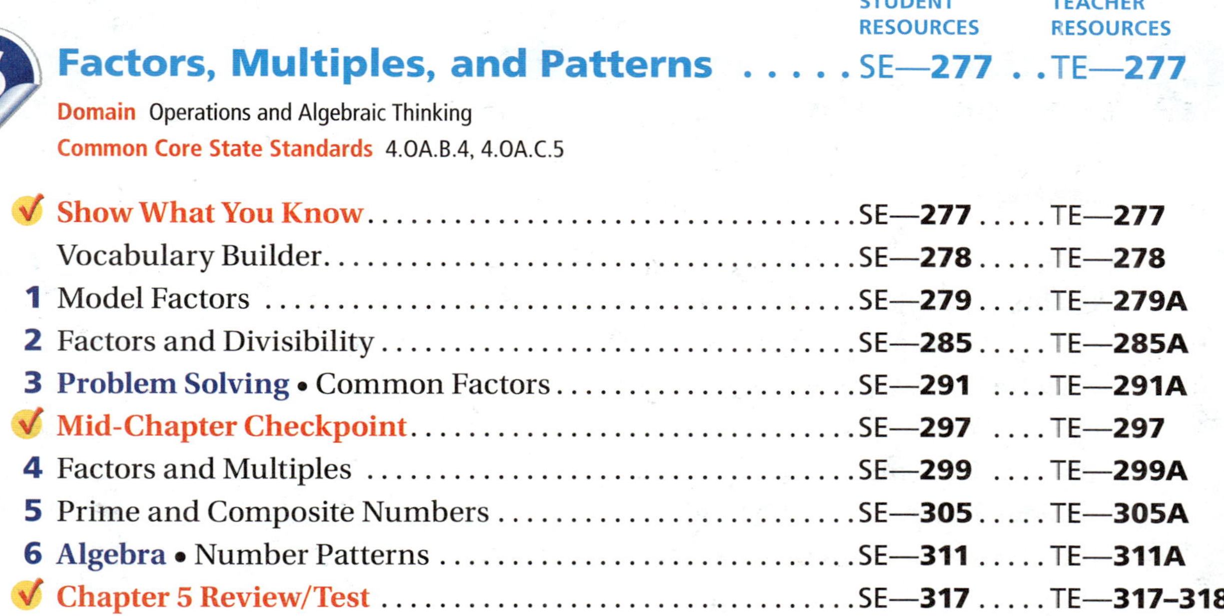

		STUDENT RESOURCES	TEACHER RESOURCES
5	**Factors, Multiples, and Patterns**	SE—**277**	TE—**277**

Domain Operations and Algebraic Thinking

Common Core State Standards 4.OA.B.4, 4.OA.C.5

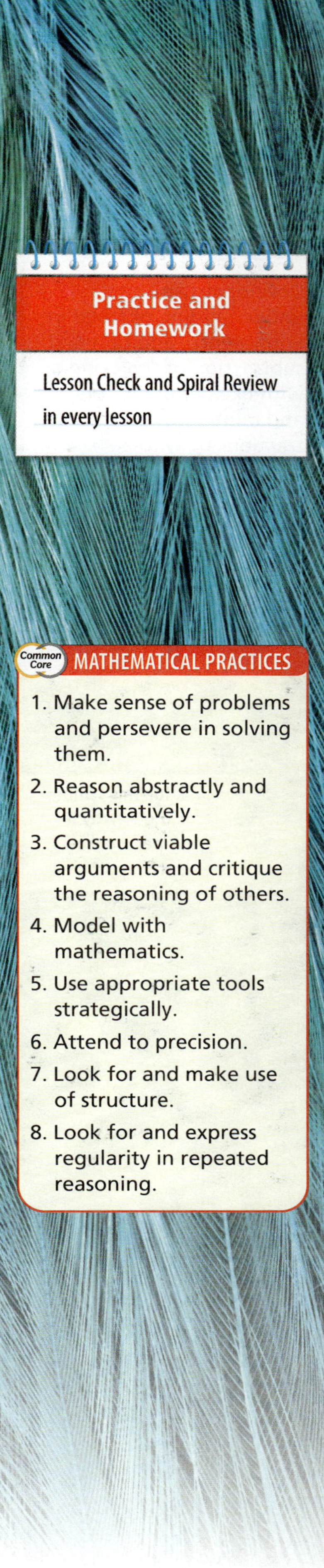

Key: SE—Student Edition; **TE**—Teacher Edition

Critical Area

Common Core CRITICAL AREA

Developing an understanding of fraction equivalence, addition and subtraction of fractions with like denominators, and multiplication of fractions by whole numbers

Personal Math Trainer

Look for this symbol for a gateway to your personalized learning path!

Fractions and Decimals

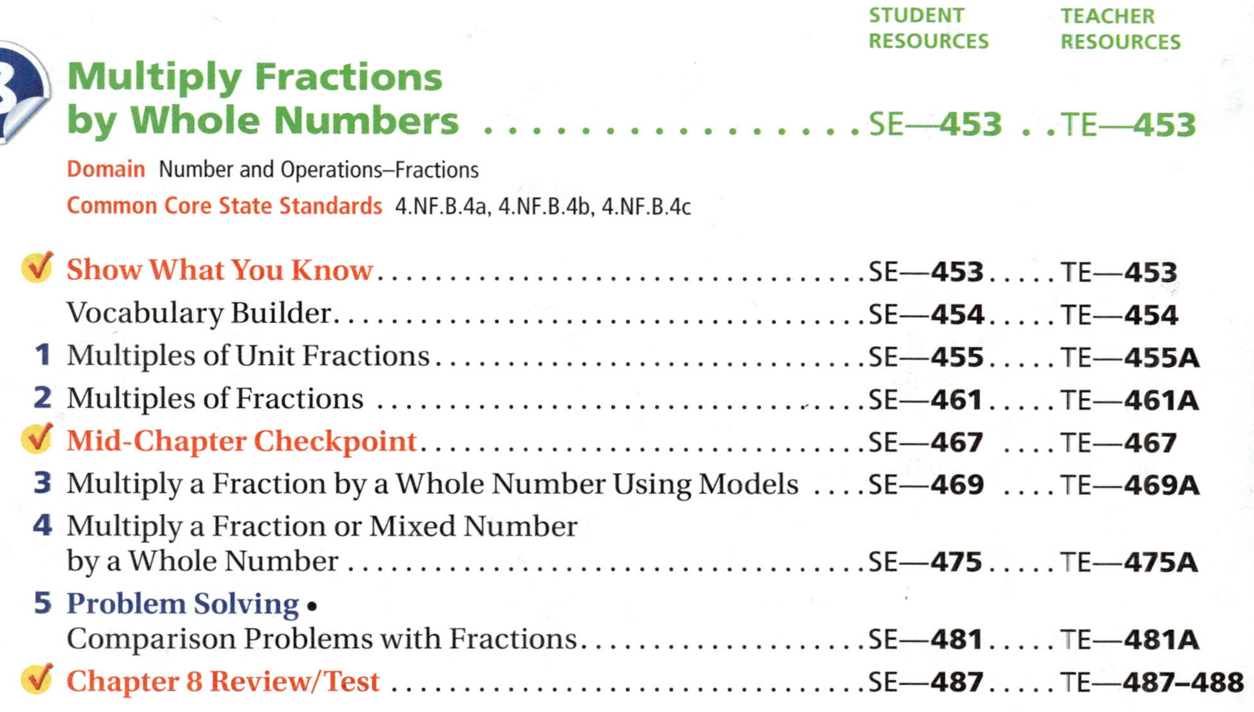

	STUDENT RESOURCES	TEACHER RESOURCES

8 Multiply Fractions by Whole Numbers . . . SE—453 . . TE—453

Domain Number and Operations–Fractions

Common Core State Standards 4.NF.B.4a, 4.NF.B.4b, 4.NF.B.4c

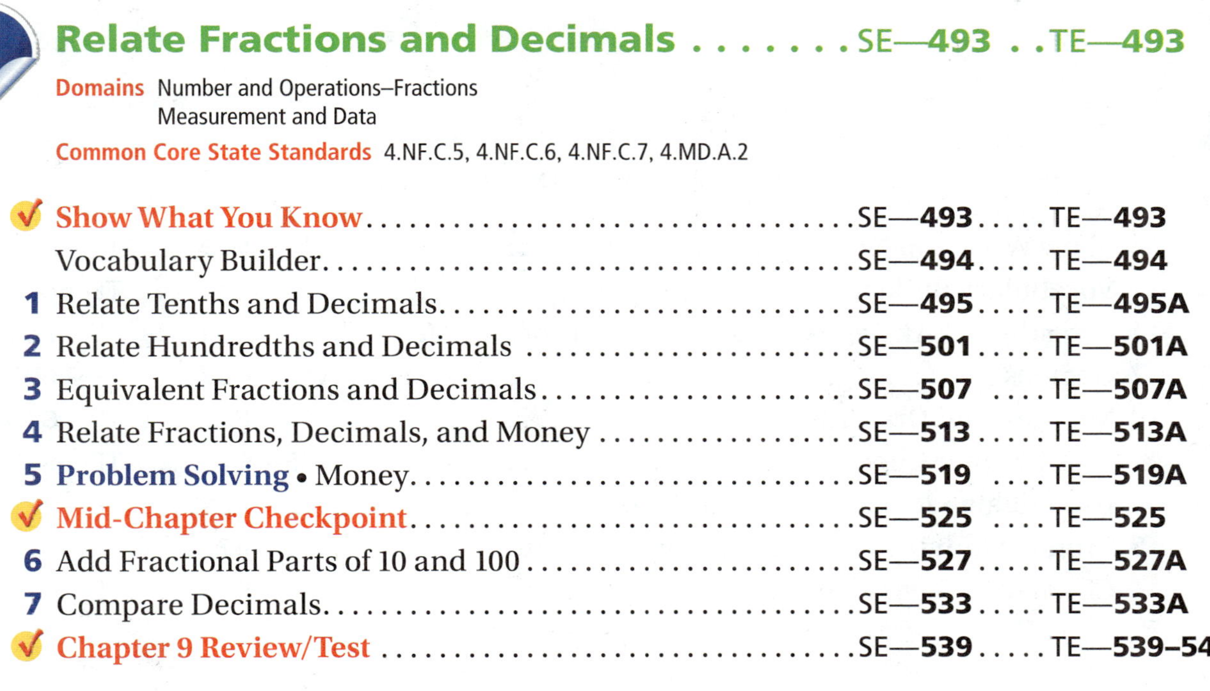

9 Relate Fractions and Decimals . . . SE—493 . . TE—493

Domains Number and Operations–Fractions
Measurement and Data

Common Core State Standards 4.NF.C.5, 4.NF.C.6, 4.NF.C.7, 4.MD.A.2

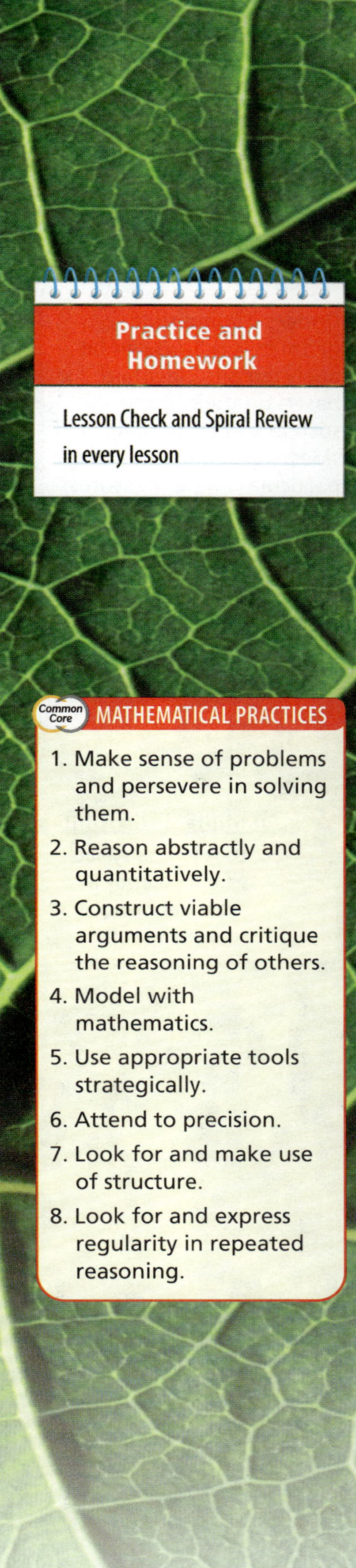

Practice and Homework

Lesson Check and Spiral Review in every lesson

MATHEMATICAL PRACTICES

1. Make sense of problems and persevere in solving them.
2. Reason abstractly and quantitatively.
3. Construct viable arguments and critique the reasoning of others.
4. Model with mathematics.
5. Use appropriate tools strategically.
6. Attend to precision.
7. Look for and make use of structure.
8. Look for and express regularity in repeated reasoning.

Key: SE—Student Edition; **TE**—Teacher Edition

Critical Area

Common Core **CRITICAL AREA**

Understanding that geometric figures can be analyzed and classified based on their properties, such as having parallel sides, perpendicular sides, particular angle measures, and symmetry

Geometry, Measurement, and Data

Personal Math Trainer

Look for this symbol for a gateway to your personalized learning path!

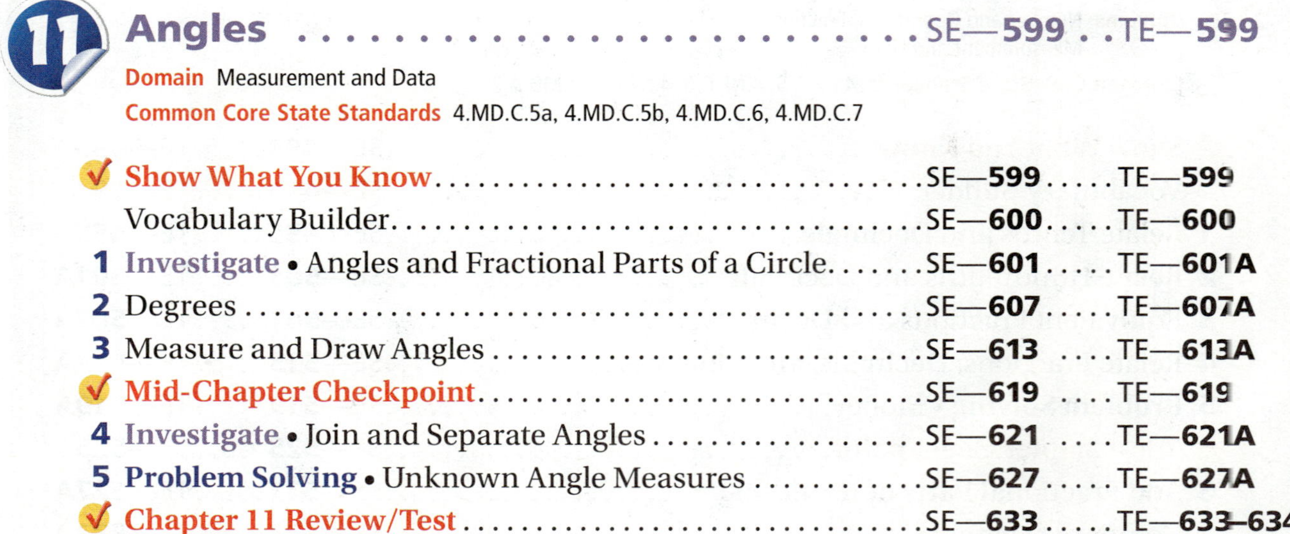

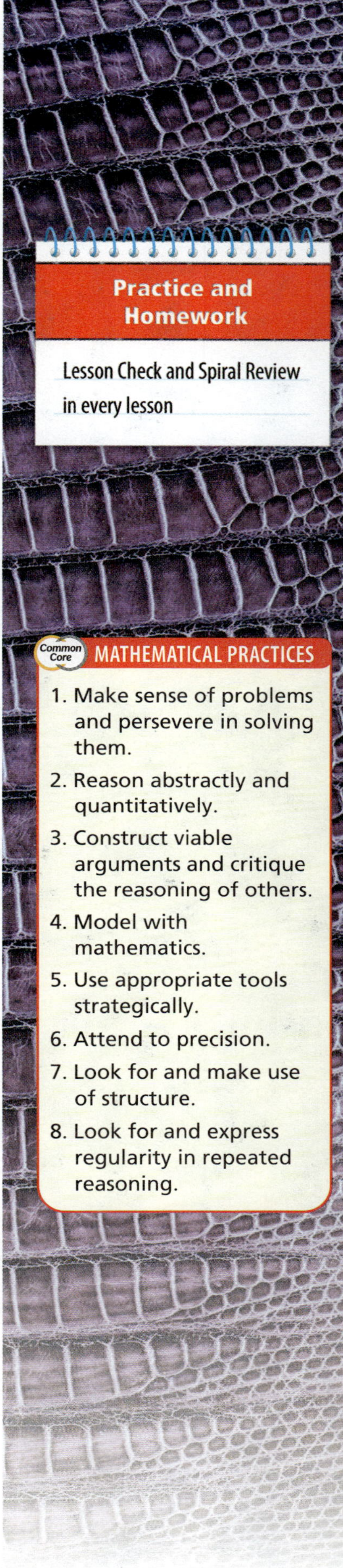

Practice and Homework

Lesson Check and Spiral Review in every lesson

MATHEMATICAL PRACTICES

1. Make sense of problems and persevere in solving them.
2. Reason abstractly and quantitatively.
3. Construct viable arguments and critique the reasoning of others.
4. Model with mathematics.
5. Use appropriate tools strategically.
6. Attend to precision.
7. Look for and make use of structure.
8. Look for and express regularity in repeated reasoning.

Key: SE—Student Edition; **TE**—Teacher Edition

End-of-Year Resources

Review Projects

Getting Ready for Grade 5

Key: P—Online Projects; **PG**—Planning Guide

Teacher Notes

Online Projects 

Review Project:
The Black-Footed Ferret

CRITICAL AREA Developing understanding and fluency with multi-digit multiplication, and developing understanding of dividing to find quotients involving multi-digit dividends

Print Resources
- Planning Guide, p. PG42

Review Project:
Fundraiser

CRITICAL AREA Developing an understanding of fraction equivalence, addition and subtraction of fractions with like denominators, and multiplication of fractions by whole numbers

Print Resources
- Planning Guide, p. PG44

Review Project:
Creating Cars

CRITICAL AREA Understanding that geometric figures can be analyzed and classified based on their properties, such as having parallel sides, perpendicular sides, particular angle measures, and symmetry

Print Resources
- Planning Guide, p. PG46

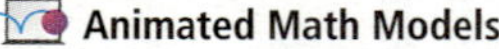

- Animated Math Models
- Assessment
- HMH Mega Math
- *i*Tools
- Projects
- Multimedia *e*Glossary

Getting Ready Lessons build on Grade 4 content and prepare students for Grade 5 content.

Daily Pacing Chart

Review Projects	Lessons	Assessment	Total
3 days	20 days	2 days	25 days

Lesson 1 Add Dollars and Cents

COMMON CORE 4.NBT.B.4, 5.NBT.B.7

Resources
- Student Lesson Pages, Online
- Planning Guide, p. PG48

Lesson 5 Model Division with 2-Digit Divisors

COMMON CORE 4.NBT.B.6, 5.NBT.B.6

Resources
- Student Lesson Pages, Online
- Planning Guide, p. PG56

Lesson 6 Place Value Through Millions

COMMON CORE 4.NBT.A.2, 5.NBT.A.1

Resources
- Student Lesson Pages, Online
- Planning Guide, p. PG58

Lesson 10 Decompose Multiples of 10, 100, 1,000

COMMON CORE 4.OA.B.4, 5.NBT.A.2

Resources
- Student Lesson Pages, Online
- Planning Guide, p. PG66

Lesson 11 Number Patterns

COMMON CORE 4.OA.C.5, 5.OA.B.3

Resources
- Student Lesson Pages, Online
- Planning Guide, p. PG68

Lesson 15 Repeated Subtraction with Fractions

COMMON CORE 4.NF.B.3d, 5.NF.B.7b

Resources
- Student Lesson Pages, Online
- Planning Guide, p. PG78

Lesson 16 Fractions and Division

COMMON CORE 4.NF.B.3d, 5.NF.B.3

Resources
- Student Lesson Pages, Online
- Planning Guide, p. PG80

Lesson 20 Find Area of the Base

COMMON CORE 4.MD.A.3, 5.MD.C.5b

Resources
- Student Lesson Pages, Online
- Planning Guide, p. PG88

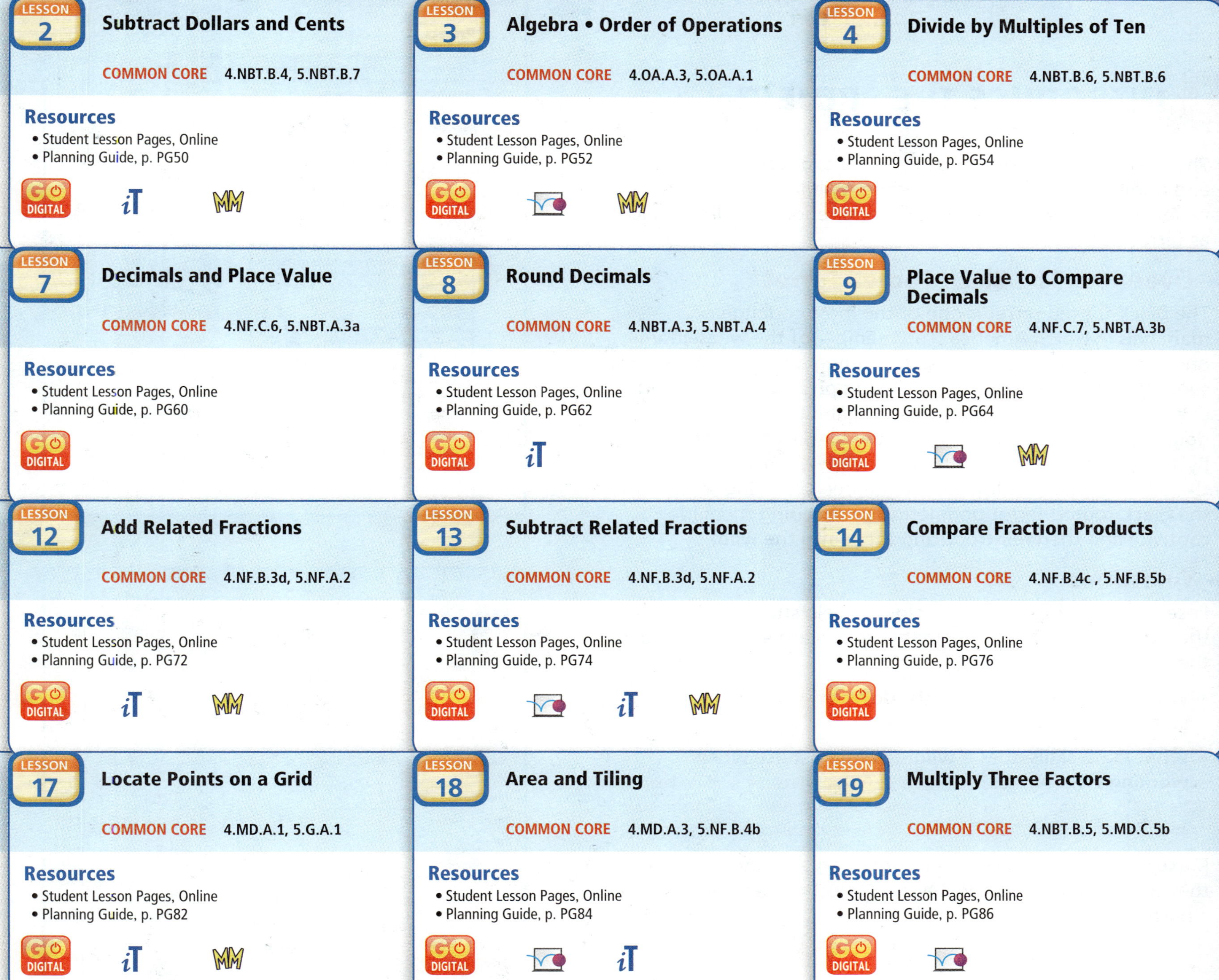

LESSON 2 Subtract Dollars and Cents

COMMON CORE 4.NBT.B.4, 5.NBT.B.7

Resources
- Student Lesson Pages, Online
- Planning Guide, p. PG50

LESSON 3 Algebra • Order of Operations

COMMON CORE 4.OA.A.3, 5.OA.A.1

Resources
- Student Lesson Pages, Online
- Planning Guide, p. PG52

LESSON 4 Divide by Multiples of Ten

COMMON CORE 4.NBT.B.6, 5.NBT.B.6

Resources
- Student Lesson Pages, Online
- Planning Guide, p. PG54

LESSON 7 Decimals and Place Value

COMMON CORE 4.NF.C.6, 5.NBT.A.3a

Resources
- Student Lesson Pages, Online
- Planning Guide, p. PG60

LESSON 8 Round Decimals

COMMON CORE 4.NBT.A.3, 5.NBT.A.4

Resources
- Student Lesson Pages, Online
- Planning Guide, p. PG62

LESSON 9 Place Value to Compare Decimals

COMMON CORE 4.NF.C.7, 5.NBT.A.3b

Resources
- Student Lesson Pages, Online
- Planning Guide, p. PG64

LESSON 12 Add Related Fractions

COMMON CORE 4.NF.B.3d, 5.NF.A.2

Resources
- Student Lesson Pages, Online
- Planning Guide, p. PG72

LESSON 13 Subtract Related Fractions

COMMON CORE 4.NF.B.3d, 5.NF.A.2

Resources
- Student Lesson Pages, Online
- Planning Guide, p. PG74

LESSON 14 Compare Fraction Products

COMMON CORE 4.NF.B.4c , 5.NF.B.5b

Resources
- Student Lesson Pages, Online
- Planning Guide, p. PG76

LESSON 17 Locate Points on a Grid

COMMON CORE 4.MD.A.1, 5.G.A.1

Resources
- Student Lesson Pages, Online
- Planning Guide, p. PG82

LESSON 18 Area and Tiling

COMMON CORE 4.MD.A.3, 5.NF.B.4b

Resources
- Student Lesson Pages, Online
- Planning Guide, p. PG84

LESSON 19 Multiply Three Factors

COMMON CORE 4.NBT.B.5, 5.MD.C.5b

Resources
- Student Lesson Pages, Online
- Planning Guide, p. PG86

Assessment

An Assessment Check Mark following a lesson title indicates that a Checkpoint or Getting Ready Test is available for assessment after completing the lesson.

Checkpoints and Getting Ready Tests can be found in the online Getting Ready Student Edition and Getting Ready Resources: Assessment, Practice, and Reteach.

Critical Area

Review Project

Developing understanding and fluency with multi-digit multiplication, and developing understanding of dividing to find quotients involving multi-digit dividends

1 INTRODUCE THE PROJECT

The Review Project for this critical area connects measurement and numbers to the study of wildlife. Wildlife biologists use a variety of math skills as they study and report on animals such as ferrets.

Overview: The Black-Footed Ferret

The black-footed ferret is one of the most endangered mammals in North America. This member of the weasel family once roamed the Great Plains, depending on prairie dogs for survival. In the early 1900s, prairie dog populations declined due to poisoning, illness, and loss of habitat. As the prairie dogs decreased in number, so did the black-footed ferrets. By 1986, black-footed ferrets were nearly extinct. Since then, the U.S. Fish and Wildlife Service has been working to increase the black-footed ferret population by breeding them in captivity and then reintroducing them into the wild.

Questions

Pose questions like the ones below to help students understand that they will use the mathematics they learn every day and in the future. Ask:

- **What does a wildlife biologist do?** Possible answer: they study the animal life of a region or environment.
- **What math skills does a wildlife biologist use when working with ferrets?** Possible answer: biologists use math to keep track of such things as how many ferrets are in the breeding program, how much food the ferrets need, and how the ferret population is growing.

Make sure students have the information and understanding they need to complete the Review Project on their own or with a partner.

Name __________

CRITICAL AREA Developing understanding and fluency with multi-digit multiplication, and developing understanding of dividing to find quotients involving multi-digit dividends

Review Project
The Black-Footed Ferret

Project

You are a wildlife biologist. You are interested in saving the black-footed ferret from becoming extinct. Your job is to establish a new ferret-breeding program at a zoo. You will keep records about your ferrets to share with other breeders.

Plan

You attend a class at the Black-Footed Ferret Conservation Center. The instructor provides the following data about ferrets. Use the data to help you answer these questions.

Ferret Population
- In 1987, there were only 18 black-footed ferrets left in the world.
- Now there are about 5,500 black-footed ferrets in captivity plus others in the wild.

History of Ferrets at the Conservation Center
- Began with 160 ferrets
- About 420 ferrets born each year
- Released to the wild: about 200 per year

A. There are about 36 times as many black-footed ferrets in the wild now as in 1987. About how many black-footed ferrets are there in the wild now? 648

B. If there are about 3 ferrets born in each litter, about how many litters are born at the Conservation Center each year? 140

C. About how many black-footed ferrets does the Conservation Center release to the wild in 5 years? 1,000

Put It Together

A. Several western states have black-footed ferret release programs. When released, each adult black-footed ferret needs about 120 acres of space to find food. Complete the table to show how many total acres of space each program needs to release the black-footed ferrets successfully.

FERRET RELEASE PROGRAMS

State	Number of Ferrets per Program	Total Number of Acres Needed
Arizona	8	960
Montana	6	720
South Dakota	7	840
Utah	9	1,080
Wyoming	5	600

B. Suppose that you have now been working on your program for several years. You have kept track of the number of kits that were born. Complete this table to show how many kits were born.

KITS BORN

Number of Litters	Kits per Litter	Total Kits
13	6	78
12	2	24
14	5	70
24	4	96
22	3	66
	Total Number of Kits:	334

Online Projects, pp. B7–B8

Name ______________________

Reflect

Eventually, you hope to produce between 300 and 350 healthy ferrets each year. Use what you have learned from the Black-Footed Ferret Conservation Center to answer these questions.

A. About how many ferrets do you expect to reintroduce to the wild each year? Explain.

Possible answer: about 420 ferrets are born at the Black-Footed Ferret Conservation Center each year. They reintroduce about 200 ferrets to the wild each year. That's about half of the number of ferrets born each year. If there are about 300 to 350 ferrets born in my program each year, I would expect to reintroduce to the wild 150 to 175 ferrets each year.

B. About how many ferrets would you be able to reintroduce to the wild in 5 years? Explain.

Possible answer: if I can reintroduce 150 to 175 ferrets to the wild each year, I can expect to reintroduce between 750 and 875 ferrets in 5 years.

$5 \times 150 = 750$

$5 \times 175 = 875$

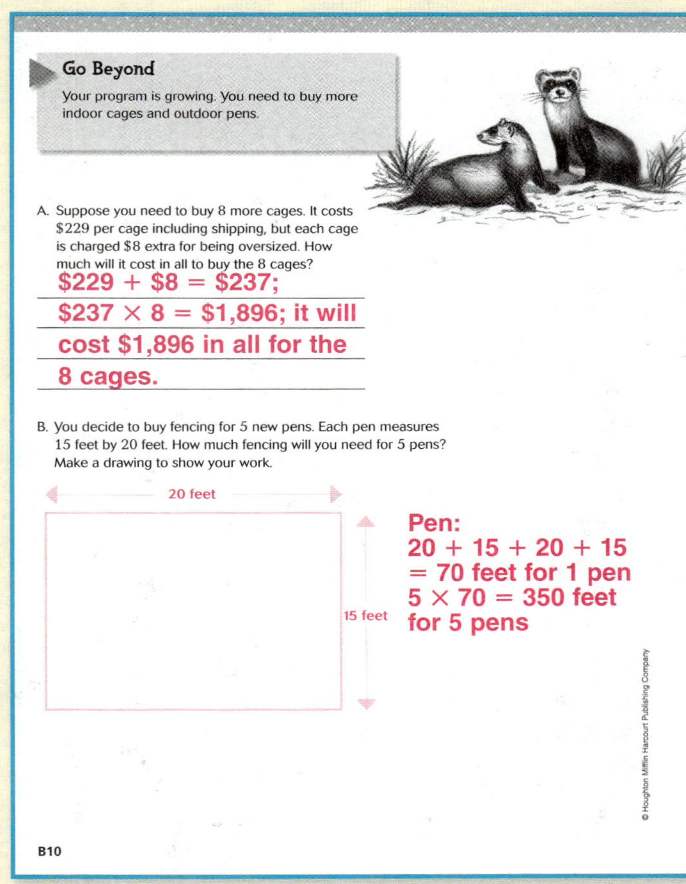

Go Beyond

Your program is growing. You need to buy more indoor cages and outdoor pens.

A. Suppose you need to buy 8 more cages. It costs \$229 per cage including shipping, but each cage is charged \$8 extra for being oversized. How much will it cost in all to buy the 8 cages?

$229 + $8 = $237;
$237 × 8 = $1,896; it will cost $1,896 in all for the 8 cages.

B. You decide to buy fencing for 5 new pens. Each pen measures 15 feet by 20 feet. How much fencing will you need for 5 pens? Make a drawing to show your work.

Pen:
$20 + 15 + 20 + 15 = 70$ feet for 1 pen
$5 \times 70 = 350$ feet for 5 pens

2 DO THE PROJECT

The Black-Footed Ferret

- Before students begin work, have them read the opening sentences of the Project and preview the remaining sections.
- Ask students to explain in their own words what they need to do.

3 EXTEND THE PROJECT

Have students do research to learn more about black-footed ferrets. Pose the following questions to get them started.

- **About how many prairie dogs does a black-footed ferret eat in 1 year?** A ferret eats about 100 prairie dogs in a year. **About how many prairie dogs is that per month?** $100 \div 12$ is 8 r4; about 8 prairie dogs per month
- **How fast does a black-footed ferret move?** A ferret moves in jumps at a speed of about 6 miles per hour. **If it could run constantly at that speed for 3 hours, how far could it run?** 3 hours × 6 miles per hour = 18 miles
- **How much does an adult black-footed ferret weigh?** An adult's average weight is 2 pounds. **About how much would a group of 7 adults weigh?** 7 adults × 2 pounds per adult = 14 pounds

You may suggest that students place completed Review Projects in their portfolios.

Project Scoring Rubric

Score	Description
3	Demonstrates full understanding of the project. Uses the important facts to produce a complete response with no errors. Presents the project clearly and completely.
2	Demonstrates a thorough understanding of the project. Uses the important facts to produce a complete response that may contain one or two errors. Presents the project clearly, without noticing errors.
1	Demonstrates a partial understanding of the project. Uses the important facts, but makes errors applying them. Makes a good, but incomplete attempt at presenting the project.
0	Demonstrates little understanding of the project. Fails to use the important facts and to present accurate and complete conclusions.

Online Projects, pp. B9–B10

Review Project

Developing an understanding of fraction equivalence, addition and subtraction of fractions with like denominators, and multiplication of fractions by whole numbers

1 INTRODUCE THE PROJECT

The Review Project for this critical area connects the understanding of fractions and operations with fractions to adapting a recipe for a bake-sale fundraising project. Bakers and merchants use a variety of math skills to bake, to organize their time, and to sell goods.

Overview: Fundraiser

Fundraising events have a long history in the United States, from the making and selling of quilt blankets during the Civil War in the 1860s, to youth groups making and/or selling baked goods to support local projects.

Recipes for baked goods in the United States often show the amount of ingredients needed using customary measurement units such as cup and teaspoon, or fractions of a cup or a teaspoon. These are measures of volume, or how much a container can hold. A cup of flour, for example, is the amount of flour that a cup measure can hold. Fractions of the cup unit, or fractions of the teaspoon unit, involve a part of the whole unit. For example, $\frac{1}{2}$ of a cup stands for 1 of 2 equal parts of a cup.

Questions

Pose questions like the ones below to help students understand that they will use the mathematics they learn every day and in the future. Ask:

- **What do you need to plan when you organize a fundraiser?** Possible answer: the amount of money that needs to be raised, how the money will be raised, how much you will sell goods for
- **If you were a baker, how might you use fractions and operations?** Possible answer: I would measure ingredients using fractions of a cup or a teaspoon. I would need to add or multiply fractions to find the amount needed to make different numbers of batches. I would need to subtract fractions if I am making only part of a whole batch and need to know the new amount of ingredients I need.

Make sure students have the information and understanding they need to complete the Review Project on their own or with a partner.

Name ______________________

CRITICAL AREA Developing an understanding of fraction equivalence, addition and subtraction of fractions with like denominators, and multiplication of fractions by whole numbers

Review Project
Fundraiser

Project

Students at your school have organized a bake sale to raise money for charity. You have decided to bake 8 batches of banana muffins to sell at the bake sale.

Plan

Your recipe for 1 batch of banana muffins is shown. Complete the chart to show how much of each ingredient you need for 4 batches.

Banana Muffin Recipe

1 Batch	4 Batches
$1\frac{1}{2}$ cups flour	6 cups
1 tsp baking powder	4 tsp baking powder
1 tsp baking soda	4 tsp baking soda
3 large bananas	12 large bananas
$\frac{3}{4}$ cup sugar	3 cups sugar
1 egg	4 eggs
$\frac{1}{3}$ cup butter	$1\frac{1}{3}$ cups butter

Bake at 350° for $\frac{3}{6}$ hour. Makes 12 muffins.

A. You check what ingredients you have. You discover you have $3\frac{1}{8}$ cups of sugar. Do you have enough sugar to make 4 batches of banana muffins? If not, how much more sugar do you need? Explain.

Yes; possible explanation: since 3 cups $< 3\frac{1}{8}$ cups, there is enough sugar.

Put It Together

It takes $\frac{1}{6}$ hour to prepare each batch and $\frac{3}{6}$ hour to cook each batch. Complete the table to find the amount of time it takes to make each batch of banana muffins.

Batch	Time to Mix and Bake	Total Time
1	$\frac{1}{6}$ hour + $\frac{3}{6}$ hour = $\frac{4}{6}$ or $\frac{2}{3}$ hour	$\frac{4}{6}$ or $\frac{2}{3}$ hour
2	$\frac{1}{6}$ hour + $\frac{3}{6}$ hour = $\frac{4}{6}$ or $\frac{2}{3}$ hour	$\frac{8}{6}$ or $1\frac{2}{6}$ or $1\frac{1}{3}$ hours
3	$\frac{1}{6}$ hour + $\frac{3}{6}$ hour = $\frac{4}{6}$ or $\frac{2}{3}$ hour	$\frac{12}{6}$ or 2 hours
4	$\frac{1}{6}$ hour + $\frac{3}{6}$ hour = $\frac{4}{6}$ or $\frac{2}{3}$ hour	$\frac{16}{6}$ or $2\frac{4}{6}$ or $2\frac{2}{3}$ hours

A. Suppose you have only $2\frac{1}{2}$ hours to make the muffins. How many batches of muffins can you make? Explain.

3 batches; possible explanation: it takes $2\frac{2}{3}$ hours to make 4 batches. Since $2\frac{2}{3} > 2\frac{1}{2}$, there is not enough time to make 4 batches. 2 hours $< 2\frac{1}{2}$ hours, so there is enough time to make 3 batches.

B. Suppose you have 1 hour in the morning and 2 hours in the afternoon to make muffins. Can you make all 4 batches? Explain.

Yes; possible explanation: I can make 1 batch in the morning, which takes $\frac{2}{3}$ of an hour. Then I need $2\frac{2}{3}$ hours $- 1$ hour $= 1\frac{2}{3}$ hours to make the remaining batches. $1\frac{2}{3}$ hours < 2 hours, so there is enough time to make all 4 batches.

Online Projects, pp. B11–B12

Name ______________________

Reflect

You made all 4 batches of banana muffins for the bake sale. You hope to sell each muffin for $1. Find the total amount you can raise if you sell all the muffins. Then complete the table to find how much you can raise if you sell only a fraction of the muffins. You decide to set a goal for the amount that you wish to raise at the bake sale.

Each batch makes 12 muffins.

Total number of muffins in 4 batches: **48 muffins**

Total amount raised if all muffins are sold: **$48**

Fraction of Total Muffins Sold	Amount Raised
$\frac{1}{4}$	$12
$\frac{1}{2}$	**$24**
$\frac{5}{8}$	**$30**
$\frac{3}{4}$	**$36**

A. How many muffins do you need to sell to reach your goal at the bake sale? Explain.

Answers will vary. Possible answer: I need to sell $\frac{1}{2}$ of the muffins, or 24 muffins to reach my goal. I decided I wanted to raise half of the possible $48, which is $24. If I sell 24 muffins, I will raise $24.

B. What can you do to be sure you sell the most muffins possible?

Possible answer: sell the muffins for less money or be sure to advertise about the bake sale and the reason for the bake sale.

Review Project B13

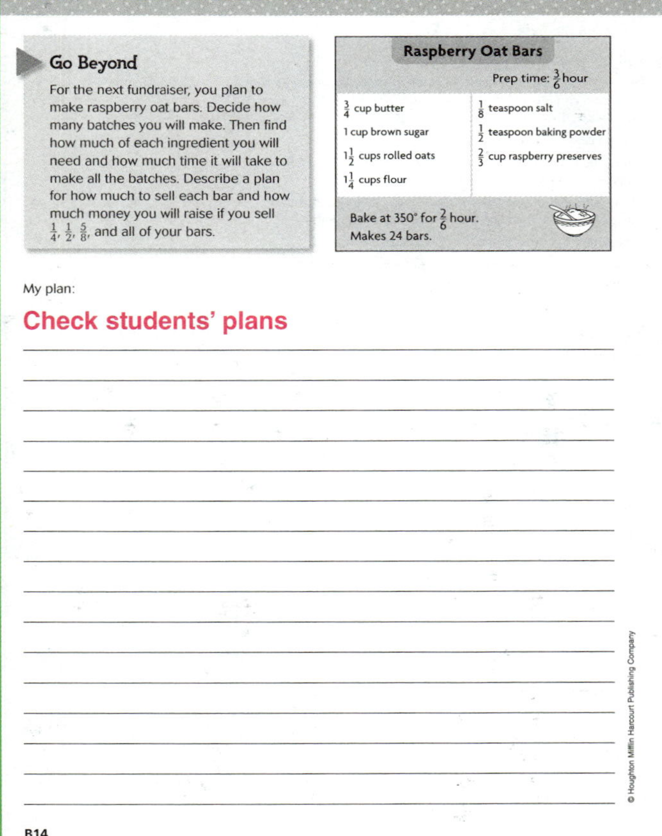

Go Beyond

For the next fundraiser, you plan to make raspberry oat bars. Decide how many batches you will make. Then find how much of each ingredient you will need and how much time it will take to make all the batches. Describe a plan for how much to sell each bar and how much money you will raise if you sell $\frac{1}{4}$, $\frac{1}{2}$, $\frac{5}{8}$, and all of your bars.

Raspberry Oat Bars

Prep time: $\frac{3}{6}$ hour

$\frac{3}{4}$ cup butter
1 cup brown sugar
$1\frac{1}{2}$ cups rolled oats
$1\frac{1}{4}$ cups flour
$\frac{1}{8}$ teaspoon salt
$\frac{1}{2}$ teaspoon baking powder
$\frac{2}{3}$ cup raspberry preserves

Bake at 350° for $\frac{2}{6}$ hour.
Makes 24 bars.

My plan:

Check students' plans

B14

2 DO THE PROJECT

▶ Fundraiser

- Before students begin work, have them read the opening sentences of the Review Project and preview the remaining sections.
- Ask students to explain in their own words what they need to do.

3 EXTEND THE PROJECT

Have students research other fractions used in measurement. For example, measuring lengths for sewing or for distances. Pose these questions to get them started.

- **What fractions of a yard are used to measure fabric?** Possible answer: $\frac{1}{3}$ yard, $\frac{1}{2}$ yard, $\frac{2}{3}$ yard
- **What fractions of a mile are used to measure distances from one place to another?** Possible answer: $\frac{1}{2}$ mile, $\frac{1}{4}$ mile, $\frac{3}{4}$ mile
- **If you need to travel round-trip from your home to the library and the distance for a one-way trip is $\frac{1}{4}$ mile, how would you find the total amount of miles you need to travel?** Possible answer: could multiply $2 \times \frac{1}{4}$ mile to get $\frac{1}{2}$ mile.

You may suggest that students place completed Review Projects in their portfolios.

Project Scoring Rubric

3	Demonstrates full understanding of the project. Uses the important facts to produce a complete response with no errors. Presents the project clearly and completely.
2	Demonstrates a thorough understanding of the project. Uses the important facts to produce a complete response that may contain one or two errors. Presents the project clearly, without noticing errors.
1	Demonstrates a partial understanding of the project. Uses the important facts, but makes errors applying them. Makes a good, but incomplete attempt at presenting the project.
0	Demonstrates little understanding of the project. Fails to use the important facts and to present accurate and complete conclusions.

Online Projects, pp. B13–B14

Critical Area

Review Project

Understanding that geometric figures can be analyzed and classified based on their properties, such as having parallel sides, perpendicular sides, particular angle measures, and symmetry

1 INTRODUCE THE PROJECT

The Review Project for this critical area connects the understanding of area of rectangles and drawing rectangles on grid paper to the study of car designs. Car designers and engineers need to consider the size of the cars they design. They use models and drawings to help them design cars that will have the look and size that customers want.

▶ Overview: Creating Cars

Designers and engineers at automobile companies design cars of the future. They use geometry, color, and imagination to create concept cars. These are presented to consumers for feedback. The designers always ask, "What do people want in a car that they don't have already?" Initial feedback is often collected at auto shows around the world. If people like what they see, the concept car may be put into production and then seen on the road in five to ten years.

▶ Questions

Pose questions like the ones below to help students understand that they will use the mathematics they learn every day and in the future. Ask:

- **How is math used in the design of future cars?** Possible answer: geometry plays a big part in creating a design for a car that is both functional and attractive. A successful design uses symmetry and a variety of shapes and angles that repeat in pleasing patterns.
- **What information about a car would you need in order to design a showroom to display several cars?** Possible answer: you would need to know the car's measurements so you could figure out how big the showroom needs to be.

Make sure students have the information and understanding they need to complete the Review Project on their own or with a partner.

Name ____________________

CRITICAL AREA Understanding that geometric figures can be analyzed and classified based on their properties, such as having parallel sides, perpendicular sides, particular angle measures, and symmetry

Review Project
Creating Cars

Project

You are on the sales and marketing team at an automobile company. Design a showroom to display three new model cars. Include an information booth. Arrange the cars so visitors can walk all around them and get into and out of them. Use as little space as necessary.

Plan

Here are the new model cars and their specifications.

Vehicle	Dimensions	Other Information
Sporty Compact	Length: 15 ft Width: 6 ft	Doors: open out 3 ft
Midsize Sedan	Length: 16 ft Width: 6 ft	Doors: open out 3 ft
SUV	Length: 17 ft Width: 7 ft	Doors: open out 3 ft

Put It Together

Decide how much space you will need in your showroom for the three cars and the information booth shown on the next page.

A. For each car:

- draw and label the footprint with the *doors closed*. Then find the area of that footprint in square feet.
- draw and label dotted lines to enlarge the footprint to show the *doors open*. Then find the area of the larger footprint.

(The footprint of the Sporty Compact is drawn for you.)

Each square on the grid represents 1 square foot. Use the area formula for a rectangle to find each area: $A = b \times h$.

Car's Footprint	Area: Doors Closed	Area: Doors Open
Sporty Compact 3 ft, 6 ft, 3 ft; 15 ft	$15 \times 6 = 90$, 90 square feet	$15 \times 12 = 180$, 180 square feet
Midsize Sedan 3 ft, 6 ft, 3 ft; 16 ft	$16 \times 6 = 96$, 96 square feet	$16 \times 12 = 192$, 192 square feet
SUV 3 ft, 7 ft, 3 ft; 17 ft	$17 \times 7 = 119$, 119 square feet	$17 \times 13 = 221$, 221 square feet

Online Projects, pp. B15–B16

Name ______________________

B. How much floor space will this information booth need?
- Use the area formula for a rectangle to find the footprint of the booth in square feet.

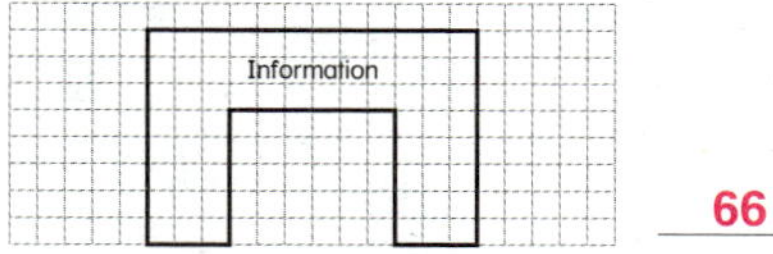

1 square = 1 square foot

66 square feet

- Decide how much more floor space you need to leave around the booth so people can get close to it.

Check students' answers.

Think...
- Where will the door to the showroom be?
- Where should you put the information booth?
- How will you position the cars?
- How much room should you leave between cars so people can move around them?

C. Now, design your own showroom on grid paper. Remember to leave enough space around the cars and information booth for visitors to walk around. Use this key:
1 square = 1 square foot

D. Find the total area of your showroom. Show your work.

Check students' answers based on their designs.

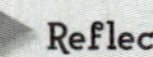

Reflect

Dimensions for cars are usually given in inches instead of in feet. For example, the SUV is 208 in. long and 79 in. wide. For the showroom design, it makes more sense to submit your designs in feet instead of inches. Explain why.

Possible answer: inches are too small for measuring large spaces such as showrooms.

Go Beyond

Suppose it is your job to judge the showroom designs. Look at this design. Explain how and why you might change it.

Answers will vary. Students should point out that the design does not allow enough room for opening car doors. It also would be hard for people to get to the information booth with a car only 2 ft away from it. The information booth looks like it is against a wall, so no one could stand behind it.

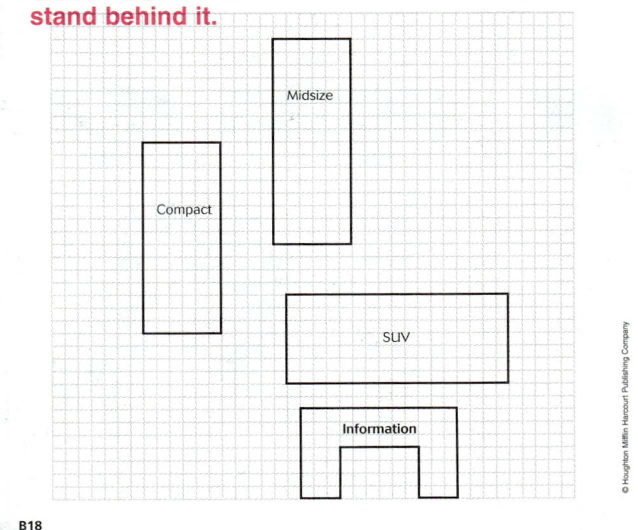

Online Projects, pp. B17–B18

2 DO THE PROJECT

Design a Car Showroom

- Have grid paper, scissors, and tape or glue available for students' use in designing their showrooms. Before students begin work, have them read the opening sentences of the Project and preview the remaining sections.
- Ask students to explain in their own words what they need to do.
- Direct students' attention to the Sporty Compact diagram on the second page. Discuss the concept of a car's "footprint."
  - **How can you find the area of this car with the doors closed?** Possible answer: count the squares.
  - **What shortcut can you use instead of counting squares?** Use the formula $A = b \times h$. **Why does this shortcut work?** because you are multiplying rows of equal numbers of squares

3 EXTEND THE PROJECT

Have students display their showroom designs. Encourage them to compare their work and discuss the advantages and disadvantages of each design.

- **Which showroom uses the least amount of floor space?** Answers will vary.
- **Which showroom seems to allow for the greatest number of people to view the cars at once?** Answers will vary.

You may suggest that students place completed Review Projects in their portfolios.

Project Scoring Rubric

Performance Assessment

3	Demonstrates full understanding of the project. Uses the important facts to produce a complete response with no errors. Presents the project clearly and completely.
2	Demonstrates a thorough understanding of the project. Uses the important facts to produce a complete response that may contain one or two errors. Presents the project clearly, without noticing errors.
1	Demonstrates a partial understanding of the project. Uses the important facts, but makes errors applying them. Makes a good, but incomplete attempt at presenting the project.
0	Demonstrates little understanding of the project. Fails to use the important facts and to present accurate and complete conclusions.

LESSON 1

Add Dollars and Cents

LESSON AT A GLANCE

Common Core Standards

Use place value understanding and properties of operations to perform multi-digit arithmetic.
4.NBT.B.4 Fluently add and subtract multi-digit whole numbers using the standard algorithm.

Perform operations with multi-digit whole numbers and with decimals to hundredths.
5.NBT.B.7 Add, subtract, multiply, and divide decimals to hundredths, using concrete models or drawings and strategies based on place value, properties of operations, and/or the relationship between addition and subtraction; relate the strategy to a written method and explain the reasoning used.

Lesson Objective
Find sums of decimal amounts in dollars and cents.

Materials
MathBoard

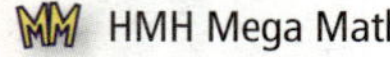
HMH Mega Math

1 TEACH and TALK

• Mega Math

Unlock the Problem

MATHEMATICAL PRACTICES

Have students read the problem.

- **How do you know which operation to use?** Possible answer: since you need to find the total amount Carlos spent in all, you add the amount he spent on a new skateboard, and on a helmet and pads.

Direct students' attention to Step 1.

- **Why is it important to line up the decimal points?** Possible answer: by lining up the decimal points, you are making sure the place values are correctly lined up.
- **How do you record the sum of the pennies?** 6 + 9 = 15; regroup 15 pennies as 1 dime 5 pennies. Write 5 in the pennies place of the sum and 1 above the dimes column to show the regrouped dime.

Allow students time to discuss why they add from right to left, and then work with students through the remaining steps.

This lesson builds on adding whole numbers presented in Chapter 1 and prepares students for adding decimals taught in Grade 5.

Name ______________________

Add Dollars and Cents

Essential Question How can you find sums of decimal amounts in dollars and cents?

Unlock the Problem

Carlos bought a new skateboard for $99.46 and a helmet and pads for $73.49. How much did Carlos spend in all?

- What operation can you use to find the amount Carlos spent? **addition**

You add money amounts in the same way as you add whole numbers. Use the decimal point to line up the digits.

Use place value.

Add. $99.46 + $73.49

STEP 1	STEP 2	STEPS 3 and 4	STEP 5
Add the pennies. Regroup 15 pennies.	Add the dimes.	Add the ones. Add the tens.	Insert the decimal point and dollar sign.
1 $ 99.46 + $ 73.49 5	1 $ 99.46 + $ 73.49 95	1 1 $ 99.46 + $ 73.49 172 95	1 1 $ 99.46 + $ 73.49 $172 95

So, Carlos spent $172.95.

Try This! Find the sum.

A.

	1			1	
$	2	3	.	1	8
+ $	5	7	.	4	5
$	8	0	.	6	3

B.

	1			1	
$	1	9	.	0	7
+ $	6	5	.	2	8
$	8	4	.	3	5

Possible explanation: if the sum of the digits in a given place is greater than 9, you need to regroup.

Math Talk Mathematical Practices

Explain how you know when to regroup.

Getting Ready for Grade 5 GR1

GR: Practice, p. GRP1

Name ______________________ Lesson 1

Add Dollars and Cents

Find the sum.

1. $58.36 + $ 5.87 = $64.23
2. $7.96 + $3.08 = $11.04
3. $98.45 + $ 4.76 = $103.21
4. $14.66 + $30.76 = $45.42
5. $26.71 + $ 5.09 = $31.80
6. $30.25 + $27.42 = $57.67
7. $54.01 + $85.23 = $139.24
8. $42.49 + $30.73 = $73.22
9. $ 7.76 + $54.02 = $61.78
10. $21.06 + $63.48 = $84.54
11. $34.59 + $ 7.45 = $42.04
12. $53.97 + $60.00 = $113.97
13. $71.25 + $ 5.90 = $77.15
14. $40.39 + $17.25 = $57.64
15. $14.99 + $ 5.23 = $20.22
16. $22.85 + $40.25 = $63.10
17. $ 5.23 + $30.55 = $35.78
18. $43.32 + $86.85 = $130.17
19. $31.26 + $88.90 = $120.16
20. $83.77 + $60.35 = $144.12

Problem Solving Real World

21. The bill for tonight's dinner is $56.85. Mr. Asham adds a $10.50 tip. How much does Mr. Asham pay in all? **$67.35**

22. Maria buys a video game for $25.99 and batteries for $7.30. What is the total cost for these two items? **$33.29**

Getting Ready for Grade 5 GRP1

GR: Reteach, p. GRR1

Name ______________________ Lesson 1 Reteach

Add Dollars and Cents

To add money amounts, line up the decimal points and then add as with whole numbers.

Find the sum.

$38.37 + $41.47

Step 1 Write the problem on grid paper. Align the digits by place value. Think of pennies as hundredths and dimes as tenths.

		T	O		T	H
	$	3	8	.	3	7
+	$	4	1	.	4	7

Step 2 Add the hundredths. Regroup 14 hundredths as 1 tenth 4 hundredths. Write 1 in the tenths column.

Then add the tenths.

		T	O		T	H
					1	
	$	3	8	.	3	7
+	$	4	1	.	4	7
					8	4

Step 3 Add the ones and then add the tens. Regroup if necessary.

Write the decimal point and dollar sign.

		T	O		T	H
					1	
	$	3	8	.	3	7
+	$	4	1	.	4	7
	$	7	9	.	8	4

So, $38.37 + $41.47 = $79.84.

Find the sum.

1. $7.81 + $5.09 = $12.90
2. $35.06 + $51.48 = $86.54
3. $ 5.32 + $85.44 = $90.76
4. $40.36 + $17.45 = $57.81
5. $37.60 + $ 9.04 = $46.64
6. $80.26 + $19.31 = $99.57
7. $48.04 + $64.65 = $112.69
8. $52.66 + $50.48 = $103.14
9. $8.47 + $7.33 = $15.80
10. $69.19 + $ 4.95 = $74.14
11. $24.70 + $62.33 = $87.03
12. $10.00 + $25.75 = $35.75

Reteach GRR1 Grade 4

*GR – Getting Ready Lessons and Resources (*www.thinkcentral.com*)

Share and Show 

1. Explain what is happening in Step 2.
Possible explanation: in Step 2, you add the dimes and regroup 13 dimes as 1 dollar 3 dimes.

STEPS 1 and 2	STEPS 3 AND 4	STEP 5
1 $84.60 + $35.70 30	11 $84.60 + $35.70 120 30	11 $84.60 + $35.70 $ 120 30

Find the sum.

2. $ 3.09 + $ 8.92 = $12.01
3. $ 26.08 + $ 41.39 = $67.47
4. $ 7.27 + $ 26.43 = $33.69
5. $ 30.47 + $ 28.56 = $59.03

On Your Own

Find the sum.

6. $ 9.57 + $ 4.09 = $13.66
7. $ 89.36 + $ 3.85 = $93.21
8. $ 23.75 + $ 10.98 = $34.73
9. $ 8.52 + $ 36.07 = $44.59
10. $ 48.92 + $ 7.08 = $56.00
11. $ 60.45 + $ 17.42 = $77.87
12. $ 58.02 + $ 73.54 = $131.56
13. $ 61.74 + $ 60.57 = $122.31

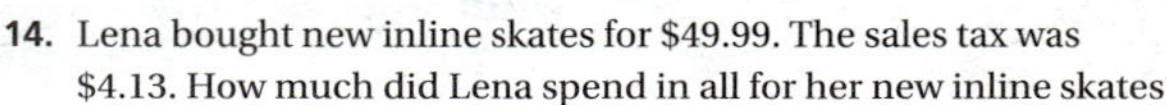

14. Lena bought new inline skates for $49.99. The sales tax was $4.13. How much did Lena spend in all for her new inline skates?
$54.12

Try This!

Have students solve A and B. Ask student volunteers to share their work and explain each step they took to find each sum.

Use **Math Talk** to check students' understanding of adding dollars and cents.

2 PRACTICE

Share and Show • Guided Practice

For Exercise 1, discuss what is happening in Step 2. Be sure students understand that they are adding 6 dimes + 7 dimes, or 13 dimes. 13 dimes is then regrouped as 1 dollar 3 dimes. Continue with what is happening in Steps 3–5.

Work with students to complete Exercises 2–5. Discuss when it is and is not necessary to regroup and why.

On Your Own • Independent Practice

For Exercises 6–13, make sure students are inserting the decimal point and dollar sign in each sum.

Problem Solving

UNLOCK THE PROBLEM For Exercise 14, explain *sales tax* to students. Be sure students understand it is an amount that is added to the cost of an item.

3 SUMMARIZE

Common Core MATHEMATICAL PRACTICES

Essential Question

How can you find the sums of decimal amounts in dollars and cents? Possible answer: I line up each addend by the digits and decimal point. I add the pennies and regroup if necessary. Then I add the dimes and any regrouped dimes, regrouping if necessary. Next, I add the ones and then the tens, regrouping if necessary. Last, I place the decimal point and dollar sign in the sum.

Math Journal WRITE Math

Explain how adding with dollars and cents is similar to and different from adding with whole numbers.

LESSON 2

Subtract Dollars and Cents

LESSON AT A GLANCE

Common Core Standards

Use place value understanding and properties of operations to perform multi-digit arithmetic.
4.NBT.B.4 Fluently add and subtract multi-digit whole numbers using the standard algorithm.

Perform operations with multi-digit whole numbers and with decimals to hundredths.
5.NBT.B.7 Add, subtract, multiply, and divide decimals to hundredths, using concrete models or drawings and strategies based on place value, properties of operations, and/or the relationship between addition and subtraction; relate the strategy to a written method and explain the reasoning used.

Lesson Objective
Find differences between decimal amounts in dollars and cents.

Materials
MathBoard

*i*Tools: Measurement
HMH Mega Math

1 TEACH and TALK

Unlock the Problem

MATHEMATICAL PRACTICES

Have students read the problem. Ask them to underline the information needed to solve the problem and to name the operation that can be used to find the amount that Sandi saved.

- **In Step 1, why do you need to regroup?** Possible answer: I cannot subtract 7 pennies from 4 pennies. So, I need to regroup 2 dimes 4 pennies as 1 dime 14 pennies. Now I can subtract 7 pennies from 14 pennies.

Direct students' attention to Step 2.

- **Explain how to regroup 4 dollars 1 dime.** Possible explanation: I cannot subtract 4 dimes from 1 dime. So, 4 dollars 1 dime is regrouped as 3 dollars 11 dimes.

Work with students through Steps 3–5. Remind students to place the decimal point and dollar sign in their answer.

Use Math Talk to check students' understanding of regrouping to subtract.

This lesson builds on subtracting whole numbers presented in Chapter 1 and prepares students for subtracting decimals taught in Grade 5.

Name ____________________

Subtract Dollars and Cents

Essential Question How can you find differences between decimal amounts in dollars and cents?

Unlock the Problem

Sandi wanted to buy a new coat online. She figured out that the cost of the coat, with shipping, would be $84.24. The next week, Sandi bought the same coat in a local store on sale for a total of $52.47. How much did Sandi save by buying the coat on sale?

You subtract money amounts in the same way as you subtract whole numbers.

- Underline the information you need to solve the problem.
- What operation can you use to find the difference between the two prices? subtraction

Use place value.

Subtract. $84.24 − $52.47

Use the decimal point to line up the digits. Work from right to left. Check each place to see if you need to regroup to subtract.

STEP 1	STEP 2	STEPS 3 and 4	STEP 5
Regroup 2 dimes and 4 pennies as 1 dime and 14 pennies. Subtract the pennies.	Regroup 4 dollars and 1 dime as 3 dollars and 11 dimes. Subtract the dimes.	Subtract the ones. Subtract the tens.	Insert the decimal point and dollar sign.
114 $84.24 − $52.47 7	11 3 1 14 $84.24 − $52.47 77	11 3 1 14 $84.24 − $52.47 31 77	11 3 1 14 $84.24 − $52.47 $31 77

So, Sandi saved $31.77.

Possible explanation: if the digit to be subtracted in any place is greater than the digit being subtracted from, I need to regroup.

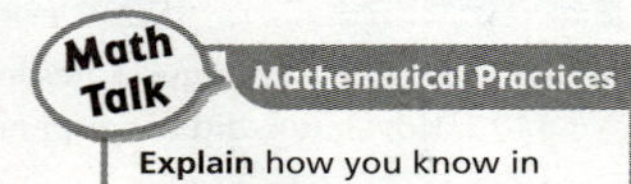

Mathematical Practices
Explain how you know in which places to regroup to subtract.

GR: Practice, p. GRP2

Name ____________________ Lesson 2

Subtract Dollars and Cents

Find the difference.

1. $58.36 − $26.87 = $31.49
2. $3.05 − $1.18 = $1.87
3. $9.43 − $7.08 = $2.35
4. $6.25 − $4.88 = $1.37
5. $15.20 − $ 9.47 = $5.73
6. $64.66 − $ 3.85 = $60.81
7. $80.00 − $ 9.99 = $70.01
8. $52.03 − $ 7.46 = $44.57
9. $73.18 − $18.42 = $54.76
10. $21.64 − $10.95 = $10.69
11. $48.57 − $20.69 = $27.88
12. $60.35 − $39.54 = $20.81
13. $91.32 − $ 8.79 = $82.53
14. $23.06 − $ 6.97 = $16.09
15. $58.30 − $ 9.41 = $48.89
16. $41.45 − $ 7.59 = $33.86
17. $34.20 − $18.15 = $16.05
18. $56.20 − $20.50 = $35.70
19. $43.17 − $30.09 = $13.08
20. $95.44 − $78.56 = $16.88

Problem Solving Real World

21. A soccer ball costs $17.99. Karla hands the cashier $20.00. How much change does she get back? $2.01

22. Hal earned $56.50 dog sitting last month. Liz earned $87.00. How much more did Liz earn than Hal? $30.50

Getting Ready for Grade 5 GRP2

GR: Reteach, p. GRR2

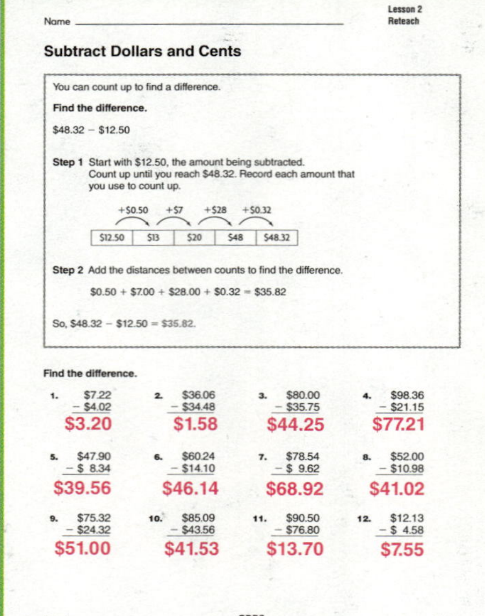

Name ____________________ Lesson 2 Reteach

Subtract Dollars and Cents

You can count up to find a difference.

Find the difference.

$48.32 − $12.50

Step 1 Start with $12.50, the amount being subtracted. Count up until you reach $48.32. Record each amount that you use to count up.

+$0.50 +$7 +$28 +$0.32

$12.50	$13	$20	$48	$48.32

Step 2 Add the distances between counts to find the difference.

$0.50 + $7.00 + $28.00 + $0.32 = $35.82

So, $48.32 − $12.50 = $35.82.

Find the difference.

1. $7.22 − $4.02 = $3.20
2. $36.06 − $34.48 = $1.58
3. $80.00 − $35.75 = $44.25
4. $98.36 − $21.15 = $77.21
5. $47.90 − $ 8.34 = $39.56
6. $60.24 − $14.10 = $46.14
7. $78.54 − $ 9.62 = $68.92
8. $52.00 − $10.98 = $41.02
9. $75.32 − $24.32 = $51.00
10. $85.09 − $43.56 = $41.53
11. $90.50 − $76.80 = $13.70
12. $12.13 − $ 4.58 = $7.55

Reteach GRR2 Grade 4
© Houghton Mifflin Harcourt Publishing Company

*GR – Getting Ready Lessons and Resources (*www.thinkcentral.com*)

Share and Show

1. Find the difference. Regroup as needed.

	10
	6 ~~0~~ 14
	$ ~~7.14~~
	$ 4.38
	$2.76

Find the difference.

2.	3.	4.	5.
$5.89	$30.07	$60.00	$99.08
− $3.16	− $11.32	− $42.75	− $91.36
$2.73	**$18.75**	**$17.25**	**$7.72**

On Your Own

Find the difference.

6.	7.	8.	9.
$9.08	$73.45	$90.00	$80.03
− $7.26	− $12.13	− $42.17	− $49.53
$1.82	**$61.32**	**$47.83**	**$30.50**

10.	11.	12.	13.
$15.36	$84.00	$74.19	$79.62
− $ 2.73	− $27.85	− $ 8.46	− $23.58
$12.63	**$56.15**	**$65.73**	**$56.04**

Problem Solving

14. Bert earned $78.70 last week. This week he earned $93.00. How much more did he earn this week than last week?

$14.30 more

GR4

2 PRACTICE

Share and Show • Guided Practice

For Exercise 1, be sure students understand that since you cannot subtract 3 dimes from 0 dimes, you must regroup 7 dollars 0 dimes as 6 dollars 10 dimes. Then you can take away 3 dimes from 10 dimes.

Work with students through Exercises 2–5 to make sure they understand when it is necessary to regroup.

On Your Own • Independent Practice

For Exercises 6–13, make sure students are carefully recording any regrouped amounts in the proper position.

Problem Solving

MATHEMATICAL PRACTICES

UNLOCK THE PROBLEM For Exercise 14, students should recognize that the amount Bert earned last week should be subtracted from the amount he earned this week.

3 SUMMARIZE

MATHEMATICAL PRACTICES

Essential Question

How can you find differences between decimal amounts in dollars and cents?

Possible answer: I line up each amount by the digits and decimal point, placing the greater value on top. I start by subtracting the pennies and work right to left. If there are not enough pennies to subtract, I regroup a dime as 10 pennies and then subtract. Then, I move on to the dimes, dollars, and so on, regrouping if necessary. Last, I place the decimal point and dollar sign in the final answer.

Math Journal

Write a word problem with dollars and cents that can be solved using subtraction. Include the solution.

LESSON 3

Algebra • Order of Operations

LESSON AT A GLANCE

Common Core Standards
Use the four operations with whole numbers to solve problems.
4.OA.A.3 Solve multistep word problems posed with whole numbers and having whole-number answers using the four operations, including problems in which remainders must be interpreted. Represent these problems using equations with a letter standing for the unknown quantity. Assess the reasonableness of answers using mental computation and estimation strategies including rounding.

Write and interpret numerical expressions.
5.OA.A.1 Use parentheses, brackets, or braces in numerical expressions, and evaluate expressions with these symbols.

Lesson Objective
Use the order of operations to find the value of expressions.

Vocabulary
order of operations

Materials
MathBoard

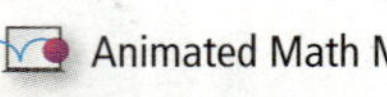
Animated Math Models
HMH Mega Math

This lesson builds on number theory and operations presented in Chapter 2 and prepares students for using the order of operations taught in Grade 5.

Name ____________________

Order of Operations

Essential Question How can you use the order of operations to find the value of expressions?

Unlock the Problem Real World

At a visit to the Book Fair, Jana buys 7 hardcover books and 5 paperback books. She is going to give an equal number of books to each of her three cousins. How many books will each of Jana's cousins get?

- What operation can you use to find the total number of books that Jana buys? addition
- What operation can you use to find how many books each of Jana's cousins gets? division

To find the value of an expression involving parentheses, you can use the order of operations. Remember, the order of operations is a special set of rules that give you the order in which calculations are done in an expression.

First, perform operations inside the parentheses.

Then, multiply and divide from left to right.

Finally, add and subtract from left to right.

Use the order of operations to find the value of $(7 + 5) \div 3$.

STEP 1
Perform operations in parentheses.
$(7 + 5) \div 3$
$12 \div 3$

STEP 2
Use the order of operations. In this case, divide.
$12 \div 3$
4

So, each of Jana's cousins will get 4 books.

- **What if** Jana decides to keep 3 books for herself? How will this change the expression? How many books will each of Jana's cousins get?
The new expression would be $(7 + 5 - 3) \div 3$. Each of Jana's cousins will get 3 books.

Math Talk Mathematical Practices
What operation should you do first to find the values of $(6 + 2) \times 3$ and $6 + (2 \times 3)$? What is the value of each expression?
add, multiply; 24, 12

Getting Ready for Grade 5 GR5

1 TEACH and TALK

• Animated Math Models

Unlock the Problem

MATHEMATICAL PRACTICES

Read the problem together. Use the questions to help students understand that this is a multistep problem.

Explain that when we use an expression to represent this problem, it is important to perform the operations in the correct order.

Use the expression $2 + 3 \times 4$ to illustrate what can happen if we perform operations in the incorrect order.

- **What is the value of the expression if you add first, and then multiply?** 20 ($2 + 3 = 5$; $5 \times 4 = 20$)
- **What is the value if you multiply first, and then add?** 14 ($3 \times 4 = 12$; $2 + 12 = 14$)

Because we multiply before we add, the second answer is correct.

GR: Practice, p. GRP3

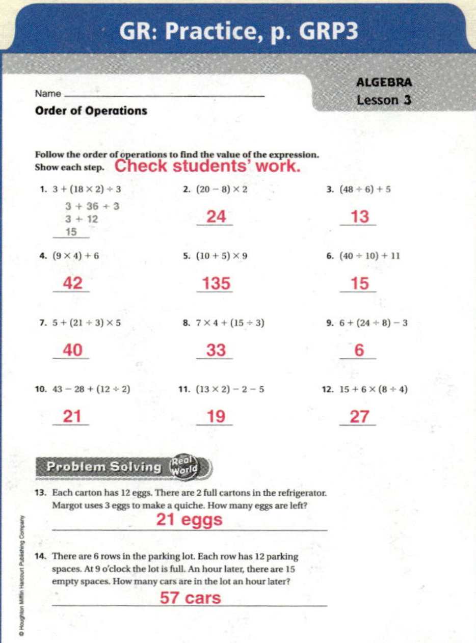
Name ____________________ ALGEBRA Lesson 3

Order of Operations

Follow the order of operations to find the value of the expression. Show each step. Check students' work.

1. $3 + (18 \times 2) \div 3$ — $3 + 36 \div 3$; $3 + 12$; 15
2. $(20 - 8) \times 2$ — 24
3. $(48 \div 6) + 5$ — 13
4. $(9 \times 4) + 6$ — 42
5. $(10 + 5) \times 9$ — 135
6. $(40 \div 10) + 11$ — 15
7. $5 + (21 \div 3) \times 5$ — 40
8. $7 \times 4 + (15 \div 3)$ — 33
9. $6 + (24 \div 8) - 3$ — 6
10. $43 - 28 + (12 \div 2)$ — 21
11. $(13 \times 2) - 2 - 5$ — 19
12. $15 + 6 \times (8 \div 4)$ — 27

Problem Solving Real World

13. Each carton has 12 eggs. There are 2 full cartons in the refrigerator. Margot uses 3 eggs to make a quiche. How many eggs are left? 21 eggs
14. There are 6 rows in the parking lot. Each row has 12 parking spaces. At 9 o'clock the lot is full. An hour later, there are 15 empty spaces. How many cars are in the lot an hour later? 57 cars

© Houghton Mifflin Harcourt Publishing Company

Getting Ready for Grade 5 GRP3

GR: Reteach, p. GRR3

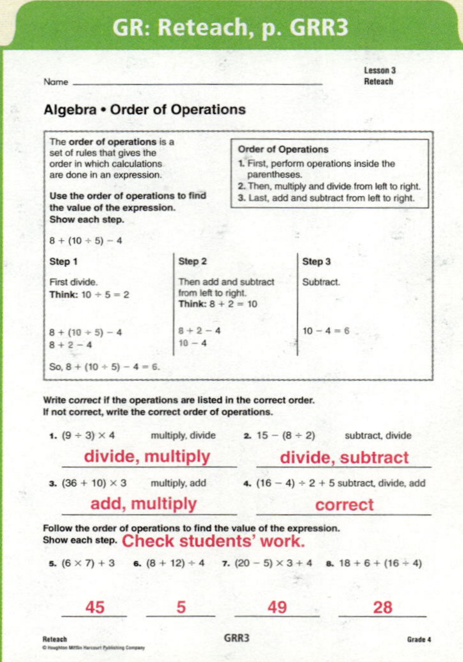
Name ____________________ Lesson 3 Reteach

Algebra • Order of Operations

The **order of operations** is a set of rules that gives the order in which calculations are done in an expression.

Order of Operations
1. First, perform operations inside the parentheses.
2. Then, multiply and divide from left to right.
3. Last, add and subtract from left to right.

Use the order of operations to find the value of the expression. Show each step.

$8 + (10 \div 5) - 4$

Step 1	Step 2	Step 3
First divide. **Think:** $10 \div 5 = 2$	Then add and subtract from left to right. **Think:** $8 + 2 = 10$	Subtract.
$8 + (10 \div 5) - 4$; $8 + 2 - 4$	$8 + 2 - 4$; $10 - 4$	$10 - 4 = 6$

So, $8 + (10 \div 5) - 4 = 6$.

Write *correct* if the operations are listed in the correct order. If not correct, write the correct order of operations.

1. $(9 \div 3) \times 4$ multiply, divide — divide, multiply
2. $15 - (8 \div 2)$ subtract, divide — divide, subtract
3. $(36 + 10) \times 3$ multiply, add — add, multiply
4. $(16 - 4) \div 2 + 5$ subtract, divide, add — correct

Follow the order of operations to find the value of the expression. Show each step. Check students' work.

5. $(6 \times 7) + 3$ — 45
6. $(8 + 12) \div 4$ — 5
7. $(20 - 5) \times 3 + 4$ — 49
8. $18 + 6 + (16 \div 4)$ — 28

Reteach © Houghton Mifflin Harcourt Publishing Company GRR3 Grade 4

*GR – Getting Ready Lessons and Resources (*www.thinkcentral.com*)

Share and Show 

Write *correct* if the operations are listed in the correct order. If not correct, write the correct order of operations.

1. (4 + 5) × 2 multiply, add
   add, multiply
2. 8 ÷ (4 × 2) multiply, divide
   correct
3. 12 + (16 ÷ 4) add, divide
   divide, add
4. 9 + 2 × (3 − 1) add, multiply, subtract
   subtract, multiply, add

Follow the order of operations to find the value of the expression. Show each step. Check students' work.

5. 6 + (2 × 5) **16**
6. 18 − (12 ÷ 4) **15**
7. 8 × (9 − 3) **48**
8. (12 + 8) ÷ 2 × 3 **30**

On Your Own

Follow the order of operations to find the value of the expression. Show each step. Check students' work.

9. 6 + (9 ÷ 3) **9**
10. (3 × 6) ÷ 2 **9**
11. (49 ÷ 7) + 5 **12**
12. 9 × (8 − 2) **54**
13. 45 ÷ (17 − 2) **3**
14. (32 + 4) ÷ 9 − 2 **2**
15. 8 × 9 − (12 − 8) **68**
16. (36 − 4) + 8 ÷ 4 **34**

Problem Solving 

17. Mr. Randall bought 4 shirts, which were on sale. The shirts were originally priced $20. The sales price of the shirts was $5 less than the original price. Write and find the value of an expression for the total amount that Mr. Randall paid for the shirts.
    Possible answer: 4 × (20 − 5); $60

GR6

For the **What if** question, have students find the value of the expression. Discuss the order of operations they used.

Use Math Talk to check students' understanding of the order of operations.

2 PRACTICE 

Share and Show • Guided Practice

Discuss Exercises 1–4 with students. Be sure students understand that you do not simply calculate from left to right. Guide students through Exercises 5–8.

On Your Own • Independent Practice

For Exercises 9–16, students may refer to the order of operations rules on page GR5.

Problem Solving MATHEMATICAL PRACTICES

UNLOCK THE PROBLEM For Exercise 17, some students may benefit from drawing a picture to represent the problem.

3 SUMMARIZE

MATHEMATICAL PRACTICES

Essential Question

How can you use the order of operations to find the value of expressions? Possible answer: when an expression has more than one type of operation, you first perform operations inside parentheses. Then you multiply and divide from left to right. Then you add and subtract from left to right.

Math Journal 

Explain why it is important to follow the order of operations. Include an example in your explanation.

LESSON 4

Divide by Multiples of Ten

LESSON AT A GLANCE

Common Core Standards
Use place value understanding and properties of operations to perform multi-digit arithmetic.
4.NBT.B.6 Find whole-number quotients and remainders with up to four-digit dividends and one-digit divisors, using strategies based on place value, the properties of operations, and/or the relationship between multiplication and division. Illustrate and explain the calculation by using equations, rectangular arrays, and/or area models.

Perform operations with multi-digit whole numbers and with decimals to hundredths.
5.NBT.B.6 Find whole-number quotients of whole numbers with up to four-digit dividends and two-digit divisors, using strategies based on place value, the properties of operations, and/or the relationship between multiplication and division. Illustrate and explain the calculation by using equations, rectangular arrays, and/or area models.

Lesson Objective
Use patterns to divide by multiples of ten.

Materials
MathBoard

1 TEACH and TALK

Unlock the Problem

MATHEMATICAL PRACTICES

Have students read the problem and discuss Example 1.

- **Why is the expression 2,000 ÷ 10 used to solve the problem?** Possible answer: there are 2,000 flyers, and they will be divided equally between 10 volunteers.
- **Why did we start with the basic fact 2 ÷ 1 = 2?** Possible answer: 2 ÷ 1 = 2 is the basic fact related to the division problem 2,000 ÷ 10.
- **Explain why 20 ÷ 10 = 2 is the next step in the solution.** Possible explanation: the quotient is the same as the quotient in the basic fact, and the divisor is the same as the divisor in the problem I am trying to solve.

Invite students to share their descriptions of the pattern used to solve the problem.

Direct students' attention to Example 2.

Discuss the basic fact and pattern used to find 2,800 ÷ 40.

This lesson builds on division presented in Chapter 4 and prepares students for dividing by two-digit numbers taught in Grade 5.

Name ______________________

Divide by Multiples of Ten

Essential Question How can you use patterns to divide by multiples of ten?

Unlock the Problem

A charity asked 10 volunteers to hand out 2,000 flyers about a fund-raising event. Each volunteer will get the same number of flyers. How many flyers will each volunteer hand out?

You can use patterns and a basic fact to divide by multiples of ten.

Example 1 Find 2,000 ÷ 10.

Think: I know that 2 ÷ 1 = 2, so 20 ÷ 10 = 2.

20 ÷ 10 = 2
200 ÷ 10 = 20
2,000 ÷ 10 = 200

So, each volunteer will hand out __200__ flyers.

Describe the pattern used to divide 2,000 by 10.
Possible answer: as the number of zeros in the dividend increases, the number of zeros in the quotient increases by the same number.

Example 2 Find 2,800 ÷ 40.

28 ÷ 4 = 7, so 280 ÷ 40 = __7__.
2,800 ÷ 40 = __70__

Possible explanation: find the basic fact related to the division problem. Use patterns of zeros to solve.

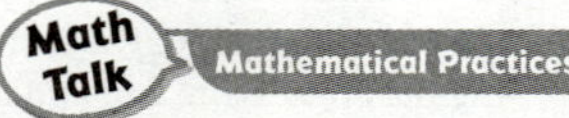

Explain how you can use basic facts to help divide by multiples of ten.

Getting Ready for Grade 5 GR7

GR: Practice, p. GRP4

Name ______________________ Lesson 4

Divide by Multiples of Ten

Divide. Use a pattern to help.

1. 1,500 ÷ 30 = __50__
   15 ÷ 3 = 5, so 150 ÷ 30 = 5.
   1,500 ÷ 30 = 50
2. 2,000 ÷ 20 = __100__
3. 4,000 ÷ 80 = __50__
4. 6,000 ÷ 30 = __200__
5. 9,000 ÷ 30 = __300__
6. 8,000 ÷ 40 = __200__
7. 1,000 ÷ 20 = __50__
8. 3,500 ÷ 50 = __70__
9. 8,100 ÷ 90 = __90__
10. 6,400 ÷ 80 = __80__
11. 2,400 ÷ 60 = __40__
12. 6,000 ÷ 60 = __100__
13. 2,100 ÷ 70 = __30__
14. 5,400 ÷ 90 = __60__
15. 2,700 ÷ 30 = __90__

Problem Solving Real World

16. A food bank has 3,600 boxes of food. The boxes will be loaded equally onto 60 trucks. How many boxes of food will be on each truck?
    60 boxes of food
17. A stadium has a seating capacity of 8,000. Suppose it is divided into 20 equal sections. How many seats are in each section? **Explain.**
    400 seats; possible explanation: I know 8 ÷ 2 = 4 and 80 ÷ 20 = 4. I used patterns of zeros to find that 8,000 ÷ 20 = 400.

Getting Ready for Grade 5 GRP4

GR: Reteach, p. GRR4

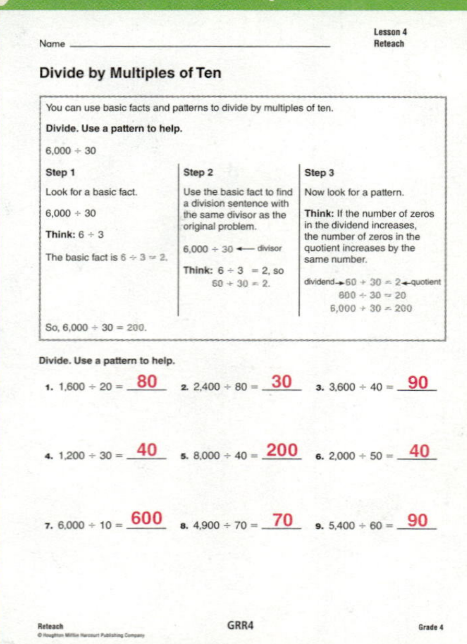

Name ______________________ Lesson 4 Reteach

Divide by Multiples of Ten

You can use basic facts and patterns to divide by multiples of ten.

Divide. Use a pattern to help.

6,000 ÷ 30

Step 1	Step 2	Step 3
Look for a basic fact. 6,000 ÷ 30 **Think:** 6 ÷ 3 The basic fact is 6 ÷ 3 = 2.	Use the basic fact to find a division sentence with the same divisor as the original problem. 6,000 ÷ 30 ← divisor **Think:** 6 ÷ 3 = 2, so 60 ÷ 30 = 2.	Now look for a pattern. **Think:** If the number of zeros in the dividend increases, the number of zeros in the quotient increases by the same number. dividend → 60 ÷ 30 = 2 ← quotient 600 ÷ 30 = 20 6,000 ÷ 30 = 200

So, 6,000 ÷ 30 = 200.

Divide. Use a pattern to help.

1. 1,600 ÷ 20 = __80__
2. 2,400 ÷ 80 = __30__
3. 3,600 ÷ 40 = __90__
4. 1,200 ÷ 30 = __40__
5. 8,000 ÷ 40 = __200__
6. 2,000 ÷ 50 = __40__
7. 6,000 ÷ 10 = __600__
8. 4,900 ÷ 70 = __70__
9. 5,400 ÷ 60 = __90__

Reteach GRR4 Grade 4

*GR – Getting Ready Lessons and Resources (*www.thinkcentral.com*)

Share and Show

1. Find 6,000 ÷ 20.
Think: I can use patterns to divide, starting with 60 ÷ 20.

6 ÷ 2 = 3, so 60 ÷ 20 = 3.
600 ÷ 20 = 30
6,000 ÷ 20 = 300

Divide. Use a pattern to help.

2. 8,000 ÷ 20 = 400
3. 4,000 ÷ 40 = 100
4. 1,200 ÷ 60 = 20

On Your Own

Divide. Use a pattern to help.

5. 9,000 ÷ 30 = 300
6. 5,000 ÷ 50 = 100
7. 1,800 ÷ 60 = 30
8. 7,000 ÷ 10 = 700
9. 3,200 ÷ 80 = 40
10. 6,300 ÷ 90 = 70

Problem Solving

11. A group of musicians wants to sell a total of 1,000 tickets for 20 concerts. Suppose they sell the same number of tickets for each concert. How many tickets will they sell for each concert? Explain how you solved the problem.
50; Possible explanation: I used a basic fact and patterns to solve. I know 10 ÷ 2 = 5, so 100 ÷ 20 = 5; 1,000 ÷ 20 = 50.

GR8

Use Math Talk to check students' understanding of how they can use patterns and basic facts to divide by multiples of ten.

2 PRACTICE

Share and Show • Guided Practice

Guide students through each step in the solution of Exercise 1. For Exercises 2–4, ask students to write the basic fact that they will use to find the quotient.

On Your Own • Independent Practice

When students are using a pattern to help them divide in Exercises 5–10, remind them that as the number of zeros in the dividend increases, the number of zeros in the quotient increases by the same number.

Problem Solving

Common Core MATHEMATICAL PRACTICES

UNLOCK THE PROBLEM For Exercise 11, ask students how they can use a basic fact and patterns to solve the problem.

3 SUMMARIZE

Common Core MATHEMATICAL PRACTICES

Essential Question

How can you use patterns to divide by multiples of ten? Possible answer: I find a basic fact related to the division problem I am trying to solve. Then I use patterns of zeros to solve. As the number of zeros in the dividend increases, the number of zeros in the quotient increases by the same number.

Math Journal

WRITE Math

Explain how to divide 4,500 by 90 using a basic fact and patterns.

LESSON 5

Model Division with 2-Digit Divisors

This lesson builds on division with 1-digit divisors presented in Chapter 4 and prepares students to divide with 2-digit divisors taught in Grade 5.

LESSON AT A GLANCE

Common Core Standards

Use place value understanding and properties of operations to perform multi-digit arithmetic.

4.NBT.B.6 Find whole-number quotients and remainders with up to four-digit dividends and one-digit divisors, using strategies based on place value, the properties of operations, and/or the relationship between multiplication and division. Illustrate and explain the calculation by using equations, rectangular arrays, and/or area models.

Perform operations with multi-digit whole numbers and with decimals to hundredths.

5.NBT.B.6 Find whole-number quotients of whole numbers with up to four-digit dividends and two-digit divisors, using strategies based on place value, the properties of operations, and/or the relationship between multiplication and division. Illustrate and explain the calculation by using equations, rectangular arrays, and/or area models.

Materials

MathBoard, base-ten blocks

Lesson Objective

Use base-ten blocks to divide with 2-digit divisors.

*i*Tools: Base-Ten Blocks

1 TEACH and TALK

• *i*Tools

Unlock the Problem

MATHEMATICAL PRACTICES

Have students read the problem. Help them to understand the steps for solving the problem.

- **Why is division used to solve the problem?** Possible answer: 154 children need to be placed on 11 equal-sized teams.
- **In Step 2, why are there 15 tens?** Possible answer: there were 5 tens to begin with. After the hundred block was regrouped as 10 tens, I added 10 tens and 5 tens to get 15 tens.
- **In Step 3, why do you draw 4 ones in each oval?** Possible answer: there were 4 ones to begin with. To these are added the 40 ones obtained by regrouping 4 leftover tens, for a total of $4 + 40 = 44$. When these are shared among 11 ovals, each oval gets 4 ones.

Use **Math Talk** to check students' understanding of the inverse relationship between dividing and multiplying.

Name ______________________

Model Division with 2-Digit Divisors

Essential Question How can you use models to divide?

CONNECT You have used base-ten blocks to divide whole numbers by 1-digit divisors. You can follow the same steps to divide whole numbers by 2-digit divisors.

Unlock the Problem

Activity **Materials** ■ base-ten blocks

There are 154 children participating in a soccer tournament. There are 11 equal-sized teams of children. How many children are on each team?

- What do you need to find? the number of children on each team
- What is the dividend? the divisor? 154; 11

STEP 1

Use base-ten blocks to model 154 children. Show 154 as 1 hundred 5 tens 4 ones. Draw 11 ovals for the teams.

STEP 2

Share the base-ten blocks equally among 11 groups. Since there are not enough hundreds to share equally, regroup 1 hundred as 10 tens. There are now 15 tens. Share the tens and draw a vertical line segment for each ten.

STEP 3

If there are any tens left over, regroup each as 10 ones. Share the ones equally among 11 groups. Draw a small circle for each one.

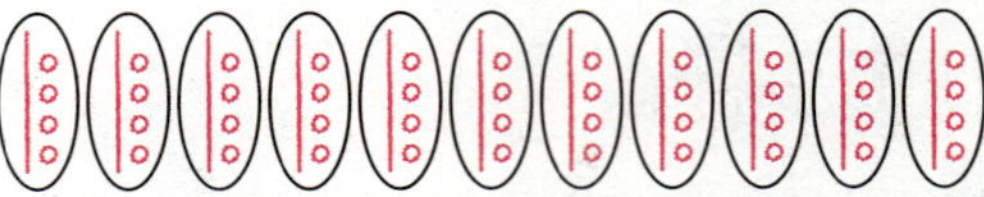

There are 1 ten(s) and 4 one(s) in each group.

So, there are 14 children on each team.

- Explain why you need to regroup in Step 3.

Possible explanation: there were 4 tens left over after I shared the tens. In order to share the leftover tens, I needed to regroup them as ones.

Math Talk Mathematical Practices

Explain how you can check your answer.

Possible explanation: I can multiply to check my division. If $14 \times 11 = 154$, then my answer is correct.

Getting Ready for Grade 5 GR9

GR: Practice, p. GRP5

Name ______________________ Lesson 5

Model Division with 2-Digit Divisors

Use base-ten blocks to divide. Check students' work.

1. 154 ÷ 11 14
2. 48 ÷ 16 3
3. 95 ÷ 19 5
4. 288 ÷ 16 18
5. 120 ÷ 15 8
6. 140 ÷ 10 14
7. 132 ÷ 12 11
8. 204 ÷ 12 17
9. 250 ÷ 10 25
10. 154 ÷ 11 14
11. 39 ÷ 13 3
12. 165 ÷ 11 15

Problem Solving Real World

13. A theater has 126 seats. The theater has 14 rows with the same number of seats in each row. How many seats are in each row? 9
14. Leila has $360 in twenty-dollar bills. How many twenty-dollar bills does she have? 18

Getting Ready for Grade 5 GRP5

GR: Reteach, p. GRR5

Name ______________________ Lesson 5 Reteach

Model Division with 2-Digit Divisors

You can use models to divide a whole number by a 2-digit divisor.

Use base-ten blocks to find 143 ÷ 13.

Step 1 Use base-ten blocks to model the dividend, 143. Show 143 as 1 hundred 4 tens 3 ones.

Remember: Each large square represents 100, each line represents 10, and each small circle represents 1.

Step 2 The divisor is 13. Divide the blocks equally between 13 groups. Since you cannot share the one-hundred square equally between the 13 groups, first break it into 10 tens. Then you will have 14 tens, altogether. Share the tens equally among 13 groups.

Step 3 After completing Step 2, you will have 1 ten and 3 ones left over. Since you cannot share the 10 equally between the 13 groups, break it into 10 ones. Then you will have 13 ones, altogether. Share the 13 ones equally among the 13 groups.

Each group contains 1 ten and 1 one, or 11. So 143 ÷ 13 = 11.

Use base-ten blocks to divide.

1. 65 ÷ 5 = 13
2. 84 ÷ 14 = 6
3. 120 ÷ 8 = 15
4. 96 ÷ 16 = 6
5. 168 ÷ 12 = 14
6. 99 ÷ 33 = 3

Reteach GRR5 Grade 4

*GR – Getting Ready Lessons and Resources (*www.thinkcentral.com*)

Share and Show 

1. Use base-ten blocks to find 182 ÷ 14. Describe the steps you took to find your answer.
   13; Possible answer: I modeled 182 and regrouped 1 hundred to give me 18 tens 2 ones. Then I shared the tens equally among 14 groups. I regrouped the leftover tens as ones and shared them equally among 14 groups.

Use base-ten blocks to divide.

2. 60 ÷ 12 = 5
3. 135 ÷ 15 = 9

On Your Own

Use base-ten blocks to divide.

4. 180 ÷ 10 = 18
5. 150 ÷ 15 = 10
6. 88 ÷ 11 = 8
7. 96 ÷ 16 = 6
8. 176 ÷ 11 = 16
9. 156 ÷ 13 = 12

Problem Solving 

10. Nicole has $250 in ten-dollar bills. How many ten-dollar bills does Nicole have?
    25
11. At Dante's party, 16 children share 192 crayons. At Maria's party, 13 children share 234 crayons. Each party splits the crayons up equally among the children attending. How many more crayons does each child at Maria's party get than each child at Dante's party? Explain.
    6; At Maria's party, each child gets 234 ÷ 13 = 18 crayons. At Dante's party, each child gets 192 ÷ 16 = 12 crayons; 18 − 12 = 6

GR10

Getting Ready Lessons and Resources, pp. GR11–GR12

Checkpoint

Name ____________

Checkpoint

Concepts and Skills

Find the sum or difference.

1. $2.87 + $8.09 = $10.96
2. $7.65 − $5.23 = $2.42
3. $37.05 + $14.95 = $52.00
4. $30.00 − $12.69 = $17.31

Use base-ten blocks to divide.

5. 143 ÷ 11 — 13
6. 224 ÷ 16 — 14
7. 108 ÷ 18 — 6

Follow the order of operations to find the value of the expression. Show each step. Check students' work.

8. (8 × 2) + 4 — 20
9. 16 − (3 × 5) — 1
10. 24 ÷ (15 − 7) — 3
11. 15 ÷ (9 − 4) × 4 — 12

Divide. Use a pattern to help.

12. 6,000 ÷ 30 — 200
13. 2,000 ÷ 20 — 100
14. 3,200 ÷ 40 — 80
15. 8,100 ÷ 90 — 90

Problem Solving Real World

16. Ellis bought groceries that were worth $99.86. After using coupons, the bill was $84.92. How much did Ellis save by using coupons?
    $14.94

Getting Ready for Grade 5 GR11

Fill in the bubble completely to show your answer.

17. Taby buys a dog leash for $18.50 and a dog collar for $12.75. What is the total cost of the leash and the collar?
    - Ⓐ $5.75
    - Ⓑ $6.25
    - Ⓒ $30.25
    - Ⓓ $31.25
18. Mr. Martin pays $35.93 for shoes for himself and $18.67 for shoes for his son. How much more do Mr. Martin's shoes cost than his son's?
    - Ⓐ $17.26
    - Ⓑ $17.36
    - Ⓒ $23.24
    - Ⓓ $54.60
19. Chris and Susan each collect baseball cards. Chris has 75 cards and Susan has 93 cards. They want to combine their collections and divide the cards evenly between them. Which expression can they use to find the number of cards each of them should have?
    - Ⓐ 75 + 93 ÷ 2
    - Ⓑ 75 + (93 ÷ 2)
    - Ⓒ (75 + 93) × 2
    - Ⓓ (75 + 93) ÷ 2
20. A store expects 4,000 customers during its 20-hour sale. Suppose the same number of customers arrives each hour. How many customers come each hour?
    - Ⓐ 20
    - Ⓑ 200
    - Ⓒ 2,000
    - Ⓓ 8,000

GR12

2 PRACTICE 

Share and Show • Guided Practice

For Exercise 1, make sure students understand why it is necessary to regroup. For Exercises 2–3, encourage students to plan their solutions using the steps they took in Exercise 1 as a model.

On Your Own • Independent Practice

After students have solved Exercise 4, you may wish to review with them the steps they took to solve problems like this in Lesson 4, when they used patterns to divide by multiples of 10.

Problem Solving

Common Core MATHEMATICAL PRACTICES

UNLOCK THE PROBLEM Help students see that to solve Exercise 10, they must divide 250 by 10. Exercise 11 is a multi-step problem. To solve it, students must first find the number of crayons each guest received at each party, and then find the difference of the two amounts.

3 SUMMARIZE

Common Core MATHEMATICAL PRACTICES

Essential Question

How can you use models to divide? Possible answer: model the dividend with base-ten blocks. Share the blocks equally among the number of groups represented by the divisor, regrouping as necessary.

Math Journal

WRITE Math

Explain how you can use a model to find the quotient 168 ÷ 12.

GETTING READY FOR GRADE 5

LESSON 6

Place Value Through Millions

LESSON AT A GLANCE

Common Core Standards
Generalize place value understanding for multi-digit whole numbers.
4.NBT.A.2 Read and write multi-digit whole numbers using base-ten numerals, number names, and expanded form. Compare two multi-digit numbers based on meanings of the digits in each place, using >, =, and < symbols to record the results of comparisons.

Understand the place value system.
5.NBT.A.1 Recognize that in a multi-digit number, a digit in one place represents 10 times as much as it represents in the place to its right and 1/10 of what it represents in the place to its left.

Lesson Objective
Read and write whole numbers through millions.

Materials
MathBoard

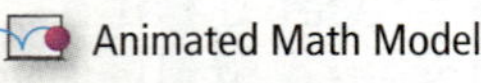
Animated Math Models
HMH Mega Math

This lesson builds on reading and writing numbers through hundred thousands presented in Chapter 1 and prepares students to read and write numbers through millions taught in Grade 5.

1 TEACH and TALK

Animated Math Models

Unlock the Problem

MATHEMATICAL PRACTICES

Draw attention to the place-value chart. Review the facts that *ones* and *thousands* are called *periods*, and that each period is made up of ones, tens, and hundreds.

Point out that in this lesson, students will extend the place-value chart one period to the left, the millions period. Reassure students that they can use the same methods to read, write, and represent numbers in the millions as they used with numbers in the thousands and the ones.

- **In the number 123,456, what digit is in the ten thousands place? In what place is the digit 4?** 2; hundreds

Have students read the problem.

- **In the number 1,550,000, what digit is in the millions place?** 1

Use **Math Talk** to check students' understanding of place value.

Name ______

Place Value Through Millions

Essential Question How can you read, write, and represent whole numbers through millions?

Unlock the Problem 

The population of Idaho is about 1,550,000. Write 1,550,000 in standard form, word form, and expanded form.

- What is the value of the ten thousands place? 50,000

You know how to read and write numbers through hundred thousands. The place-value chart can be expanded to help you read and write greater numbers, like 1,550,000.

One million is 1,000 thousands and is written as 1,000,000. The millions period is to the left of the thousands period on a place-value chart.

PERIODS

MILLIONS			THOUSANDS			ONES		
Hundreds	Tens	Ones	Hundreds	Tens	Ones	Hundreds	Tens	Ones
		1,	5	5	0,	0	0	0
		$1 \times 1{,}000{,}000$	$5 \times 100{,}000$	$5 \times 10{,}000$	$0 \times 1{,}000$	0×100	0×10	0×1
		1,000,000	500,000	50,000	0	0	0	0

The place value of the 1 in 1,550,000 is millions.

Standard form: 1,550,000

Word Form: One million, five hundred fifty thousand

Expanded Form: 1,000,000 + 500,000 + 50,000

Math Talk Mathematical Practices

Explain how 8,000,000 is different than 800,000.

Possible explanation: 8,000,000 has 80 hundred thousands, but 800,000 only has 8 hundred thousands.

Try This! Use place value to read and write the number.

Standard Form: 62,080,126

Word Form: Sixty-two million, eighty thousand, one hundred twenty-six

Expanded Form: 60,000,000 + 2,000,000 + 80,000 + 100 + 20 + 6

Getting Ready for Grade 5 GR13

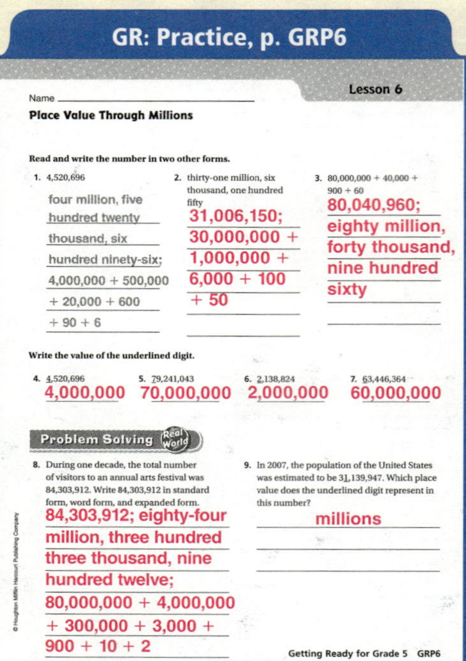
GR: Practice, p. GRP6

Name ______ Lesson 6

Place Value Through Millions

Read and write the number in two other forms.

1. 4,520,696
four million, five hundred twenty thousand, six hundred ninety-six; 4,000,000 + 500,000 + 20,000 + 600 + 90 + 6

2. thirty-one million, six thousand, one hundred fifty
31,006,150; 30,000,000 + 1,000,000 + 6,000 + 100 + 50

3. 80,000,000 + 40,000 + 900 + 60
80,040,960; eighty million, forty thousand, nine hundred sixty

Write the value of the underlined digit.

4. 4,520,696 4,000,000
5. 79,241,043 70,000,000
6. 2,138,824 2,000,000
7. 63,446,364 60,000,000

Problem Solving Real World

8. During one decade, the total number of visitors to an annual arts festival was 84,303,912. Write 84,303,912 in standard form, word form, and expanded form.
84,303,912; eighty-four million, three hundred three thousand, nine hundred twelve; 80,000,000 + 4,000,000 + 300,000 + 3,000 + 900 + 10 + 2

9. In 2007, the population of the United States was estimated to be 31,139,947. Which place value does the underlined digit represent in this number?
millions

© Houghton Mifflin Harcourt Publishing Company

Getting Ready for Grade 5 GRP6

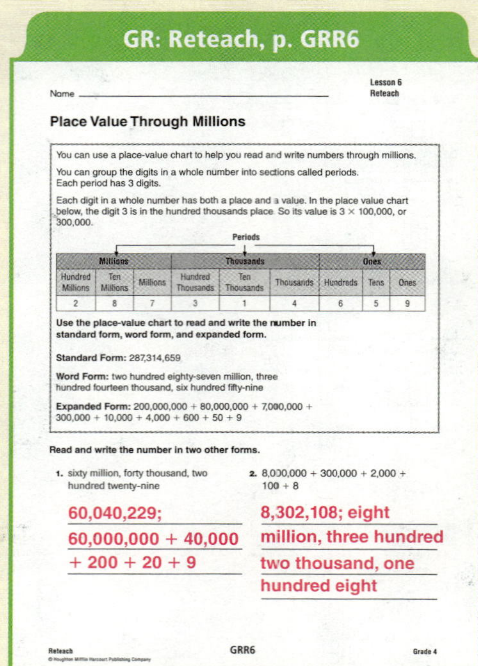
GR: Reteach, p. GRR6

Name ______ Lesson 6 Reteach

Place Value Through Millions

You can use a place-value chart to help you read and write numbers through millions.

You can group the digits in a whole number into sections called periods. Each period has 3 digits.

Each digit in a whole number has both a place and a value. In the place value chart below, the digit 3 is in the hundred thousands place. So its value is $3 \times 100{,}000$, or 300,000.

Periods

Millions			Thousands			Ones		
Hundred Millions	Ten Millions	Millions	Hundred Thousands	Ten Thousands	Thousands	Hundreds	Tens	Ones
2	8	7	3	1	4	6	5	9

Use the place-value chart to read and write the number in standard form, word form, and expanded form.

Standard Form: 287,314,659

Word Form: two hundred eighty-seven million, three hundred fourteen thousand, six hundred fifty-nine

Expanded Form: 200,000,000 + 80,000,000 + 7,000,000 + 300,000 + 10,000 + 4,000 + 600 + 50 + 9

Read and write the number in two other forms.

1. sixty million, forty thousand, two hundred twenty-nine
60,040,229; 60,000,000 + 40,000 + 200 + 20 + 9

2. 8,000,000 + 300,000 + 2,000 + 100 + 8
8,302,108; eight million, three hundred two thousand, one hundred eight

Reteach GRR6 Grade 4
© Houghton Mifflin Harcourt Publishing Company

*GR – Getting Ready Lessons and Resources (*www.thinkcentral.com*)

Share and Show 

1. Write the number 3,298,076 in word form and expanded form.

Word Form: three million, two hundred ninety-eight thousand, seventy-six

Expanded Form: 3,000,000 + 200,000 + 90,000 + 8,000 + 70 + 6

Read and write the number in two other forms.

2. fifty million, three thousand, eighty-seven
   50,003,087; 50,000,000 + 3,000 + 80 + 7

3. 60,000,000 + 400,000 + 200 + 30 + 9
   60,400,239; sixty million, four hundred thousand, two hundred thirty-nine

On Your Own

Read and write the number in two other forms.

4. 70,000,000 + 8,000,000 + 20,000 + 8
   78,020,008; seventy-eight million, twenty thousand, eight

5. twenty million, eleven thousand, twelve
   20,011,012; 20,000,000 + 10,000 + 1,000 + 10 + 2

Write the value of the underlined digit.

6. 3,3<u>5</u>6,000 — 50,000
7. 45,687,<u>9</u>09 — 900
8. <u>7</u>0,000,044 — 70,000,000
9. <u>3</u>0,051,218 — 30,000,000

Problem Solving 

10. According to one organization, there are about 93,600,000 pet cats and about 77,500,000 pet dogs in the U.S. Are there more pet cats or pet dogs? **Explain** how you know.
    Cats; possible explanation: the greatest place value in both numbers is ten millions. Since the number of cats has a 9 in the ten millions place and the number of dogs has a 7, the number of pet cats is greater.

GR14

2 PRACTICE 

Share and Show • Guided Practice

For Exercise 1, check that students do not use the word *and* when writing numbers in word form ("two hundred *and* ninety-eight thousand") and that they hyphenate correctly (*ninety-eight*, *seventy-six* but not *two-hundred*).

On Your Own • Independent Practice

In Exercises 6–9, encourage students to refer to the place-value chart to solve the problems. First, they should find the place value of the underlined digit. Then they should write the digit with zeros to its right to indicate the value of the digit.

Problem Solving 

UNLOCK THE PROBLEM Help students see that to solve Exercise 10, they must find and compare the place values of the first digits of the numbers. So, 9 ten millions is greater than 7 ten millions.

3 SUMMARIZE

Common Core MATHEMATICAL PRACTICES

Essential Question

How can you read, write, and represent whole numbers through millions? Possible answer: find the place value of each digit in a number using a place-value chart through millions. Use the place values to read, write, and represent the numbers.

Math Journal 

Choose a number in the ten millions. Show how to write the number in standard form, word form, and expanded form.

LESSON 7

Decimals and Place Value

LESSON AT A GLANCE

Common Core Standards
Understand decimal notation for fractions, and compare decimal fractions.
4.NF.C.6 Use decimal notation for fractions with denominators 10 or 100.

Understand the place value system.
5.NBT.A.3a Read, write, and compare decimals to thousandths. Read and write decimals to thousandths using base-ten numerals, number names, and expanded form, e.g., $347.392 = 3 \times 100 + 4 \times 10 + 7 \times 1 + 3 \times (1/10) + 9 \times (1/100) + 2 \times (1/1000)$.

Lesson Objective
Read and write decimals using place value.

Materials
MathBoard

1 TEACH and TALK

Unlock the Problem

MATHEMATICAL PRACTICES

Have students read the problem.

- **How do you read the number 1.06? How do you read the number 1.28?** one and six hundredths; one and twenty-eight hundredths

Explain that in this lesson, students will extend the place-value chart two places to the *right* of the place-value chart to millions they have used before. Point out that the ones place in the chart on page GR15 is the same as the ones place at the right end of the chart on page GR13.

Remind students that the value of each place in place-value charts they have used before is always one-tenth of the value of the place to its left. For example, the value of the hundreds place is one-tenth of the value of the thousands place.

- **How does the value of the tenths place compare to the value of the ones place?** It is one-tenth of the value. **How does the value of the hundredths place compare to the value of the tenths place?** It is one-tenth of the value.

Use **Math Talk** to check students' understanding of the difference between standard form and word form.

This lesson builds on understanding decimal notation to hundredths presented in Chapter 9 and prepares students to use place value to hundredths taught in Grade 5.

Name ____________

Decimals and Place Value

Essential Question How can you use place value to read, write, and represent decimals?

CONNECT Decimals, like whole numbers, can be written in standard form, word form, and expanded form.

Unlock the Problem 

One of the world's tiniest frogs lives in Asia. Adult males range in length from about 1.06 to 1.28 centimeters, about the size of a pea.

- What decimals do you see in the problem? **1.06 and 1.28**
- The numbers 1.06 and 1.28 are between which two whole numbers? **1 and 2**

You can use a place-value chart to help you understand decimals. Whole numbers are to the left of the decimal point in the place-value chart, and decimal amounts are to the right of the decimal point. The value of each place is one-tenth of the place to its left.

Use a place-value chart.

Write each of the decimals on a place-value chart. Be sure to line up each place and the decimal point.

Ones		Tenths	Hundredths
1	.	0	6
1	.	2	8

The place-value position of the digit 8 in 1.28 is hundredths. The value of the digit 8 in 1.28 is 8 hundredths, or $8 \times \frac{1}{100}$ or 0.08.

You can also write 1.28 in word form and expanded form.

Word form: one and twenty-eight hundredths

Expanded form: $1 + 0.2 + 0.08$

Math Talk Mathematical Practices
Explain why 1.28 is not one and twenty-eight tenths in word form.

Try This! Use place value to read and write the decimal.

Standard Form: 3.46

Word Form: three and forty-six hundredths

Expanded Form: 3 + 0.4 + 0.06

Possible explanation: because the last digit is in the hundredths place, so it's one and twenty-eight hundredths, not tenths.

Getting Ready for Grade 5 GR15

GR: Practice, p. GRP7

Lesson 7

Name ____________

Decimals and Place Value

Read and write the decimal in two other forms.

1. 7.32 — seven and thirty-two hundredths; 7 + 0.3 + 0.02
2. two and six tenths — 2.6; 2 + 0.6
3. 20 + 5 + 0.8 + 0.01 — 25.81; twenty-five and eighty-one hundredths
4. 86.04 — eighty-six and four hundredths; 80 + 6 + 0.04

Write the value of the underlined digit.

5. 6.2<u>4</u> — 0.04
6. 3.<u>2</u> — 0.2
7. <u>9</u>.07 — 9
8. 0.4<u>8</u> — 0.08
9. <u>1</u>.65 — 1
10. 0.<u>9</u> — 0.9
11. 5.1<u>3</u> — 0.03
12. 10.<u>8</u>2 — 0.8

Problem Solving Real World

Use the table below for 13 and 14.

Three runners finished a foot race with the following times.

Foot Race Times

Runner	Time (in seconds)
Erika	15.46
Andre	14.89
Conner	15.08

13. Which runner finished the race with a time that has the digit 8 in the hundredths place? Conner
14. What is Erika's time written in expanded form? 10 + 5 + 0.4 + 0.06

Getting Ready for Grade 5 GRP7

GR: Reteach, p. GRR7

Lesson 7
Reteach

Name ____________

Decimals and Place Value

You can write decimals, like whole numbers, in standard form, word form, and expanded form.

In a place-value chart, whole numbers are to the left of the decimal point. Decimal amounts are to the right of the decimal point. The value of each place is one-tenth, or $\frac{1}{10}$, of the place to its left.

When you write a decimal in word form, write the decimal point as "and."

Write the decimal 12.34 in word form and expanded form.

Start by writing 12.34 in a place-value chart. First, align the decimal point with the decimal in the chart. Then place the digits.

Hundreds	Tens	Ones	.	Tenths	Hundredths
	1	2	.	3	4
	1 × 10	2 × 1	.	$3 \times \frac{1}{10}$	$4 \times \frac{1}{100}$
	10	2	.	$\frac{3}{10}$	$\frac{4}{100}$

Word form: 12.34 ← Two decimals indicate hundredths.

Twelve and thirty-four hundredths

Expanded Form: Use the last row of the chart to help you write the decimal in expanded form.

12.34 = 10 + 2 + 0.3 + 0.04

Read and write the decimal in two other forms.

1. eight and seven tenths — 8.7; 8 + 0.7
2. 10 + 3 + 0.9 + 0.05 — 13.95; thirteen and ninety-five hundredths

Reteach GRR7 Grade 4

*GR – Getting Ready Lessons and Resources (*www.thinkcentral.com*)

Share and Show

1. Write the decimal 4.06 in word form and expanded form.

Word Form: four and six hundredths

Expanded Form: 4 + 0.06

Read and write the decimal in two other forms.

2. five and two tenths
5.2; 5 + 0.2

3. 6 + 0.8 + 0.09
6.89; six and eighty-nine hundredths

On Your Own

Read and write the decimal in two other forms.

4. seven and three hundredths:
7.03; 7 + 0.03

5. 2 + 0.3 + 0.01
2.31; two and thirty-one hundredths

Write the value of the underlined digit.

6. 4.56 0.5

7. 5.09 0.09

8. 7.4 7

9. 1.32 0.3

Problem Solving

10. James is 1.63 meters tall. Write James's height in word form. **Explain** how you found your answer.
One and sixty-three hundredths; Possible explanation: I wrote the ones place first, and since the last number is in the hundredths place, there are sixty-three hundredths.

11. Ani was told to write the number four and eight hundredths. She wrote 4.8. **Explain** whether or not you think Ani is correct. If you think she is not correct, write the number correctly.
Possible explanation: no, she wrote the 8 in the wrong place value. The number should be 4.08.

2 PRACTICE

Share and Show • Guided Practice

For Exercise 1, help students see that since there is a zero in the tenths place, there are no tenths in either the word or expanded form of 4.06. However, the 6 in the hundredths place indicates that there are *six hundredths* in these forms of the number.

On Your Own • Independent Practice

If students have difficulty with Exercises 6–9, refer them to the place-value chart on page GR15. Have them identify the value of each digit in the given numbers. So, for Exercise 6, the value of the 4 is 4 ones or 4, the value of the 5 is 5 tenths, and the value of the 6 is 6 hundredths.

Problem Solving

UNLOCK THE PROBLEM Exercise 11 illustrates the importance of identifying the place value of each digit in a number. The 8 is supposed to be in the hundredths place, but Ani wrote it in the tenths place. There are no tenths in the number, so she should have written a zero in the tenths place.

3 SUMMARIZE

Common Core MATHEMATICAL PRACTICES

Essential Question

How can you use place value to read, write, and represent decimals? Possible answer: find the place value of each digit in a number using a place-value chart. Use the place values to read, write, and represent the numbers.

Math Journal

WRITE Math

Choose a number with a decimal in the hundredths. Show how to write the number in standard form, word form, and expanded form.

LESSON 8

Round Decimals

LESSON AT A GLANCE

Common Core Standards

Generalize place value understanding for multi-digit whole numbers.
4.NBT.A.3 Use place value understanding to round multi-digit whole numbers to any place.

Understand the place value system.
5.NBT.A.4 Use place value understanding to round decimals to any place.

Lesson Objective

Round decimal amounts, including money amounts, to the nearest whole number or dollar.

Materials

MathBoard

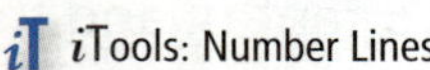

Unlock the Problem

MATHEMATICAL PRACTICES

Have students read the problem and discuss how they know a rounded answer is needed.

- **Explain how you find the two whole number benchmarks 1.35 is between.** Possible answer: I know 1.35 is greater than 1 and less than 2, so it is between the benchmarks 1 and 2.
- **How do you know 1.35 rounds to 1?** Possible answer: the point for 1.35 is between 1 and 2. The distance from 1.35 to 1 is less than the distance from 1.35 to 2, so 1.35 rounds to 1.

For Exercise 1, invite students to share their strategies with the class.

For Exercise 2, discuss with students why they can use what they know about rounding decimal amounts to rounding money amounts.

Use **Math Talk** to focus on students' understanding of lesson concepts.

This lesson builds on rounding whole numbers presented in Chapter 1 and prepares students for rounding decimals in Grade 5.

Name ____________

Round Decimals

Essential Question How can you round decimal amounts, including amounts of money, to the nearest whole number or dollar?

Unlock the Problem Real World

Ami sells fruits and nuts at an outdoor market. She sold a bag of nuts that weighed 1.35 pounds. About how much did the bag of nuts weigh, rounded to the nearest whole number?

- Underline the information that you need to find.

You know that you can use a number line or place value to round whole numbers. You can use the same strategies to round decimals.

Use a number line.

To round a decimal to the nearest whole number, find the whole numbers it is between.

1 < 1.35 < 2

Use a number line to see which whole number 1.35 is closer to.

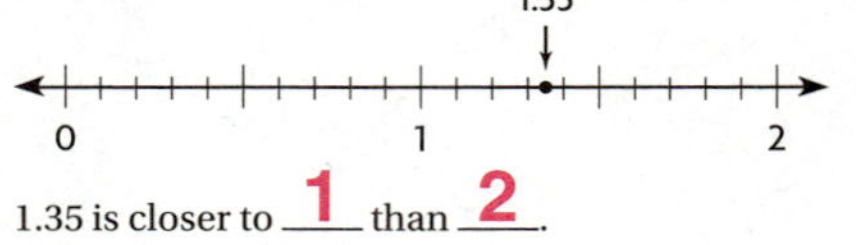

1.35 is closer to 1 than 2.

So, the bag of nuts weighed about 1 pound.

In both cases, I find two numbers the given number is between. Then I use a number line to find which of the two numbers the given number is closer to.

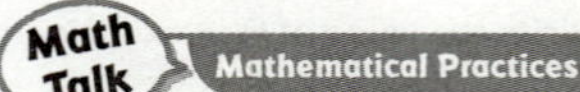

Explain how rounding decimals is like rounding whole numbers.

1. **What if** Ami sold a bag of nuts that weighed 2.82 pounds? About how much does the bag weigh, rounded to the nearest whole number?
about 3 pounds

2. **Describe** how you would round $3.90 to the nearest whole dollar.
$3.90 is between $3 and $4. On a number line I can see that $3.90 is closer to $4 than to $3. So, $3.90 rounded to the nearest dollar is $4.

Getting Ready for Grade 5 GR17

GR: Practice, p. GRP8

Lesson 8

Name ____________

Round Decimals

Round to the nearest dollar or to the nearest whole number.

1. $3.18 — $3	2. 4.7 — 5	3. $7.02 — $7	4. 8.55 — 9
5. $1.89 — $2	6. 0.2 — 0	7. $0.75 — $1	8. 9.09 — 9
9. $9.51 — $10	10. 1.01 — 1	11. $8.49 — $8	12. 6.35 — 6
13. $0.85 — $1	14. 5.9 — 6	15. $1.05 — $1	16. 4.5 — 5
17. $4.15 — $4	18. 3.65 — 4	19. $1.99 — $2	20. 5.52 — 6

Problem Solving Real World

21. Camden spends $18.25 at the driving range. How much money did Camden spend, rounded to the nearest dollar?
$18

22. Jolie bought 3.75 pounds of turkey at the deli. About how many pounds of turkey did Jolie buy?
4 pounds

© Houghton Mifflin Harcourt Publishing Company

Getting Ready for Grade 5 GRP8

GR: Reteach, p. GRR8

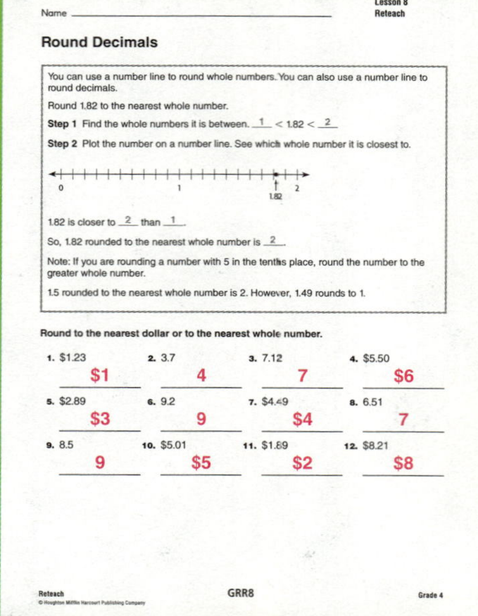

Lesson 8 Reteach

Name ____________

Round Decimals

You can use a number line to round whole numbers. You can also use a number line to round decimals.

Round 1.82 to the nearest whole number.

Step 1 Find the whole numbers it is between. 1 < 1.82 < 2

Step 2 Plot the number on a number line. See which whole number it is closest to.

0 1 1.82 2

1.82 is closer to 2 than 1.

So, 1.82 rounded to the nearest whole number is 2.

Note: If you are rounding a number with 5 in the tenths place, round the number to the greater whole number.

1.5 rounded to the nearest whole number is 2. However, 1.49 rounds to 1.

Round to the nearest dollar or to the nearest whole number.

1. $1.23 — $1	2. 3.7 — 4	3. 7.12 — 7	4. $5.50 — $6
5. $2.89 — $3	6. 9.2 — 9	7. $4.49 — $4	8. 6.51 — 7
9. 8.5 — 9	10. $5.01 — $5	11. $1.89 — $2	12. $8.21 — $8

Reteach © Houghton Mifflin Harcourt Publishing Company GRR8 Grade 4

*GR – Getting Ready Lessons and Resources (*www.thinkcentral.com*)

Share and Show

1. Round $2.67 to the nearest dollar. Locate and mark $2.67 on the number line. Which whole dollar is it closest to? **$3**

Round to the nearest dollar or to the nearest whole number.

2. $0.78 **$1**	3. 2.1 **2**	4. 3.5 **4**	5. $4.50 **$5**

On Your Own

Round to the nearest dollar or to the nearest whole number.

6. $1.70 **$2**	7. 2.2 **2**	8. $3.99 **$4**	9. 3.45 **3**
10. $1.53 **$2**	11. 0.9 **1**	12. $0.19 **$0**	13. 4.38 **4**

Problem Solving Real World

14. Candice spent $13.55 at the arts and crafts fair. How much money did Candice spend, rounded to the nearest dollar? **$14**

15. Mr. Marsh bought 2.25 pounds of American cheese. About how many pounds of cheese did Mr. Marsh buy? **2 pounds**

2 PRACTICE

▶ Share and Show • Guided Practice

Use Exercise 1 to check students' understanding of lesson concepts. Discuss with students why their answer will be a whole number dollar amount.

▶ On Your Own • Independent Practice

For Exercises 6–13, ask students to correctly place each amount on a number line before rounding. Point out that number lines can be used to show either money or decimal amounts.

▶ Problem Solving Common Core MATHEMATICAL PRACTICES

UNLOCK THE PROBLEM In Exercise 15, be sure students understand that the word "about" suggests that they can find the answer by rounding to the nearest pound.

3 SUMMARIZE

Essential Question

How can you round decimal amounts, including amounts of money, to the nearest whole number or dollar? Possible answer: I can find and label the amount on a number line by finding which benchmarks the decimal or money amount is between. I can then compare to find which benchmark the decimal or money amount is closer to.

Math Journal

Describe how to use a number line to round 3.41 to the nearest whole number.

LESSON 9

Place Value to Compare Decimals

LESSON AT A GLANCE

Common Core Standards
Understand decimal notation for fractions, and compare decimal fractions.
4.NF.C.7 Compare two decimals to hundredths by reasoning about their size. Recognize that comparisons are valid only when the two decimals refer to the same whole. Record the results of comparisons with the symbols >, =, or <, and justify the conclusions, e.g., by using a visual model.

Understand the place value system.
5.NBT.A.3b Read, write, and compare decimals to thousandths. Compare two decimals to thousandths based on meanings of the digits in each place, using >, =, and < symbols to record the results of comparisons.

Lesson Objective
Compare decimals to hundredths using place value.

Materials
MathBoard

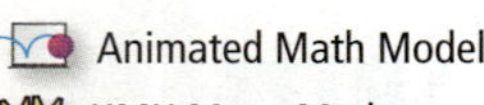
Animated Math Models
HMH Mega Math

1 TEACH and TALK

• Animated Math Models

▶ Unlock the Problem

MATHEMATICAL PRACTICES

Have students read the problem.

- **How do you read the number 0.16? How do you read the number 0.18?** sixteen hundredths; eighteen hundredths

Help students to see the importance of lining up the places when comparing decimals. Show the hummingbird weight and the nickel weight lined up incorrectly.

```
0. 1  6
   0. 1  8
```

- **A student said that since 1 is greater than the number below it, 0, and 6 is greater than the number below it, 1, then 0.16 is greater than 0.18. Was the student correct? Explain.** No. Possible answer: the student didn't line up the places correctly. As a result, the student compared digits in different places.

Use **Math Talk** to check students' understanding of using place value to compare decimals.

This lesson builds on comparing to hundredths presented in Chapter 9 and prepares students to compare decimals to thousandths taught in Grade 5.

Name ______

Place Value to Compare Decimals

Essential Question How can you use place value to compare decimals?

Unlock the Problem

Hummingbirds are small, fast, light birds that feed on flowers, trees, and insects. Suppose a particular hummingbird weighs 0.16 ounces. A nickel weighs about 0.18 ounces. Does the hummingbird weigh more or less than a nickel?

- What do you need to do to solve the problem? compare the weights
- Circle the numbers you need to compare.

Use a place-value chart.

Write each of the decimals on a place-value chart. Be sure to line up each place and the decimal point. Then compare the numbers in each place.

Ones		Tenths	Hundredths
0	.	1	6
0	.	1	8

0 = 0 1 = 1 6 < 8

Since 6 < 8, 0.16 < 0.18.

So, the hummingbird weighs less than a nickel.

Math Talk Mathematical Practices

Explain why you start comparing the decimals by comparing the ones place.

Possible explanation: I compare the ones place first because if the digits are different, then I can tell which decimal is greater or smaller. I work from left to right until I find a place with different digits.

Try This! Use a place-value chart to compare the decimals.

Write <, >, or =.

A. 1.32 < 1.34
B. 0.67 > 0.6
C. 0.99 = 0.99

Getting Ready for Grade 5 GR19

GR: Practice, p. GRP9

Name ______ Lesson 9

Place Value to Compare Decimals

Compare the decimals. Write <, >, or =.

1. 2.12 < 2.2
2. 2.6 < 2.64
3. 2.08 < 2.8
4. 2.73 < 2.77
5. 2.4 = 2.40
6. 2.89 > 2.876
7. 2.98 > 2.09
8. 2.57 < 2.75
9. 0.38 > 0.34
10. 46.2 = 46.20
11. 0.8 < 0.88
12. 25.09 < 25.48

Use a place-value chart to order the decimals from least to greatest.

13. 0.41, 0.49, 0.45 — 0.41, 0.45, 0.49
14. 8.95, 8.98, 8.9 — 8.9, 8.95, 8.98
15. 2.7, 2.77, 2.07 — 2.07, 2.7, 2.77
16. 1.23, 1.27, 1.25 — 1.23, 1.25, 1.27
17. 9.9, 9.99, 9.94 — 9.9, 9.94, 9.99
18. 3.4, 3.04, 3.44 — 3.04, 3.4, 3.44

Problem Solving Real World

19. Veronica drank 0.5 liter of water. Hector drank 0.3 liter of water. Who drank less water? Hector
20. Abby spent $6.36 on her lunch and Colby spent $6.63 on his lunch. Who spent less money on lunch—Abby or Colby? Abby

Getting Ready for Grade 5 GRP9

GR: Reteach, p. GRR9

Name ______ Lesson 9 Reteach

Place Value to Compare Decimals

You can use a place-value chart to help you compare decimals.

Use a place-value chart to compare the decimals. Write <, >, or =.

4.28 4.23

Step 1 Write both decimals in a place-value chart. Line up each place and the decimal.

Step 2 Compare the numbers in each place, starting with the numbers in the ones place and working your way right.

Ones	.	Tenths	Hundredths
4	.	2	8
4	.	2	3

4 = 4 2 = 2 8 > 3

Step 3 Since 8 is greater than 3, 4.28 is greater than 4.23.

So, 4.28 > 4.23.

1. Use the place-value chart below to compare the decimals. Write <, >, or =.

Ones	.	Tenths	Hundredths
8	.	9	2
8	.	9	7

8 = 8 9 = 9 2 < 7

So, 8.92 < 8.97.

Compare the decimals. Write <, >, or =.

2. 6.87 > 6.80
3. 9.17 < 9.19
4. 5.73 < 5.78
5. 1.23 > 1.22
6. 2.56 > 2.5
7. 3.7 = 3.70
8. 7.22 > 7.2
9. 4.4 > 4.04

Reteach GRR9 Grade 4

*GR – Getting Ready Lessons and Resources (*www.thinkcentral.com*)

Share and Show

1. Use the place-value chart below to compare the decimals. Write <, >, or =.

Ones		Tenths	Hundredths
3	.	0	5
3	.	0	1

3 = 3 0 = 0 5 (>) 1

So, 3.05 (>) 3.01.

Compare the decimals. Write <, >, =.

2. 7.24 (<) 7.42
3. 8.80 (<) 8.81
4. 0.11 (=) 0.11
5. 4.33 (>) 4.31

On Your Own

Compare the decimals. Write <, >, =.

6. 0.04 (=) 0.04
7. 1.1 (<) 1.7
8. 0.34 (<) 0.36
9. 4.04 (>) 4.01
10. 9.67 (>) 9.63
11. 1.4 (<) 1.42
12. 0.02 (<) 0.2
13. 5.4 (=) 5.40

Use a place-value chart to order the decimals from least to greatest.

14. 0.59, 0.51, 0.52 — 0.51, 0.52, 0.59
15. 7.15, 7.18, 7.1 — 7.1, 7.15, 7.18
16. 1.3, 1.33, 1.03 — 1.03, 1.3, 1.33

Problem Solving Real World

17. Jill, Ally, and Maria ran the 50-yard dash. Jill ran the race in 6.87 seconds. Ally ran the race in 6.82 seconds. Maria ran the race in 6.93. Who ran the race the fastest? **Explain** how you can use a place-value chart to find the answer.

Ally; Possible explanation: I used a place-value chart to line up the numbers. Then I compared each place.

GR20

2 PRACTICE

Share and Show • Guided Practice

For Exercise 1, be sure students understand why the numbers 3.05 and 3.01 are written in the chart as they are.

If students have difficulty with Exercises 2–5, have them compare digits left to right, reading them aloud. So, for Exercise 2, the student can say, "7 is equal to 7, 2 is less than 4," and stop there, having found the first place where the digits are not equal. Since 2 is less than 4, $7.24 < 7.42$.

On Your Own • Independent Practice

For Exercises 6–13, suggest that students use a place-value chart to compare the two numbers in each exercise.

Problem Solving MATHEMATICAL PRACTICES

UNLOCK THE PROBLEM For Exercise 17, be sure students understand that the runner who ran *fastest* was the one who completed the race in the *least* amount of time. Since $6.82 < 6.87 < 6.93$, the runner with a time of 6.82 ran the fastest race.

3 SUMMARIZE

MATHEMATICAL PRACTICES

Essential Question

How can you use place value to compare decimals? Possible answer: write the decimals in a place-value chart, being careful to line up the places correctly. Then compare the digits left to right.

Math Journal WRITE Math

Write two numbers between 2 and 3, writing each number to hundredths. Then explain how you can use place value to compare the decimals.

LESSON 10

Decompose Multiples of 10, 100, 1,000

LESSON AT A GLANCE

Common Core Standards

Gain familiarity with factors and multiples.
4.OA.B.4 Find all factor pairs for a whole number in the range 1–100. Recognize that a whole number is a multiple of each of its factors. Determine whether a given whole number in the range 1–100 is a multiple of a given one-digit number. Determine whether a given whole number in the range 1–100 is prime or composite.

Understand the place value system.
5.NBT.A.2 Explain patterns in the number of zeros of the product when multiplying a number by powers of 10, and explain patterns in the placement of the decimal point when a decimal is multiplied or divided by a power of 10. Use whole-number exponents to denote powers of 10.

Lesson Objective
Decompose multiples of 10, 100, and 1,000.

Materials
MathBoard

1 TEACH and TALK

Unlock the Problem

MATHEMATICAL PRACTICES

Have students read the problem. If they aren't sure what they are being asked to find, restate the question as, "What number must you multiply the height of the model by to produce the height of the building?"

One Way

- **What does the word "decompose" mean in the sentence "Decompose 1,200"?** Possible answer: express 1,200 as a product of its factors.

Help students write the unknown factor in each equation using mental math and a pattern.

- **Compare the total number of zeros in the factors to the number of zeros in the product 1,200.** Possible answer: for each equation, the total number of zeros in the factors is the same as the number of zeros in the product 1,200.
- **How can you decompose the following numbers: 90; 900; 9,000?** 9 × 10; 9 × 100; 9 × 1,000

Another Way

- **Decompose 120 using place value.** 120 = 12 tens = 12 × 10

Use **Math Talk** to check students' understanding of factors and multiples.

This lesson builds on relating factors and multiples presented in Chapters 2 and 5 and prepares students for multiplication patterns taught in Grade 5.

Name ____________

Decompose Multiples of 10, 100, 1,000

Essential Question How can you find factors of multiples of 10, 100, and 1,000?

Unlock the Problem

Architects make scale models of buildings before they build the real thing. The height of an actual building is going to be (1,200) feet. The scale model is (12) feet tall. How many times the height of the model is the height of the actual building?

- What do you need to find? factors of 1,200
- Circle the numbers you need to use to solve the problem.

You can decompose a multiple of 10, 100, or 1,000 by finding factors.

One Way Use mental math and a pattern.

Decompose 1,200.

1,200 = 1,200 × 1

1,200 = 120 × 10

1,200 = 12 × 100

So, the building is 100 times the height of the model.

Remember
A multiple of 10, 100, or 1,000 is a number that has a factor of 10, 100, or 1,000.

Another Way Use place value.

Decompose 1,200.

1,200 = 12 hundreds = 12 × 100

So, 1,200 = 12 × 100.

Math Talk Mathematical Practices
Explain the difference between factors and multiples.

Possible explanation: Factors are multiplied to get a product. A multiple is a product of factors.

- Explain how you use mental math and a pattern to find factors of multiples of 10, 100, or 1,000.

Possible explanation: I use mental math and a pattern to find a factor that when multiplied will result in a multiple with the correct place value.

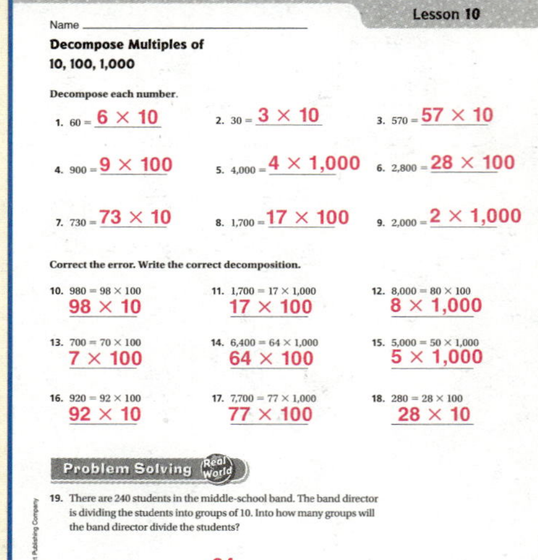
GR: Practice, p. GRP10

Name ____________ Lesson 10

Decompose Multiples of 10, 100, 1,000

Decompose each number.

1. 60 = 6 × 10
2. 30 = 3 × 10
3. 570 = 57 × 10
4. 900 = 9 × 100
5. 4,000 = 4 × 1,000
6. 2,800 = 28 × 100
7. 730 = 73 × 10
8. 1,700 = 17 × 100
9. 2,000 = 2 × 1,000

Correct the error. Write the correct decomposition.

10. 980 = 98 × 100 — 98 × 10
11. 1,700 = 17 × 1,000 — 17 × 100
12. 8,000 = 80 × 100 — 8 × 1,000
13. 700 = 70 × 100 — 7 × 100
14. 6,400 = 64 × 1,000 — 64 × 100
15. 5,000 = 50 × 1,000 — 5 × 1,000
16. 920 = 92 × 100 — 92 × 10
17. 7,700 = 77 × 1,000 — 77 × 100
18. 280 = 28 × 100 — 28 × 10

Problem Solving Real World

19. There are 240 students in the middle-school band. The band director is dividing the students into groups of 10. Into how many groups will the band director divide the students?

24

© Houghton Mifflin Harcourt Publishing Company

Getting Ready for Grade 5 GRP10

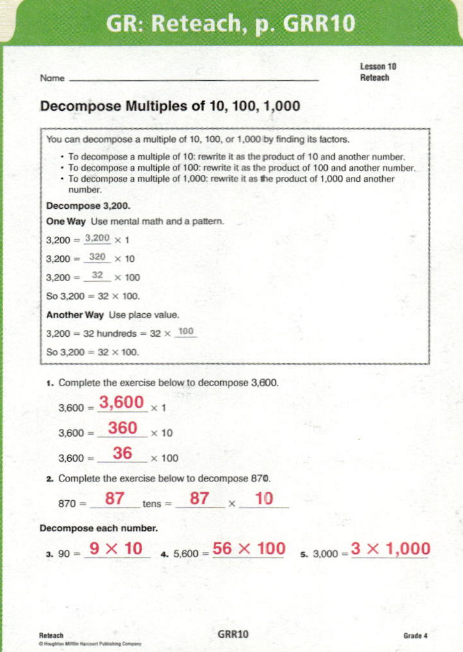
GR: Reteach, p. GRR10

Name ____________ Lesson 10 Reteach

Decompose Multiples of 10, 100, 1,000

You can decompose a multiple of 10, 100, or 1,000 by finding its factors.

- To decompose a multiple of 10: rewrite it as the product of 10 and another number.
- To decompose a multiple of 100: rewrite it as the product of 100 and another number.
- To decompose a multiple of 1,000: rewrite it as the product of 1,000 and another number.

Decompose 3,200.

One Way Use mental math and a pattern.

3,200 = 3,200 × 1
3,200 = 320 × 10
3,200 = 32 × 100
So 3,200 = 32 × 100.

Another Way Use place value.

3,200 = 32 hundreds = 32 × 100
So 3,200 = 32 × 100.

1. Complete the exercise below to decompose 3,600.
   3,600 = 3,600 × 1
   3,600 = 360 × 10
   3,600 = 36 × 100
2. Complete the exercise below to decompose 870.
   870 = 87 tens = 87 × 10

Decompose each number.

3. 90 = 9 × 10
4. 5,600 = 56 × 100
5. 3,000 = 3 × 1,000

Reteach GRR10 Grade 4
© Houghton Mifflin Harcourt Publishing Company

*GR – Getting Ready Lessons and Resources (*www.thinkcentral.com*)

Share and Show

1. Complete the exercise below to decompose 2,800.

   2,800 = **2,800** × 1

   2,800 = **280** × 10

   2,800 = **28** × 100

2. Complete the exercise below to decompose 930.

   930 = **93** tens = **93** × **10**

Decompose each number. Possible answers are given.

3. 80 = **8 × 10**
4. 320 = **32 × 10**
5. 8,000 = **8 × 1,000**

On Your Own

Decompose each number. Possible answers are given.

6. 90 = **9 × 10**
7. 40 = **4 × 10**
8. 890 = **89 × 10**
9. 300 = **3 × 100**
10. 7,000 = **7 × 1,000**
11. 3,700 = **37 × 100**

Correct the error. Write the correct decomposition. Possible answers are given.

12. 560 = 56 × 100 **56 × 10**
13. 4,300 = 43 × 1,000 **43 × 100**
14. 6,000 = 60 × 10 **6 × 1,000**

Problem Solving

15. Jon goes to the bank with $990. How many ten-dollar bills can he get? Show how you found your answer.

    99; Possible answer: 99 × 1 = 99; 99 × 10 = 990

GR22

2 PRACTICE

Share and Show • Guided Practice

For Exercise 1, help students use mental math and a pattern to find each unknown factor. Before starting, ask students to determine the total number of zeros that will be in the factors of each equation. For Exercise 3, students may wonder why the answer, 8 × 10, is not broken down further to 2 × 2 × 2 × 2 × 5. Assure them that doing so would not be wrong, but that in these exercises, they should look for just two factors, one of them a multiple of 10. A similar explanation applies to Exercises 4–5 as well.

On Your Own • Independent Practice

For Exercises 12–14, students can check their answers by confirming that there are the same number of zeros in their answers as there are in the numbers on the left side of the equations.

Problem Solving

UNLOCK THE PROBLEM Exercise 15 asks students to apply what they have learned to a real-world problem involving a multiple of 10, namely a $10 bill.

3 SUMMARIZE

Common Core MATHEMATICAL PRACTICES

Essential Question

How can you find factors of multiples of 10, 100, and 1,000? Possible answer: decompose the number using either mental math and a pattern or place value.

Math Journal WRITE Math

Decompose 5,900, where one factor is 10, 100, or 1,000. Explain your reasoning.

LESSON 11

Number Patterns

LESSON AT A GLANCE

Common Core Standards

Generate and analyze patterns.
4.OA.C.5 Generate a number or shape pattern that follows a given rule. Identify apparent features of the pattern that were not explicit in the rule itself.

Analyze patterns and relationships.
5.OA.B.3 Generate two numerical patterns using two given rules. Identify apparent relationships between corresponding terms. Form ordered pairs consisting of corresponding terms from the two patterns, and graph the ordered pairs on a coordinate plane.

Lesson Objective
Use multiplication to describe patterns.

Materials
MathBoard

Animated Math Models

1 TEACH and TALK

Animated Math Models

Unlock the Problem

MATHEMATICAL PRACTICES

Give students an opportunity to describe patterns they have seen, such as skip counting by 3s or reciting the first 5 even numbers.

Have students read the problem.

- **In Step 1, how do you know that "Multiply by 2" describes the sequence?** Possible answer: I can get from each term to the next one by multiplying by 2.
- **Give another pattern that you can describe with the rule "Multiply by 2."** Possible answer: 5, 10, 20, 40

Be sure students understand that a rule describes a pattern only if it gives a method for getting from each number in the pattern to the next number.

- **Blythe said that "Multiply by 3" describes the pattern 2, 6, 10, 14. Was she right?** No. Possible answer: it is true that you can get from 2 to 6 by multiplying by 3. But the rule fails after that. 6×3 is not equal to 10, and 10×3 is not equal to 14.

Use **Math Talk** to check students' understanding of finding rules to describe sequences.

This lesson builds on creating number patterns presented in Chapter 5 and prepares students for describing and continuing number patterns taught in Grade 5.

Name ____________

Number Patterns

Essential Question How can you use multiplication to describe a pattern?

Unlock the Problem

You know how to use a rule and a first term to write a sequence. Now, you will describe a sequence using a rule.

Describe a pattern.

A scientist counts the number of lily pads in a pond each day. She records the number of lily pads in the table below. How many lily pads will be in the pond on days 5 and 6?

Day	1	2	3	4
Lilly Pads	8	16	32	64

- Do the numbers in the sequence increase or decrease? increase
- Underline the information you need to find.

STEP 1 Describe the sequence.

THINK: How do I get from one term to the next?

Try multiplying by 2 since $8 \times 2 = 16$.

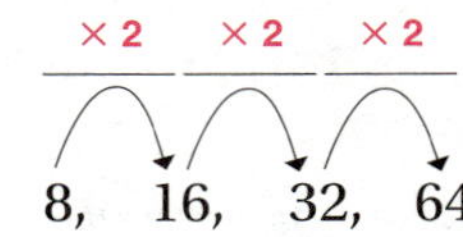

Write a rule to describe the number of lily pads in the pond.

RULE: Multiply by 2.

STEP 2 Find the next two terms in the sequence.

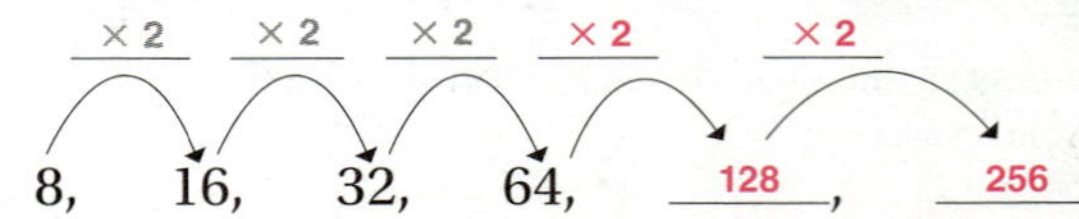

So, there will be 128 lily pads on day 5 and 256 lily pads on day 6.

Possible explanation: I can add 8 to 8 to get 16, but if I add 8 to 16, I get 24. Since the next number in the pattern is 32, adding 8 isn't the rule.

Math Talk Mathematical Practices

Explain how you know the rule isn't add 8.

Getting Ready for Grade 5 GR23

GR: Practice, p. GRP11

Name ____________ Lesson 11

Number Patterns

Describe the pattern. Then find the next two numbers in the pattern.

1. 4, 12, 36, 108, 324, 972 Multiply by 3.
2. 14, 28, 56, 112, 224, 448 Multiply by 2.
3. 2, 8, 32, 128, 512, 2,048 Multiply by 4.
4. 1, 5, 25, 125, 625, 3,125 Multiply by 5.

Determine the pattern and use it to fill in the blanks.

5. 1, 6, 36, 216, 1,296
6. 2, 6, 18, 54, 162
7. 3, 12, 48, 192, 768
8. 4, 12, 36, 108, 324
9. 1, 2, 4, 8, 16
10. 5, 20, 80, 320, 1,280

Problem Solving Real World

11. Pippen works at an aquarium. Each month, she counts the number of fish in one of the aquariums. She records the total number of fish in the table below. If the pattern continues, how many fish will be in the aquarium in Months 6 and 7?

Month	1	2	3	4	5
Number of Fish	4	8	16	32	64

128 in Month 6; 256 in Month 7

Getting Ready for Grade 5 GRP11

GR: Reteach, p. GRR11

Name ____________ Lesson 11 Reteach

Number Patterns

You already know how to use a rule and the first term to write a sequence. Now you will use multiplication to describe a pattern.

Stephen is saving his money to buy a car. The table shows how much money he has saved at the end of each month. If the pattern continues, how much money will Stephen have saved after months 5 and 6?

Number of Months	1	2	3	4
Total Amount Saved ($)	15	30	60	120

Step 1 Describe the sequence.

Think: How do I get from one term to the next?

Try multiplying by 2, since $15 \times 2 = 30$.

× 2 × 2 × 2
15, 30, 60, 120

Step 2 Write a rule that describes how much money Stephen has saved at the end of each month.

Rule: Multiply by 2.

Step 3 Use the rule to find the next two terms in the sequence.

× 2 × 2 × 2 × 2 × 2
15, 30, 60, 120 240, 480

So, at the end of month 5, Stephen will have saved $240.
At the end of month 6, have will have saved $480.

Describe the pattern. Then find the next two numbers in the pattern.

1. 2, 10, 50, 250, 1,250 Multiply by 5.
2. 2, 6, 18, 54, 162 Multiply by 3.

Reteach GRR11 Grade 4

*GR – Getting Ready Lessons and Resources (*www.thinkcentral.com*)

Share and Show

1. Find the next two numbers in the pattern below.

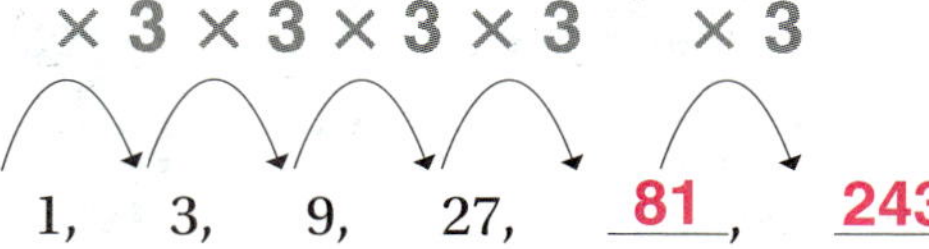

Describe the pattern. Then find the next two numbers in the pattern.

2. 1, 2, 4, 8, **16**, **32**
Multiply by 2.

3. 7, 14, 28, 56, **112**, **224**
Multiply by 2.

On Your Own

Describe the pattern. Then find the next two numbers in the pattern.

4. 1, 4, 16, 64, **256**, **1,024**
Multiply by 4.

5. 2, 6, 18, 54, **162**, **486**
Multiply by 3.

Determine the pattern and use it to fill in the blanks.

6. 1, 5, 25, **125**, 625

7. 3, 6, **12**, 24, **48**

8. 2, **8**, 32, **128**, 512

Problem Solving

9. A clothing store starts selling a new type of sneaker. The table shows the number of pairs of sneakers sold in the first four weeks. If the pattern continues, how many pairs of sneakers will the store sell in weeks 5 and 6? **Explain.**

Week	1	2	3	4
Pairs Sold	5	10	20	40

80 pairs in week 5 and 160 pairs in week 6; possible explanation: I used the pattern multiply by 2.

Getting Ready Lessons and Resources, pp. GR25–GR26

Checkpoint

Name ______________

Checkpoint

Concepts and Skills

Round to the nearest whole dollar or to the nearest whole number.

1. $7.23 **$7**
2. 2.89 **3**
3. 0.52 **1**
4. $9.49 **$9**

Compare the decimals. Write <, >, or =.

5. 0.6 (=) 0.60
6. 5.08 (<) 5.80
7. 8.14 (<) 8.17
8. 7.37 (>) 7.32

Read and write the numbers in two other forms.

9. seventy-five million, three hundred thousand, two hundred seven
75,300,207; 70,000,000 + 5,000,000 + 300,000 + 200 + 7

10. 30,000,000 + 40,000 + 6,000 + 20 + 2
30,046,022; thirty million, forty-six thousand, twenty-two

Decompose each number.

11. 20 = **2 × 10**
12. 740 = **74 × 10**
13. 6,000 = **6 × 1,000**

Problem Solving

14. A new music website is keeping track of the number of members that join. The table shows the number of members in the first four days. If the pattern continues, how many members will the website have on day 6? **Explain** how you found your answer.

Day	1	2	3	4
Members	5	15	45	135

1,215; I used the pattern "multiply by 3" to find the number of members on day 6.

15. A particular female Asian elephant weighs 4.63 tons. What is this decimal written in word form?
(A) four and sixty-three tenths
(B) four and sixty-three hundredths
(C) four hundred and sixty-three
(D) four and sixty-three thousandths

16. Joe, Adam, Michael, and Carl all work at an office. Joe earns $15.53 per hour. Adam earns $15.59 per hour. Carl earns $15.95 per hour. Michael earns $15.91. Who earns the most money per hour?
(A) Joe
(B) Adam
(C) Carl
(D) Michael

17. Which number is ninety-eight million, forty thousand, six hundred fifty three written in another form?
(A) 98,040,653
(B) 98,400,653
(C) 98,046,053
(D) 98,40,653

18. Which rule describes the pattern below?
3, 12, 48, 192
(A) Multiply by 2.
(B) Multiply by 3.
(C) Add 9.
(D) Multiply by 4.

2 PRACTICE

Share and Show • Guided Practice

As students begin Exercises 1–3, stress that the rule they find must allow them to get from each number in the sequence to the next number.

On Your Own • Independent Practice

To solve Exercise 8, students may have to try several possible rules. To help them get started, you might ask if "Multiply by 2" is the rule. Help them to see that it cannot be the rule, because $2 \times 2 = 4$ and $4 \times 2 = 8$. So, for the rule "Multiply by 2," the third term in the sequence is 8, not 32. Encourage them to try other possible rules until they find the one that allows them to get from each term in the sequence to the next term.

Problem Solving

Common Core MATHEMATICAL PRACTICES

UNLOCK THE PROBLEM Exercise 9 asks students to apply what they have learned to a real-world problem. They should try possible rules until they find the correct one, "Multiply by 2," then use it to find the fifth and sixth terms of the sequence.

3 SUMMARIZE

Essential Question

How can you use multiplication to describe a pattern? Possible answer: I look for a factor that allows me to get from each term in the sequence to the next term. The pattern is to multiply by the factor that I find.

Math Journal

WRITE Math

Find the next term in the sequence 3, 12, 48, 192. Explain how you found the term.

Getting Ready for Grade 5 Test

Lessons 1 to 11

Summative Assessment

Use the **Getting Ready Test** to assess students' progress in Getting Ready for Grade 5 Lessons 1–11.

Getting Ready Tests are provided in multiple-choice and mixed-response format in the *Getting Ready Lessons and Resources.*

Getting Ready Test is available online.

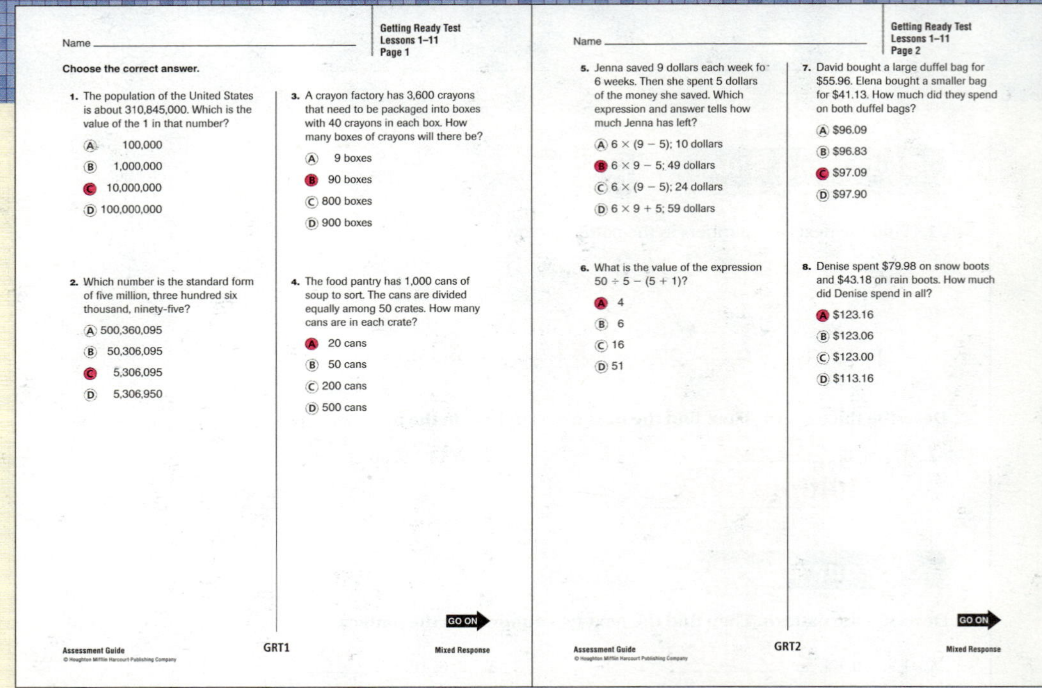

Name ____________ Getting Ready Test Lessons 1–11 Page 1

Choose the correct answer.

1. The population of the United States is about 310,845,000. Which is the value of the 1 in that number?
   - (A) 100,000
   - (B) 1,000,000
   - (C) 10,000,000
   - (D) 100,000,000

2. Which number is the standard form of five million, three hundred six thousand, ninety-five?
   - (A) 500,360,095
   - (B) 50,306,095
   - (C) 5,306,095
   - (D) 5,306,950

3. A crayon factory has 3,600 crayons that need to be packaged into boxes with 40 crayons in each box. How many boxes of crayons will there be?
   - (A) 9 boxes
   - (B) 90 boxes
   - (C) 800 boxes
   - (D) 900 boxes

4. The food pantry has 1,000 cans of soup to sort. The cans are divided equally among 50 crates. How many cans are in each crate?
   - (A) 20 cans
   - (B) 50 cans
   - (C) 200 cans
   - (D) 500 cans

GO ON

Assessment Guide © Houghton Mifflin Harcourt Publishing Company GRT1 Mixed Response

Name ____________ Getting Ready Test Lessons 1–11 Page 2

5. Jenna saved 9 dollars each week for 6 weeks. Then she spent 5 dollars of the money she saved. Which expression and answer tells how much Jenna has left?
   - (A) 6 × (9 − 5); 10 dollars
   - (B) 6 × 9 − 5; 49 dollars
   - (C) 6 × (9 − 5); 24 dollars
   - (D) 6 × 9 + 5; 59 dollars

6. What is the value of the expression 50 ÷ 5 − (5 + 1)?
   - (A) 4
   - (B) 6
   - (C) 16
   - (D) 51

7. David bought a large duffel bag for $55.96. Elena bought a smaller bag for $41.13. How much did they spend on both duffel bags?
   - (A) $96.09
   - (B) $96.83
   - (C) $97.09
   - (D) $97.90

8. Denise spent $79.98 on snow boots and $43.18 on rain boots. How much did Denise spend in all?
   - (A) $123.16
   - (B) $123.06
   - (C) $123.00
   - (D) $113.16

GO ON

Assessment Guide © Houghton Mifflin Harcourt Publishing Company GRT2 Mixed Response

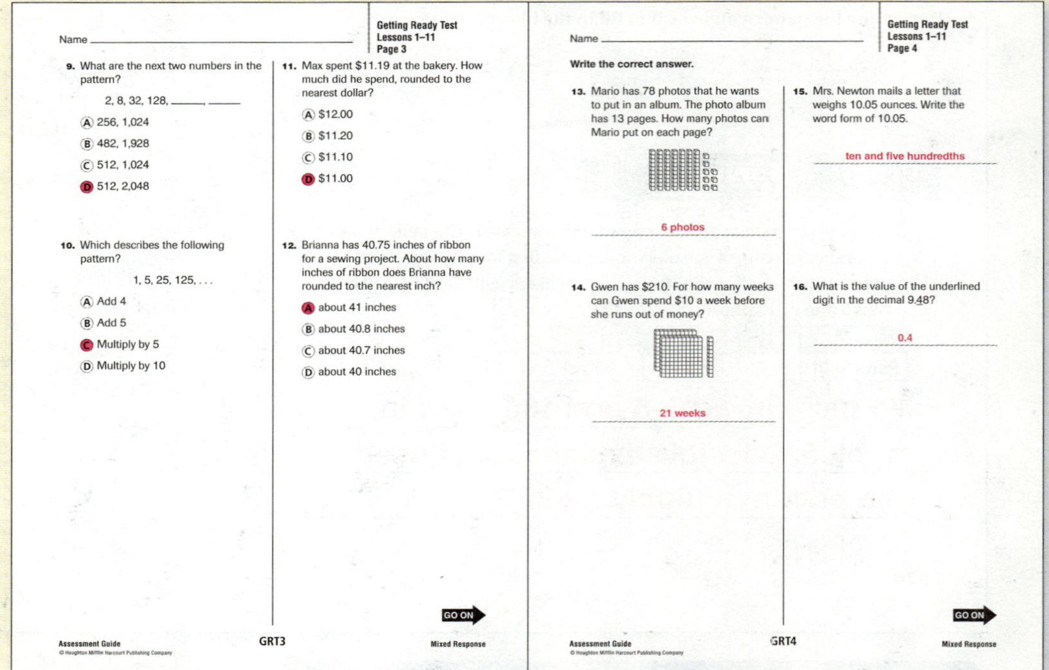

Name ____________ Getting Ready Test Lessons 1–11 Page 3

9. What are the next two numbers in the pattern?

   2, 8, 32, 128, ____, ____
   - (A) 256, 1,024
   - (B) 482, 1,928
   - (C) 512, 1,024
   - (D) 512, 2,048

10. Which describes the following pattern?

    1, 5, 25, 125, . . .
    - (A) Add 4
    - (B) Add 5
    - (C) Multiply by 5
    - (D) Multiply by 10

11. Max spent $11.19 at the bakery. How much did he spend, rounded to the nearest dollar?
    - (A) $12.00
    - (B) $11.20
    - (C) $11.10
    - (D) $11.00

12. Brianna has 40.75 inches of ribbon for a sewing project. About how many inches of ribbon does Brianna have rounded to the nearest inch?
    - (A) about 41 inches
    - (B) about 40.8 inches
    - (C) about 40.7 inches
    - (D) about 40 inches

GO ON

Assessment Guide © Houghton Mifflin Harcourt Publishing Company GRT3 Mixed Response

Name ____________ Getting Ready Test Lessons 1–11 Page 4

Write the correct answer.

13. Mario has 78 photos that he wants to put in an album. The photo album has 13 pages. How many photos can Mario put on each page?

    6 photos

14. Gwen has $210. For how many weeks can Gwen spend $10 a week before she runs out of money?

    21 weeks

15. Mrs. Newton mails a letter that weighs 10.05 ounces. Write the word form of 10.05.

    ten and five hundredths

16. What is the value of the underlined digit in the decimal 9.48?

    0.4

GO ON

Assessment Guide © Houghton Mifflin Harcourt Publishing Company GRT4 Mixed Response

Data-Driven Decision Making RtI

Item	Lesson	Common Error	Intervene With
1, 2	6	May not understand the place value of numbers to ten millions	**R**—GRR6
3, 4	4	May not understand how to use patterns to divide by multiples of ten	**R**—GRR4
5, 6, 23	3	May not understand how to use the order of operations to find the value of expressions	**R**—GRR3
7, 8	1	May not understand how to find sums of decimal amounts in dollars and cents	**R**—GRR1
9, 10	11	May not understand how to use multiplication to describe a pattern	**R**—GRR11
11, 12	8	May be unable to round decimals, including amounts of money, to the nearest whole number or dollar	**R**—GRR8

Key: R—Getting Ready Lessons and Resources: Reteach

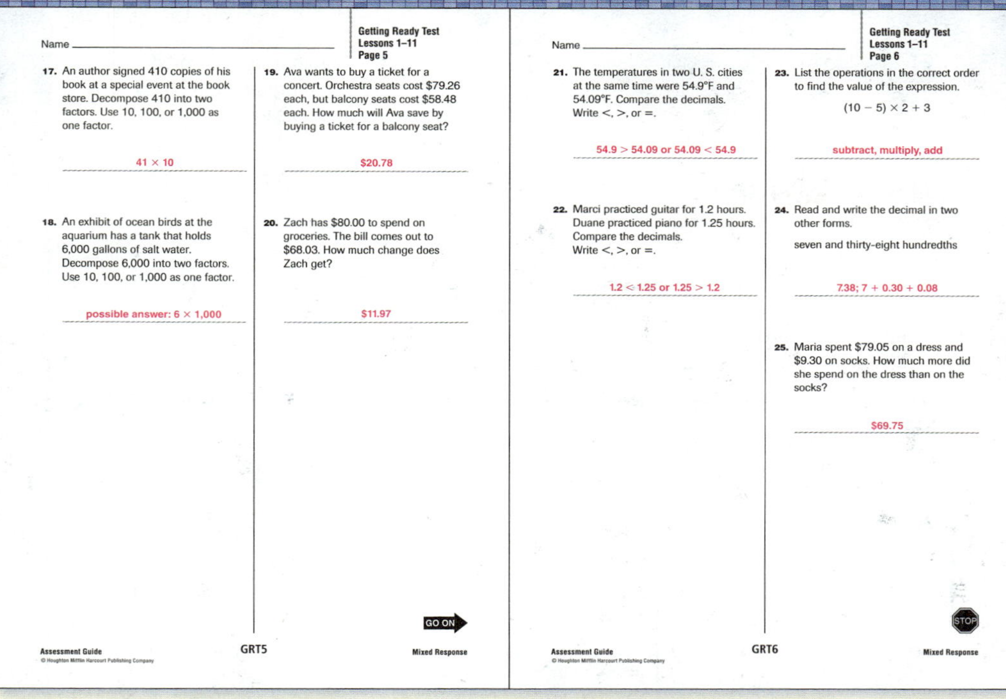

Name ______

Getting Ready Test
Lessons 1–11
Page 5

17. An author signed 410 copies of his book at a special event at the book store. Decompose 410 into two factors. Use 10, 100, or 1,000 as one factor.

41×10

18. An exhibit of ocean birds at the aquarium has a tank that holds 6,000 gallons of salt water. Decompose 6,000 into two factors. Use 10, 100, or 1,000 as one factor.

possible answer: $6 \times 1{,}000$

19. Ava wants to buy a ticket for a concert. Orchestra seats cost $79.26 each, but balcony seats cost $58.48 each. How much will Ava save by buying a ticket for a balcony seat?

$20.78

20. Zach has $80.00 to spend on groceries. The bill comes out to $68.03. How much change does Zach get?

$11.97

GO ON

Assessment Guide
© Houghton Mifflin Harcourt Publishing Company
GRT5
Mixed Response

Name ______

Getting Ready Test
Lessons 1–11
Page 6

21. The temperatures in two U. S. cities at the same time were 54.9°F and 54.09°F. Compare the decimals. Write <, >, or =.

$54.9 > 54.09$ or $54.09 < 54.9$

22. Marci practiced guitar for 1.2 hours. Duane practiced piano for 1.25 hours. Compare the decimals. Write <, >, or =.

$1.2 < 1.25$ or $1.25 > 1.2$

23. List the operations in the correct order to find the value of the expression.

$(10 - 5) \times 2 + 3$

subtract, multiply, add

24. Read and write the decimal in two other forms.

seven and thirty-eight hundredths

7.38; $7 + 0.30 + 0.08$

25. Maria spent $79.05 on a dress and $9.30 on socks. How much more did she spend on the dress than on the socks?

$69.75

STOP

Assessment Guide
© Houghton Mifflin Harcourt Publishing Company
GRT6
Mixed Response

Portfolio Suggestions The portfolio represents the growth, talents, achievements, and reflections of the mathematics learner. Students might spend a short time selecting work samples for their portfolios.

You may want to have students respond to the following questions:

- What new understanding of math have I developed in the past several weeks?
- What growth in understanding or skills can I see in my work?
- What can I do to improve my understanding of math ideas?
- What would I like to learn more about?

For information about how to organize, share, and evaluate portfolios, see the *Chapter Resources*.

Data-Driven Decision Making

Item	Lesson	Common Error	Intervene With
13, 14	5	May not understand how to use models to divide	R—GRR5
15, 16, 24	7	May not understand how to use place value to read, write, and represent decimals	R—GRR7
17, 18	10	May not be able to find the factors of multiples of 10, 100, and 1,000	R—GRR10
19, 20, 25	2	May not understand how to find differences of decimal amounts in dollars and cents	R—GRR2
21, 22	9	May not understand how to use place value to compare decimals	R—GRR9

Key: R—Getting Ready Lessons and Resources: Reteach

GETTING READY FOR GRADE 5

LESSON 12

Add Related Fractions

LESSON AT A GLANCE

Common Core Standards

Build fractions from unit fractions by applying and extending previous understandings of operations on whole numbers.

4.NF.B.3d Understand a fraction a/b with $a > 1$ as a sum of fractions $1/b$. Solve word problems involving addition and subtraction of fractions referring to the same whole and having like denominators, e.g., by using visual fraction models and equations to represent the problem.

Use equivalent fractions as a strategy to add and subtract fractions.

5.NF.A.2 Solve word problems involving addition and subtraction of fractions referring to the same whole, including cases of unlike denominators, e.g., by using visual fraction models or equations to represent the problem. Use benchmark fractions and number sense of fractions to estimate mentally and assess the reasonableness of answers.

Lesson Objective

Add fractions when one denominator is a multiple of the other.

Materials

MathBoard, Fraction Strips (see *eTeacher Resources*)

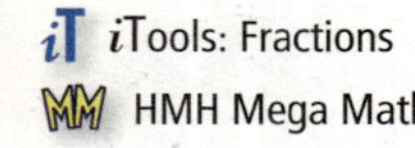

*i*Tools: Fractions

HMH Mega Math

1 TEACH and TALK

• *i*Tools

Activity MATHEMATICAL PRACTICES

Invite students to read and discuss the first paragraph. Then distribute the fraction strips and have students model the problem as shown in Step 1. Discuss Step 2.

- **Why do you need to show $\frac{1}{2}$ using $\frac{1}{6}$ strips?**
  Possible answer: I need to add equal-size pieces. I can show $\frac{1}{2}$ using $\frac{1}{6}$ pieces. Then I can find how many $\frac{1}{6}$ pieces there are in all.

Direct students' attention to Step 3.

- **Describe how you add the fractions.**
  Possible answer: add the numerators: $3 + 2 = 5$; keep the denominator the same: 6.

Have students discuss the sizes of the $\frac{1}{2}$ and the $\frac{1}{6}$ pieces and the relationship between the denominators of the fractions. They should notice that the $\frac{1}{2}$ piece is three times the size of the $\frac{1}{6}$ piece, and the $\frac{1}{6}$ piece is one third the size of the $\frac{1}{2}$ piece. Guide students to see that 6 is a multiple of 2.

This lesson builds on adding fractions with like denominators presented in Chapter 7 and prepares students for adding fractions with unlike denominators taught in Grade 5.

Name ______________________

Add Related Fractions

Essential Question How can you add fractions when one denominator is a multiple of the other?

When you add fractions, you find how many equal-size pieces there are in all. The denominator shows the size of the pieces. To add fractions with denominators that are not the same, first find equivalent fractions with the same denominator.

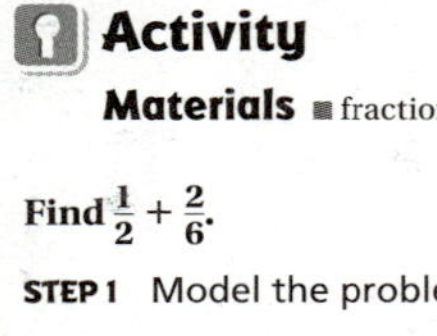

Activity

Materials ■ fraction strips

Find $\frac{1}{2} + \frac{2}{6}$.

STEP 1 Model the problem.

Think: To add fractions, you need to count equal size pieces. The $\frac{1}{2}$ strip and the $\frac{1}{6}$ strip are different sizes.

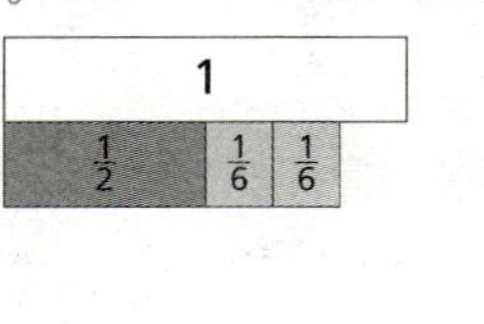

STEP 2 Show $\frac{1}{2}$ using $\frac{1}{6}$ strips.

$\frac{1}{2} = \frac{3}{6}$

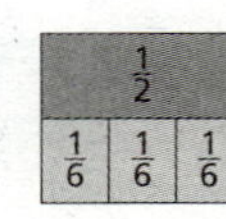

STEP 3 Add. Use the equivalent fraction you found.

Find $\frac{3}{6} + \frac{2}{6}$.

How many $\frac{1}{6}$ strips are there? 5

Write the sum. $\frac{3}{6} + \frac{2}{6} = \frac{5}{6}$

So, $\frac{1}{2} + \frac{2}{6} = \frac{5}{6}$.

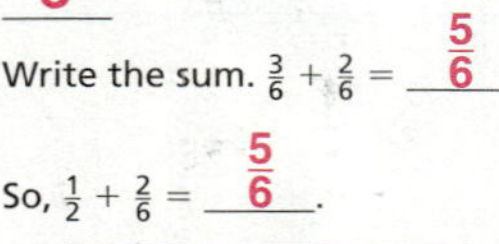

- **Describe** how the sizes of the $\frac{1}{2}$ strip and the $\frac{1}{6}$ strip compare. Then describe how the denominators of the fractions $\frac{1}{2}$ and $\frac{1}{6}$ are related.

Possible explanation: the $\frac{1}{2}$ strip is three times the size of the $\frac{1}{6}$ strip. The denominator 6 is three times the denominator 2.

Possible explanation: one $\frac{1}{2}$ strip is the same length as three $\frac{1}{6}$ strips.

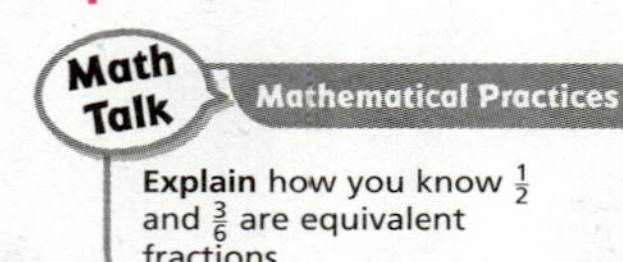

Explain how you know $\frac{1}{2}$ and $\frac{3}{6}$ are equivalent fractions.

GR: Practice, p. GRP12

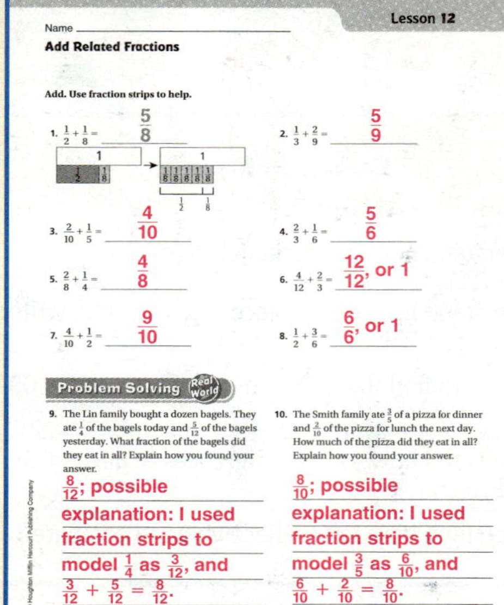

Lesson 12

Name ______________________

Add Related Fractions

Add. Use fraction strips to help.

1. $\frac{1}{2} + \frac{1}{8} = \frac{5}{8}$
2. $\frac{1}{3} + \frac{2}{9} = \frac{5}{9}$
3. $\frac{2}{10} + \frac{1}{5} = \frac{4}{10}$
4. $\frac{2}{3} + \frac{1}{6} = \frac{5}{6}$
5. $\frac{2}{8} + \frac{1}{4} = \frac{4}{8}$
6. $\frac{4}{12} + \frac{2}{3} = \frac{12}{12}$, or 1
7. $\frac{4}{10} + \frac{1}{2} = \frac{9}{10}$
8. $\frac{1}{2} + \frac{3}{6} = \frac{6}{6}$, or 1

Problem Solving Real World

9. The Lin family bought a dozen bagels. They ate $\frac{1}{4}$ of the bagels today and $\frac{5}{12}$ of the bagels yesterday. What fraction of the bagels did they eat in all? Explain how you found your answer.
   $\frac{8}{12}$; possible explanation: I used fraction strips to model $\frac{1}{4}$ as $\frac{3}{12}$, and $\frac{3}{12} + \frac{5}{12} = \frac{8}{12}$.
10. The Smith family ate $\frac{3}{5}$ of a pizza for dinner and $\frac{2}{10}$ of the pizza for lunch the next day. How much of the pizza did they eat in all? Explain how you found your answer.
   $\frac{8}{10}$; possible explanation: I used fraction strips to model $\frac{3}{5}$ as $\frac{6}{10}$, and $\frac{6}{10} + \frac{2}{10} = \frac{8}{10}$.

© Houghton Mifflin Harcourt Publishing Company

Getting Ready for Grade 5 GRP12

GR: Reteach, p. GRR12

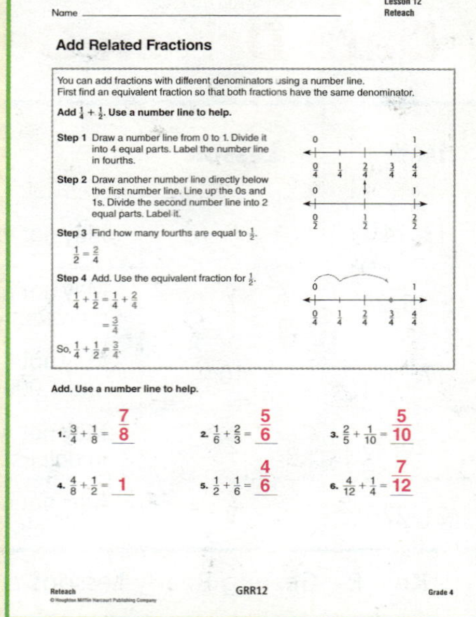

Lesson 12 Reteach

Name ______________________

Add Related Fractions

You can add fractions with different denominators using a number line. First find an equivalent fraction so that both fractions have the same denominator.

Add $\frac{1}{4} + \frac{1}{2}$. Use a number line to help.

Step 1 Draw a number line from 0 to 1. Divide it into 4 equal parts. Label the number line in fourths.

Step 2 Draw another number line directly below the first number line. Line up the 0s and 1s. Divide the second number line into 2 equal parts. Label it.

Step 3 Find how many fourths are equal to $\frac{1}{2}$.

$\frac{1}{2} = \frac{2}{4}$

Step 4 Add. Use the equivalent fraction for $\frac{1}{2}$.

$\frac{1}{4} + \frac{1}{2} = \frac{1}{4} + \frac{2}{4}$

$= \frac{3}{4}$

So, $\frac{1}{4} + \frac{1}{2} = \frac{3}{4}$.

Add. Use a number line to help.

1. $\frac{3}{4} + \frac{1}{8} = \frac{7}{8}$
2. $\frac{1}{6} + \frac{2}{3} = \frac{5}{6}$
3. $\frac{2}{5} + \frac{1}{10} = \frac{5}{10}$
4. $\frac{4}{8} + \frac{1}{2} = 1$
5. $\frac{1}{2} + \frac{1}{6} = \frac{4}{6}$
6. $\frac{4}{12} + \frac{1}{4} = \frac{7}{12}$

Reteach © Houghton Mifflin Harcourt Publishing Company GRR12 Grade 4

*GR – Getting Ready Lessons and Resources (*www.thinkcentral.com*)

Share and Show

1. **Explain** which fraction strips you could use to add $\frac{1}{3}$ and $\frac{3}{6}$.

Possible explanation: $\frac{1}{6}$ strips because the $\frac{1}{3}$ strip and the $\frac{1}{6}$ strip are different sizes. I need to show $\frac{1}{3}$ using $\frac{1}{6}$ strips and then add.

2. Use fraction strips to add $\frac{1}{4} + \frac{2}{8}$.

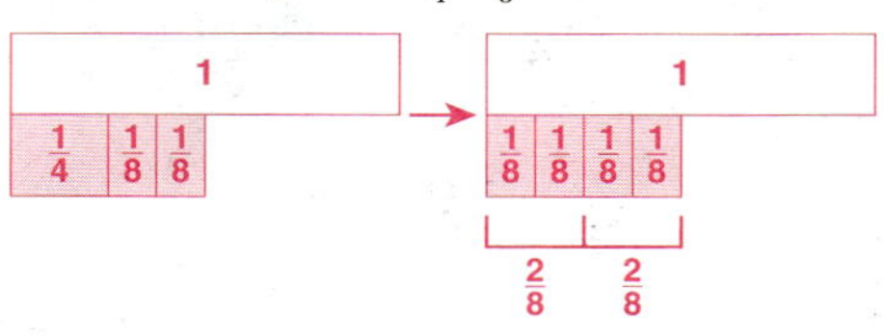

$\frac{1}{4} + \frac{2}{8} = \frac{4}{8}$

Add. Use fraction strips to help.

3. $\frac{1}{4} + \frac{1}{2} = \frac{3}{4}$

4. $\frac{1}{2} + \frac{3}{8} = \frac{7}{8}$

5. $\frac{1}{2} + \frac{3}{10} = \frac{8}{10}$

On Your Own

Add. Use fraction strips to help.

6. $\frac{1}{3} + \frac{2}{6} = \frac{4}{6}$

7. $\frac{1}{5} + \frac{3}{10} = \frac{5}{10}$

8. $\frac{3}{8} + \frac{1}{4} = \frac{5}{8}$

9. $\frac{5}{12} + \frac{1}{3} = \frac{9}{12}$

10. $\frac{1}{3} + \frac{8}{12} = \frac{12}{12}$ or 1

11. $\frac{8}{10} + \frac{1}{5} = \frac{10}{10}$ or 1

Problem Solving

12. Paola used $\frac{1}{4}$ of a carton of eggs today and $\frac{4}{12}$ of the carton yesterday. What fraction of the carton of eggs did she use in all? **Explain** how you found your answer.

$\frac{7}{12}$; Possible explanation: I used fraction strips to model $\frac{1}{4}$ as $\frac{3}{12}$. Then I added $\frac{3}{12}$ to $\frac{4}{12}$ to get $\frac{7}{12}$.

GR28

Use **Math Talk** to check students' understanding of why $\frac{1}{2}$ and $\frac{3}{6}$ are equivalent fractions.

2 PRACTICE

Share and Show • Guided Practice

Use Exercises 1–5 to check students' understanding of lesson concepts. For Exercise 1, elicit from students that the $\frac{1}{3}$ piece and the $\frac{1}{6}$ piece are different sizes. They must find an equivalent fraction to add equal-size pieces. In Exercise 2, make sure students correctly use the fraction strips to rename $\frac{1}{4}$ as $\frac{2}{8}$.

On Your Own • Independent Practice

For Exercises 6–11, have students who need extra support rewrite the addition exercises using the equivalent fractions.

Problem Solving

UNLOCK THE PROBLEM For Exercise 12, students have to find equivalent fractions to add $\frac{1}{4}$ and $\frac{4}{12}$. Have students check their work to be sure they are adding fractions with the same denominator and that they are not adding the denominators.

3 SUMMARIZE

Common Core MATHEMATICAL PRACTICES

Essential Question

How can you add fractions when one denominator is a multiple of the other? Possible answer: I can use fraction strips to find an equivalent fraction so both fractions have the same denominator. Then I add the numerators. The denominator stays the same.

Math Journal

WRITE Math

Draw a diagram that shows how to add $\frac{1}{10}$ and $\frac{1}{2}$ using fraction strips. Explain each step.

GETTING READY FOR GRADE 5

LESSON 13

Subtract Related Fractions

LESSON AT A GLANCE

Common Core Standards

Build fractions from unit fractions by applying and extending previous understandings of operations on whole numbers.

4.NF.B.3d Understand a fraction a/b with $a > 1$ as a sum of fraction $1/b$. Solve word problems involving addition and subtraction of fractions referring to the same whole and having like denominators, e.g., by using visual fraction models and equations to represent the problem.

Use equivalent fractions as a strategy to add and subtract fractions.

5.NF.A.2 Solve word problems involving addition and subtraction of fractions referring to the same whole, including cases of unlike denominators, e.g., by using visual fraction models or equations to represent the problem. Use benchmark fractions and number sense of fractions to estimate mentally and assess the reasonableness of answers.

Lesson Objective

Subtract fractions when one denominator is a multiple of the other.

Materials

MathBoard, Fraction Strips (see *eTeacher Resources*)

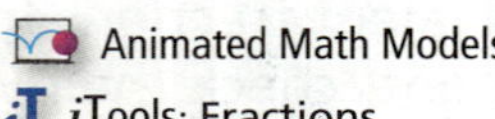
Animated Math Models

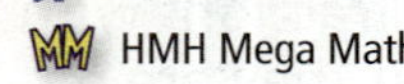
*i*Tools: Fractions

HMH Mega Math

1 TEACH and TALK

Animated Math Models

Activity

MATHEMATICAL PRACTICES

Read and discuss the first paragraph with students.

One Way

Distribute the fraction strips. Have students model the problem.

- **Why do you need to show $\frac{1}{4}$ using $\frac{1}{8}$ strips?** Possible answer: I need to subtract equal-size pieces. Both fractions can be shown using $\frac{1}{8}$ pieces.
- **Describe how you subtract the fractions.** Possible answer: subtract the numerators: $5 - 2 = 3$; keep the denominator the same: 8.

Another Way

Guide students through the example.

- **Explain how you compared the $\frac{1}{4}$ piece to the five $\frac{1}{8}$ pieces.** Possible answer: $\frac{1}{4}$ is equivalent to $\frac{2}{8}$. There are three more eighths in $\frac{5}{8}$ than in $\frac{1}{4}$.

This lesson builds on subtracting fractions with like denominators presented in Chapter 7 and prepares students for subtracting fractions with unlike denominators taught in Grade 5.

Name ______________________

Subtract Related Fractions

Essential Question How can you subtract fractions when one denominator is a multiple of the other?

When you subtract fractions, you must use equal-size pieces. To subtract fractions with different denominators, first find equivalent fractions with the same denominator. You can also compare to find the difference.

Activity

Materials ■ fraction strips

Find $\frac{5}{8} - \frac{1}{4}$.

One Way Find an equivalent fraction.

Model the problem.

Think: You need to subtract $\frac{1}{4}$ from $\frac{5}{8}$, but the $\frac{1}{4}$ strip and the $\frac{1}{8}$ strips are different sizes.

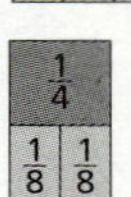

Show $\frac{1}{4}$ using $\frac{1}{8}$ strips.

$\frac{1}{4} = \frac{2}{8}$

Subtract. Use the equivalent fraction you found.

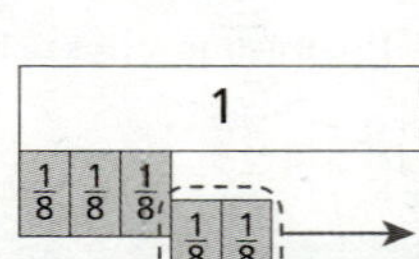

Find $\frac{5}{8} - \frac{2}{8}$.

Write the difference. $\frac{5}{8} - \frac{2}{8} = \frac{3}{8}$

So, $\frac{5}{8} - \frac{1}{4} = \frac{3}{8}$

Another Way Compare to find the difference.

Model the problem.

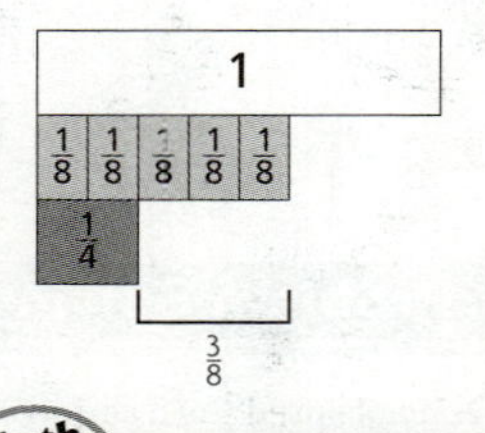

Think: The $\frac{1}{4}$ strip is the same size as two $\frac{1}{8}$ strips.

Compare the $\frac{1}{4}$ strip to the five $\frac{1}{8}$ strips. Find the difference.

$\frac{5}{8} - \frac{1}{4} = \frac{3}{8}$.

Math Talk Mathematical Practices

Explain how the $\frac{1}{4}$ strip is related to the $\frac{1}{8}$ strip. Then describe how the denominators 4 and 8 are related.

Possible explanation: the $\frac{1}{4}$ strip is equivalent to two $\frac{1}{8}$ strips. The denominator 8 is 2 times the denominator 4.

Getting Ready for Grade 5 GR29

GR: Practice, p. GRP13

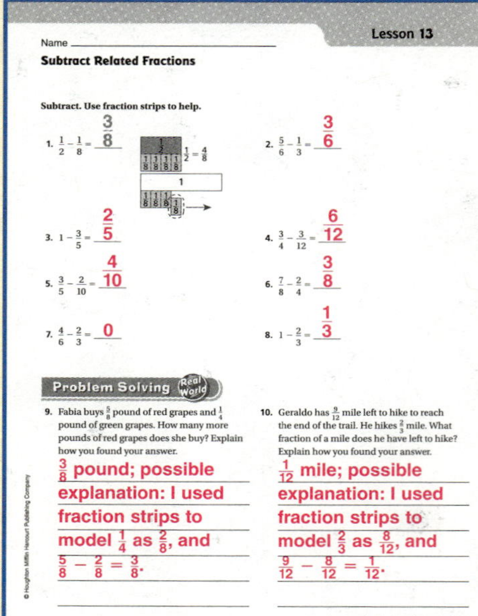

Lesson 13

Name ______________________

Subtract Related Fractions

Subtract. Use fraction strips to help.

1. $\frac{1}{2} - \frac{1}{8} = \frac{3}{8}$ ($\frac{1}{2} = \frac{4}{8}$)
2. $\frac{5}{6} - \frac{1}{3} = \frac{3}{6}$
3. $1 - \frac{3}{5} = \frac{2}{5}$
4. $\frac{3}{4} - \frac{3}{12} = \frac{6}{12}$
5. $\frac{3}{5} - \frac{2}{10} = \frac{4}{10}$
6. $\frac{7}{8} - \frac{2}{4} = \frac{3}{8}$
7. $\frac{4}{6} - \frac{2}{3} = 0$
8. $1 - \frac{2}{3} = \frac{1}{3}$

Problem Solving Real World

9. Fabia buys $\frac{5}{8}$ pound of red grapes and $\frac{1}{4}$ pound of green grapes. How many more pounds of red grapes does she buy? Explain how you found your answer.
$\frac{3}{8}$ pound; possible explanation: I used fraction strips to model $\frac{1}{4}$ as $\frac{2}{8}$, and $\frac{5}{8} - \frac{2}{8} = \frac{3}{8}$.

10. Geraldo has $\frac{9}{12}$ mile left to hike to reach the end of the trail. He hikes $\frac{2}{3}$ mile. What fraction of a mile does he have left to hike? Explain how you found your answer.
$\frac{1}{12}$ mile; possible explanation: I used fraction strips to model $\frac{2}{3}$ as $\frac{8}{12}$, and $\frac{9}{12} - \frac{8}{12} = \frac{1}{12}$.

Getting Ready for Grade 5 GRP13

GR: Reteach, p. GRR13

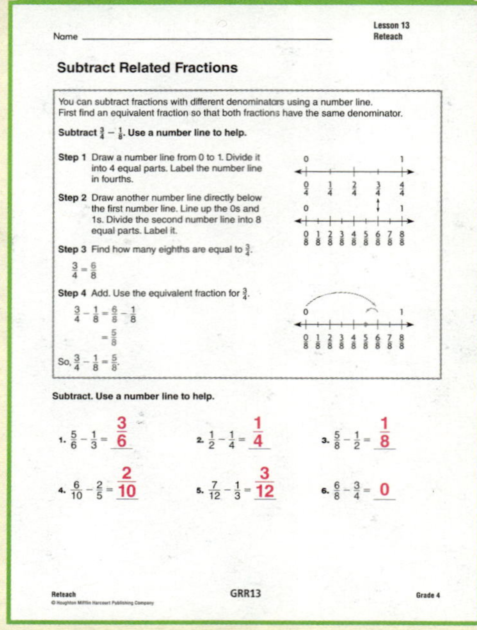

Lesson 13 Reteach

Name ______________________

Subtract Related Fractions

You can subtract fractions with different denominators using a number line. First find an equivalent fraction so that both fractions have the same denominator.

Subtract $\frac{3}{4} - \frac{1}{8}$. Use a number line to help.

Step 1 Draw a number line from 0 to 1. Divide it into 4 equal parts. Label the number line in fourths.

Step 2 Draw another number line directly below the first number line. Line up the 0s and 1s. Divide the second number line into 8 equal parts. Label it.

Step 3 Find how many eighths are equal to $\frac{3}{4}$.

$\frac{3}{4} = \frac{6}{8}$

Step 4 Add. Use the equivalent fraction for $\frac{3}{4}$.

$\frac{3}{4} - \frac{1}{8} = \frac{6}{8} - \frac{1}{8}$

$= \frac{5}{8}$

So, $\frac{3}{4} - \frac{1}{8} = \frac{5}{8}$.

Subtract. Use a number line to help.

1. $\frac{5}{6} - \frac{1}{3} = \frac{3}{6}$
2. $\frac{1}{2} - \frac{1}{4} = \frac{1}{4}$
3. $\frac{5}{8} - \frac{1}{2} = \frac{1}{8}$
4. $\frac{6}{10} - \frac{2}{5} = \frac{2}{10}$
5. $\frac{7}{12} - \frac{1}{3} = \frac{3}{12}$
6. $\frac{6}{8} - \frac{3}{4} = 0$

Reteach GRR13 Grade 4

*GR – Getting Ready Lessons and Resources (*www.thinkcentral.com*)

Share and Show 

1. A student subtracted $\frac{2}{3}$ from 1 whole as shown at the right. Explain the student's method. Then find the difference.
Possible explanation: the student knows that 1 whole is equivalent to $\frac{3}{3}$. He compared $\frac{3}{3}$ to $\frac{2}{3}$ to find the difference of $\frac{1}{3}$.

2. Use fraction strips to subtract $\frac{5}{6} - \frac{1}{2}$.

$\frac{5}{6} - \frac{1}{2} = \frac{2}{6}$

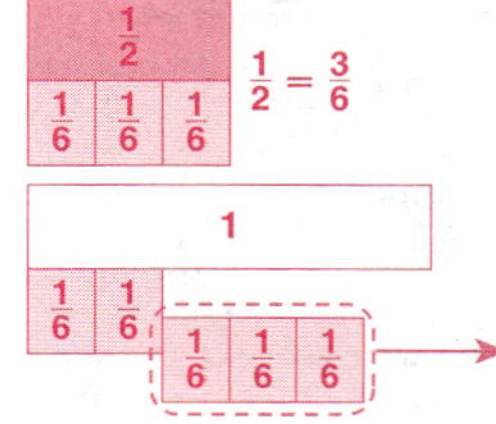

Subtract. Use fraction strips to help.

3. $\frac{1}{2} - \frac{3}{8} = \frac{1}{8}$
4. $1 - \frac{2}{5} = \frac{3}{5}$
5. $\frac{2}{4} - \frac{2}{12} = \frac{4}{12}$

On Your Own

Subtract. Use fraction strips to help.

6. $\frac{4}{5} - \frac{2}{10} = \frac{6}{10}$
7. $\frac{7}{8} - \frac{3}{4} = \frac{1}{8}$
8. $\frac{5}{6} - \frac{2}{3} = \frac{1}{6}$
9. $\frac{7}{10} - \frac{2}{5} = \frac{3}{10}$
10. $\frac{2}{6} - \frac{1}{3} = 0$
11. $\frac{6}{8} - \frac{1}{2} = \frac{2}{8}$

Problem Solving 

12. Boris had $\frac{2}{3}$ of a book left to read. He read $\frac{1}{6}$ of the book today. What fraction of the book does he have left to read now? Explain how you found your answer.
$\frac{3}{6}$; Possible explanation: I used fraction strips to model $\frac{2}{3}$ as $\frac{4}{6}$. Then I took $\frac{1}{6}$ away, which left $\frac{3}{6}$.

GR30

2 PRACTICE 

Share and Show • Guided Practice

Use Exercises 1–5 to check students' understanding of lesson concepts. For Exercise 1, students should identify that the comparison method is being used to solve the problem. In Exercise 2, make sure students are able to use the fraction strips to rename $\frac{1}{2}$ as $\frac{3}{6}$.

On Your Own • Independent Practice

For Exercises 6–11, encourage students to try both solution methods shown in the learning model.

Problem Solving

Common Core MATHEMATICAL PRACTICES

UNLOCK THE PROBLEM For Exercise 12, have students look for important words to help them determine what operation to use to solve the problem.

3 SUMMARIZE

Common Core MATHEMATICAL PRACTICES

Essential Question

How can you subtract fractions when one denominator is a multiple of the other? Possible answer: I can use fraction strips to find an equivalent fraction so both fractions have the same denominator. Then I subtract the numerators. The denominator stays the same. I can also compare with fraction strips to find the difference.

Math Journal WRITE Math

Describe how you would use fraction strips to compare $\frac{1}{10}$ and 1 to find the difference.

LESSON 14

Compare Fraction Products

LESSON AT A GLANCE

Common Core Standards

Build fractions from unit fractions by applying and extending previous understandings of operations on whole numbers.

4.NF.B.4c Apply and extend previous understandings of multiplication to multiply a fraction by a whole number. Solve word problems involving multiplication of a fraction by a whole number, e.g., by using visual fraction models and equations to represent the problem.

Apply and extend previous understandings of multiplication and division to multiply and divide fractions.

5.NF.B.5b Interpret multiplication as scaling (resizing), by: Explaining why multiplying a given number by a fraction greater than 1 results in a product greater than the given number (recognizing multiplication by whole numbers greater than 1 as a familiar case); explaining why multiplying a given number by a fraction less than 1 results in a product smaller than the given number; and relating the principle of fraction equivalence $a/b = (n \times a)/(n \times b)$ to the effect of multiplying a/b by 1.

Lesson Objective

Compare the size of the product to the size of each factor when multiplying fractions in real-world situations.

Materials

MathBoard

1 TEACH and TALK

▶ Unlock the Problem

MATHEMATICAL PRACTICES

▶ One Way

Have students shade the models to represent each problem.

Complete the problems with students. They should make the generalization that when a fraction less than 1 is multiplied by a whole number, the product is greater than the fraction. Also, when a whole number is multiplied by a fraction less than 1, the product is less than the whole number.

- **Compare the model for Problem B to the model for Problem A.** Possible answer: they look the same, but the model in Problem A is showing 3 groups of $\frac{2}{3}$ and the model in Problem B is showing $\frac{2}{3}$ of 3 wholes.
- **How are the expressions you wrote for each problem alike and how are they different?** Possible answer: alike: the factors in both expressions are the same. Different: the factors are ordered differently.

This lesson builds on multiplying fractions by whole numbers presented in Chapter 8 and prepares students for multiplying fractions and mixed numbers taught in Grade 5.

Name ____________

Compare Fraction Products

Essential Question How does the size of the product compare to the size of each factor when multiplying fractions in real-world situations?

Unlock the Problem Real World

One Way Use a model.

A. Serena uses $\frac{2}{3}$ yard of fabric to make a pillow. How much fabric does she need to make 3 pillows?

- Shade the model to show 3 groups of $\frac{2}{3}$.
- Write an expression for three groups of $\frac{2}{3}$: 3 × $\frac{2}{3}$.
- What can you say about the product when $\frac{2}{3}$ is multiplied by a whole number? Write *greater than* or *less than*. The product is greater than $\frac{2}{3}$.

B. Serena has 3 yards of fabric. She uses $\frac{2}{3}$ of it to make a blanket. How much fabric does she use to make the blanket?

- There are 3 wholes. Each represents one yard.
- Shade $\frac{2}{3}$ of each whole.
- Write an expression for $\frac{2}{3}$ of three wholes: $\frac{2}{3}$ × 3
- What can you say about the product when 3 is multiplied by a fraction less than 1? Write *greater than* or *less than*. The product is less than 3.

Another Way Use a number line.

A. Show $\frac{2}{3} \times 2$.

0 1 2 3 4

B. Show $\frac{2}{3} \times 3$.

0 1 2 3 4

Complete each statement with *greater than* or *less than*.

- The product of $\frac{2}{3}$ and 2 is greater than $\frac{2}{3}$.
- The product of a whole number greater than 1 and $\frac{2}{3}$ will be less than the whole number factor.

Math Talk Mathematical Practices

What if a different fraction was multiplied by 2 and 3? Would your statements still be true? **Explain.**

Yes; Possible explanation: Several groups of $\frac{2}{3}$ is greater than $\frac{2}{3}$. A whole number times a fraction means part of the whole number.

Getting Ready for Grade 5 GR31

GR: Practice, p. GRP14

Name ____________ Lesson 14

Compare Fraction Products

Complete each statement with *greater than* or *less than*.

1. $\frac{2}{4} \times 3$ will be less than 3.
   0 1 2 3
2. $\frac{3}{8} \times 2$ will be greater than $\frac{3}{8}$.
3. $4 \times \frac{5}{6}$ will be greater than $\frac{5}{6}$.
4. $2 \times \frac{1}{4}$ will be less than 2.
5. $3 \times \frac{4}{9}$ will be greater than $\frac{4}{9}$.
6. $\frac{7}{10} \times 2$ will be greater than $\frac{7}{10}$.
7. $3 \times \frac{3}{5}$ will be less than 3.
8. $5 \times \frac{2}{3}$ will be greater than $\frac{2}{3}$.

Problem Solving Real World

9. Jen is making 3 loaves of banana bread. She needs $\frac{3}{4}$ cup sugar for each loaf. Will she need more or less than 3 cups of sugar to make all 3 loaves? Explain.
   Less than 3 cups; possible explanation: I know the product of $3 \times \frac{3}{4}$ will be less than 3.
10. Tafua exercises for $\frac{5}{6}$ hour every day. After 2 days, will Tafua have exercised for less than or more than $\frac{5}{6}$ hour? Explain.
    More than $\frac{5}{6}$ hour; possible explanation: a few groups of $\frac{5}{6}$ will be greater than $\frac{5}{6}$.

Getting Ready for Grade 5 GRP14

GR: Reteach, p. GRR14

Name ____________ Lesson 14 Reteach

Compare Fraction Products

When a fraction less than one is multiplied by a whole number, is the product less than or greater than the fraction?

Is the product of $\frac{3}{4} \times 2$ less than or greater than $\frac{3}{4}$?

Step 1 Show two groups of $\frac{3}{4}$.

The model shows $\frac{6}{4}$ shaded.

Step 2 Compare. The product $\frac{6}{4}$ is greater than $\frac{3}{4}$.

So, the product of $\frac{3}{4} \times 2$ is greater than $\frac{3}{4}$.

When a whole number is multiplied by a fraction less than one, is the product less than or greater than the whole number?

Is the product of $3 \times \frac{3}{5}$ less than or greater than 3?

Step 1 Show three groups of $\frac{3}{5}$.

The model shows $\frac{9}{5}$ shaded.

Step 2 Compare. The product $\frac{9}{5}$ is less than 3.

So, the product of $3 \times \frac{3}{5}$ is less than 3.

Complete each statement with *greater than* or *less than*.

1. $2 \times \frac{5}{6}$ will be greater than $\frac{5}{6}$.
2. $\frac{3}{8} \times 2$ will be less than 2.
3. $3 \times \frac{2}{5}$ will be less than 3.
4. $\frac{2}{3} \times 4$ will be greater than $\frac{2}{3}$.

Reteach GRR14 Grade 4

*GR – Getting Ready Lessons and Resources (*www.thinkcentral.com*)

Share and Show

1. Complete the statement with *greater than* or *less than*.

$2 \times \frac{3}{4}$ will be greater than $\frac{3}{4}$.

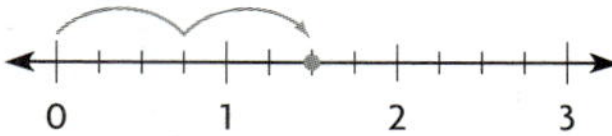

Complete each statement with *greater than* or *less than*.

2. $3 \times \frac{2}{5}$ will be less than 3.

3. $3 \times \frac{1}{3}$ will be greater than $\frac{1}{3}$

On Your Own

Complete each statement with *greater than* or *less than*.

4. $3 \times \frac{3}{8}$ will be greater than $\frac{3}{8}$.

5. $\frac{5}{6} \times 5$ will be greater than $\frac{5}{6}$.

6. $\frac{3}{10} \times 6$ will be greater than $\frac{3}{10}$.

7. $4 \times \frac{5}{9}$ will be less than 4.

Problem Solving

8. Celia wants to sew 4 pillows. She needs $\frac{3}{8}$ yard of fabric for each pillow. Will she need more than $\frac{3}{8}$ yard or less than $\frac{3}{8}$ yard of fabric to make all the pillows? Explain.

More; possible explanation: she will need more than one pillow's worth of fabric.

9. Rohan walks $\frac{3}{4}$ mile to school each day. After 5 days, will Rohan have walked more than 5 miles or less than 5 miles to school? Explain.

Less; possible explanation: $\frac{3}{4}$ is less than 1, so 5 amounts less than 1 is less than 5.

Another Way

Guide students through the examples.

- **How does the number line show that $\frac{2}{3} \times 3$ is less than 3?** Possible answer: 3 "hops" of $\frac{2}{3}$ on the number line is 2, which is less than 3.

Use Math Talk to focus on students' understanding of lesson concepts.

2 PRACTICE

Share and Show • Guided Practice

Use Exercises 1–3 to check students' understanding of lesson concepts. For Exercise 1, students should use the number line to show that the product of $2 \times \frac{3}{4}$ is greater than $\frac{3}{4}$.

On Your Own • Independent Practice

For Exercises 4–7, encourage students to use a model or a number line to help them complete each sentence.

Problem Solving

Common Core MATHEMATICAL PRACTICES

UNLOCK THE PROBLEM For Exercises 8 and 9, students have to compare the size of the product to the size of a factor in a real-world situation. Have students write a multiplication expression to help them answer each problem.

3 SUMMARIZE

Essential Question

How does the size of the product compare to the size of each factor when multiplying fractions in real-world situations? Possible answer: the product of a whole number greater than 1 and a fraction less than 1 will be greater than the fraction and less than the whole-number factor.

Math Journal

WRITE Math

Write a word problem that can be solved by comparing the size of a product and the size of a factor when multiplying a whole number and a fraction. Include the solution.

LESSON 15

Repeated Subtraction with Fractions

LESSON AT A GLANCE

Common Core Standards
Build fractions from unit fractions by applying and extending previous understandings of operations on whole numbers.
4.NF.B.3d Understand a fraction a/b with $a > 1$ as a sum of fractions $1/b$. Solve word problems involving addition and subtraction of fractions referring to the same whole and having like denominators, e.g., by using visual fraction models and equations to represent the problem.

Apply and extend previous understandings of multiplication and division to multiply and divide fractions.
5.NF.B.7b Apply and extend previous understandings of division to divide unit fractions by whole numbers and whole numbers by unit fractions. Interpret division of a whole number by a unit fraction, and compute such quotients.

Materials
MathBoard, Number Lines (see *eTeacher Resources*)

Lesson Objective
Use repeated subtraction to solve problems involving division with fractions.

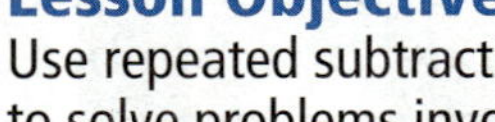

1 TEACH and TALK

Unlock the Problem

Read and discuss the problem.

- **Why can you use division to solve this problem?** Possible answer: I'm dividing a whole, 3 cups, into equal-size groups of $\frac{1}{2}$ cup, and I'm trying to find the number of equal-size groups.

Discuss how to use repeated subtraction on a number line to find the quotient.

- **How does the number line help you divide?** Possible answer: I can start with 3 and then make "hops" of $\frac{1}{2}$ until I reach 0 or get as close to it as possible. The number of "hops" is how many times I count back by $\frac{1}{2}$; it is the number of equal-size groups.
- **What does 3 represent in the division problem?** the dividend **What does $\frac{1}{2}$ represent?** the divisor

Use **Math Talk** to check students' understanding of what the number of groups of $\frac{1}{2}$ represents.

This lesson builds on dividing whole numbers presented in Chapter 4 and subtracting fractions with like denominators presented in Chapter 7 and prepares students for dividing fractions taught in Grade 5.

Name ______

Repeated Subtraction with Fractions

Essential Question How can you use repeated subtraction to solve problems involving division with fractions?

Unlock the Problem

Mr. Jones is making snacks for his family. He has 3 cups of almonds and is dividing them into $\frac{1}{2}$-cup portions. How many portions can he make?

You have used repeated subtraction to divide whole numbers. Now, you will use repeated subtraction to solve a problem involving division by a fraction.

- What do you need to find? the number of portions
- What other operation can you use instead of repeated subtraction to solve the problem? division

Use repeated subtraction to divide 3 by $\frac{1}{2}$.

STEP 1 Start at 3 and count back $\frac{1}{2}$.

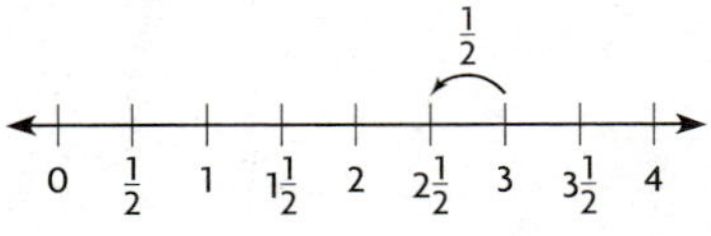

STEP 2 Subtract by $\frac{1}{2}$ until you reach 0 or get as close to it as possible.

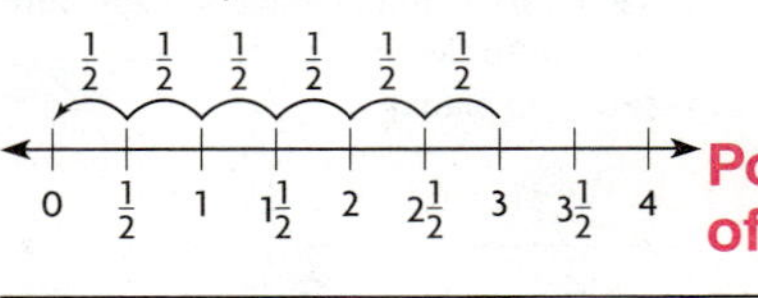

Math Talk Mathematical Practices
Explain why you count the number of groups of $\frac{1}{2}$.
Possible explanation: each group of $\frac{1}{2}$ represents one $\frac{1}{2}$-cup portion.

STEP 3 Find the number of times you counted back by $\frac{1}{2}$.

You counted 6 groups of $\frac{1}{2}$ to reach 0.

So, Mr. Jones can make 6 half-cup portions of almonds.

Getting Ready for Grade 5 GR33

GR: Practice, p. GRP15

Name ______ Lesson 15

Repeated Subtraction with Fractions

Use repeated subtraction to divide.

1. $1 \div \frac{1}{4}$ 4
2. $2 \div \frac{1}{8}$ 16
3. $4 \div \frac{1}{2}$ 8
4. $3 \div \frac{1}{3}$ 9
5. $3 \div \frac{1}{5}$ 15
6. $2 \div \frac{1}{6}$ 12
7. $6 \div \frac{1}{2}$ 12
8. $4 \div \frac{1}{4}$ 16

Problem Solving Real World

9. Harold has 4 cups of trail mix. He wants to give $\frac{1}{3}$ cup trail mix to each camper in his group. There are 8 campers in his group. Does he have enough trail mix for all the campers? Explain.
Yes; possible explanation: $4 \div \frac{1}{3} =$ 12; he has enough trail mix for 12 campers, which is more than 8.

10. Marita is cutting rolls of ribbon that are 3 feet long into $\frac{1}{2}$-foot pieces. She needs fifteen $\frac{1}{2}$-foot pieces for a project. She has 3 rolls of ribbon. Does she have enough to cut 15 pieces? Explain.
Yes; possible explanation: $3 \div \frac{1}{2} =$ 6; she has 3 rolls of ribbon, so she can cut 18 pieces. This is more than 15 pieces.

Getting Ready for Grade 5 GRP15

GR: Reteach, p. GRR15

Name ______ Lesson 15 Reteach

Repeated Subtraction with Fractions

You can use repeated subtraction to divide whole numbers.
You can also use repeated subtraction to divide a whole number by a fraction.

Use repeated subtraction to find $2 \div \frac{1}{4}$.

Step 1 Draw a number line from 0 to 2. Divide it into fourths.

Step 2 Start at 2. Count back by $\frac{1}{4}$ to subtract.

Step 3 Keep subtracting $\frac{1}{4}$ until you reach 0 or get as close to it as possible.

Step 4 Count the number of times you counted back by $\frac{1}{4}$. You counted back 8 groups of $\frac{1}{4}$.

So, $2 \div \frac{1}{4} = 8$.

Use repeated subtraction to divide.

1. $3 \div \frac{1}{2}$ 6
2. $2 \div \frac{1}{5}$ 10
3. $1 \div \frac{1}{4}$ 4
4. $4 \div \frac{1}{3}$ 12
5. $2 \div \frac{1}{6}$ 12
6. $2 \div \frac{1}{8}$ 16

Reteach GRR15 Grade 4

*GR – Getting Ready Lessons and Resources (*www.thinkcentral.com*)

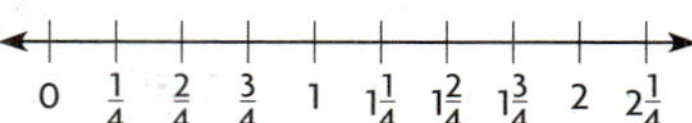

1. Use repeated subtraction and the number line to find $2 \div \frac{1}{4}$.

$0 \quad \frac{1}{4} \quad \frac{2}{4} \quad \frac{3}{4} \quad 1 \quad 1\frac{1}{4} \quad 1\frac{2}{4} \quad 1\frac{3}{4} \quad 2 \quad 2\frac{1}{4}$

Start subtracting at **2**.

Count back by groups of $\frac{1}{4}$.

How many groups did you count to reach 0? **8**

Use repeated subtraction to divide.

2. $2 \div \frac{1}{3}$ **6**

3. $5 \div \frac{1}{2}$ **10**

4. $1 \div \frac{1}{8}$ **8**

Use repeated subtraction to divide.

5. $1 \div \frac{1}{5}$ **5**

6. $2 \div \frac{1}{2}$ **4**

7. $4 \div \frac{1}{3}$ **12**

8. $2 \div \frac{1}{5}$ **10**

9. $7 \div \frac{1}{2}$ **14**

10. $3 \div \frac{1}{4}$ **12**

Problem Solving Real World

11. You are putting raisins into snack bags. You have 3 cups of raisins. You want to put $\frac{1}{3}$ cup of raisins in each bag. How many bags can you make?

9 bags

12. Margaret is cutting straws that are 4 inches long into $\frac{1}{2}$-inch pieces. She has two straws. She needs twenty $\frac{1}{2}$-inch pieces. Does she have enough to cut 20 pieces? **Explain.**

No; Possible explanation: $4 \div \frac{1}{2} = 8$; she has 2 straws, so she can cut $2 \times 8 = 16$ pieces, which is less than 20.

2 PRACTICE

Share and Show • Guided Practice

Use Exercises 1–4 to check students' understanding of lesson concepts. In Exercise 1, make sure students start at 2 on the number line and count back by $\frac{1}{4}$ until they reach 0. The number of groups of $\frac{1}{4}$ is the quotient.

On Your Own • Independent Practice

For Exercises 5–10, encourage students to use a number line to help them find each quotient.

Problem Solving MATHEMATICAL PRACTICES

UNLOCK THE PROBLEM For Exercise 11, have students explain why they need to use division to solve the problem. Exercise 12 is a multistep problem that requires students to divide, multiply the quotient by 2, and then compare the product to the given number to decide whether there are enough straws.

3 SUMMARIZE

MATHEMATICAL PRACTICES

Essential Question

How can you use repeated subtraction to solve problems involving division with fractions? Possible answer: I can subtract the divisor from the dividend repeatedly until I reach 0 or get as close to it as possible. The number of times I subtract the divisor is the quotient.

Math Journal WRITE Math

Explain how to use repeated subtraction to find the quotient of $5 \div \frac{1}{5}$.

GETTING READY FOR GRADE 5

LESSON 16

Fractions and Division

LESSON AT A GLANCE

Common Core Standards

Build fractions from unit fractions by applying and extending previous understandings of operations on whole numbers.

4.NF.B.3d Solve word problems involving addition and subtraction of fractions referring to the same whole and having like denominators, e.g., by using visual fraction models and equations to represent the problem.

Apply and extend previous understandings of multiplication and division to multiply and divide fractions.

5.NF.B.3 Interpret a fraction as division of the numerator by the denominator ($a/b = a \div b$). Solve word problems involving division of whole numbers leading to answers in the form of fractions or mixed numbers, e.g., by using visual fraction models or equations to represent the problem.

Materials

MathBoard

Lesson Objective

Write division problems as fractions.

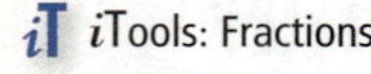

1 TEACH and TALK

▶ Unlock the Problem

MATHEMATICAL PRACTICES

Read the problem together. Students should understand that there are three sisters sharing the pizzas. Direct students' attention to the four pizzas.

- **How can the pizzas be divided equally?** Each pizza can be cut into equal-size slices. The slices can be divided equally among the sisters.
- **Why is it helpful to divide each pizza into 3 equal-size pieces?** Possible answer: it is helpful because the pizzas are being shared equally among 3 people.

Have students look at the expression $4 \div 3$ and the fraction $\frac{4}{3}$. Tell students that a fraction is a way to show division. Explain that they can think of the fraction bar as a division sign, so $\frac{4}{3}$ means the same as $4 \div 3$.

This lesson builds on division presented in Chapter 4 and fraction concepts presented in Chapters 6–8 and prepares students for fraction operations taught in Grade 5.

Name ______

Fractions and Division

Essential Question How can you write division problems as fractions?

Division and fractions both show sharing equal numbers of things or making equal-size groups. You can write division problems as fractions.

Unlock the Problem (Real World)

Mavi and her 2 sisters want to share 4 small pizzas equally. How much pizza will each person have?

- How many people want to share the pizzas? **3 people**

Think: What is 4 divided by 3, or $4 \div 3$?

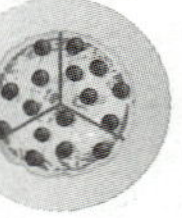
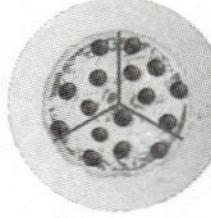
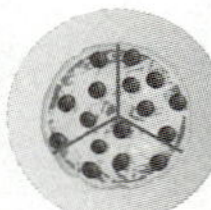
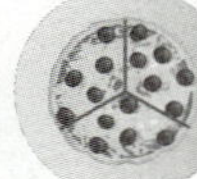

Each pizza is divided into **3** equal slices.

How many slices are in 4 pizzas? **12**

What fraction of the pizza is each slice? $\mathbf{\frac{1}{3}}$

How many $\frac{1}{3}$-size slices does each sister get? **4**

What fraction of the pizzas does each sister get? $\mathbf{\frac{4}{3}}$

So, $4 \div 3$ is the same as $\frac{4}{3}$.

Possible answer: I can write $\frac{4}{3}$ as $1\frac{1}{3}$.

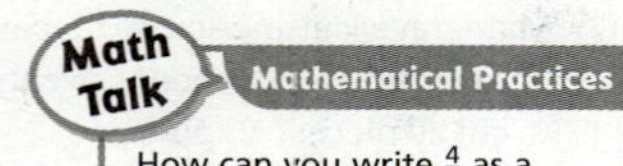

How can you write $\frac{4}{3}$ as a mixed number?

Getting Ready for Grade 5 GR35

GR: Practice, p. GRP16

Name ______ Lesson 16

Fractions and Division

Write the division problem as a fraction. Write each fraction greater than 1 as a whole number or mixed number.

1. $8 \div 2$ — $\frac{8}{2}$, 4
2. $10 \div 2$ — $\frac{10}{2}$, 5
3. $6 \div 5$ — $\frac{6}{5}$, $1\frac{1}{5}$
4. $9 \div 6$ — $\frac{9}{6}$, $1\frac{3}{6}$, or $1\frac{1}{2}$
5. $2 \div 5$ — $\frac{2}{5}$
6. $2 \div 8$ — $\frac{2}{8}$, or $\frac{1}{4}$
7. $24 \div 6$ — $\frac{24}{6}$, 4
8. $9 \div 1$ — $\frac{9}{1}$, 9
9. $15 \div 2$ — $\frac{15}{2}$, $7\frac{1}{2}$

Problem Solving (Real World)

10. There are 13 bagels in a baker's dozen. Hillary, Mark, and Tam share the bagels equally. Will each friend get more than or fewer than 4 whole bagels? Explain.
More than 4 whole bagels; possible explanation: $\frac{13}{3} = 4\frac{1}{3}$, which is greater than 4.

Getting Ready for Grade 5 GRP16

GR: Reteach, p. GRR16

Name ______ Lesson 16 Reteach

Fractions and Division

You can use division to make equal shares or to make equal-sized groups. You can use a fraction to show division.

Write the division problem as a fraction.

$3 \div 4$

Think of a division sign as a fraction bar.
numerator ÷ denominator ⟷ $\frac{\text{numerator}}{\text{denominator}}$

You can use fraction strips to model the relationship between division and fractions.

Step 1	Step 2	Step 3
Begin with 3 wholes.	Think of each whole as 4 fourth-size pieces.	Arrange the fourth-size pieces into 4 equal groups. There are 3 fourth-size pieces in each equal group.

So, $3 \div 4$ can be written as $\frac{3}{4}$.

Write the division problem as a fraction. Write each fraction greater than 1 as a whole number or mixed number.

1. $9 \div 3$ — $\frac{9}{3}$, 3
2. $1 \div 6$ — $\frac{1}{6}$
3. $2 \div 8$ — $\frac{2}{8}$, or $\frac{1}{4}$
4. $5 \div 4$ — $\frac{5}{4}$, $1\frac{1}{4}$
5. $7 \div 2$ — $\frac{7}{2}$, $3\frac{1}{2}$
6. $12 \div 8$ — $\frac{12}{8}$, $1\frac{4}{8}$, or $1\frac{1}{2}$

Reteach GRR16 Grade 4

*GR – Getting Ready Lessons and Resources (*www.thinkcentral.com*)

Share and Show

1. Alex baked a pan of corn bread and cut it into 12 equal-size pieces. Alex and his 3 sisters want to share the pieces equally.

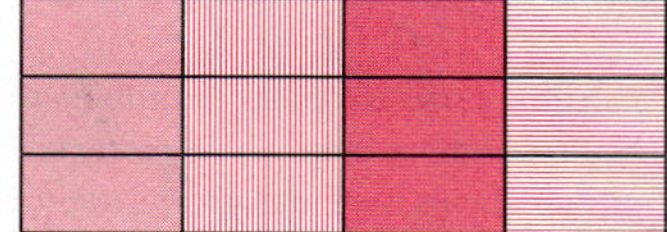

What division problem can you write to solve the problem? **Possible answer: 12 ÷ 4**

Write the division problem as a fraction. $\frac{12}{4}$

Write the division problem as a fraction. Write each fraction greater than 1 as a whole number or mixed number.

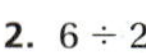

2. 6 ÷ 2 — $\frac{6}{2}$, 3
3. 1 ÷ 4 — $\frac{1}{4}$
4. 1 ÷ 3 — $\frac{1}{3}$
5. 32 ÷ 8 — $\frac{32}{8}$, 4

On Your Own

Write the division problem as a fraction. Write each fraction greater than 1 as a whole number or mixed number.

6. 5 ÷ 6 — $\frac{5}{6}$
7. 3 ÷ 2 — $\frac{3}{2}$, $1\frac{1}{2}$
8. 1 ÷ 8 — $\frac{1}{8}$
9. 2 ÷ 4 — $\frac{2}{4}$ or $\frac{1}{2}$
10. 12 ÷ 3 — $\frac{12}{3}$, 4
11. 9 ÷ 4 — $\frac{9}{4}$, $2\frac{1}{4}$
12. 11 ÷ 2 — $\frac{11}{2}$, $5\frac{1}{2}$
13. 8 ÷ 6 — $\frac{8}{6}$, $1\frac{2}{6}$ or $1\frac{1}{3}$

Problem Solving

14. Stefan and his 2 friends want to share 16 muffins equally. Will each friend get more than or less than 5 whole muffins? **Explain** how you know.

More; possible explanation: $\frac{16}{3} = 5\frac{1}{3}$, so everyone gets 5 whole muffins and $\frac{1}{3}$ of the remaining muffin.

GR36

Generalize that they can think of the division of two whole numbers as a fraction. Therefore, students can write the answer to the problem on page GR35 as a mixed number instead of a quotient with a remainder.

Use **Math Talk** to check students' understanding of writing a fraction greater than 1 as a mixed number and vice versa.

2 PRACTICE

Share and Show • Guided Practice

Discuss Exercise 1 with students. Students should understand that 4 people will share the 12 pieces of corn bread. Suggest that students shade the diagram to model the problem.

As students complete Exercises 2–5, reinforce that they can think of the division of two whole numbers as a fraction whether they are dividing a lesser number by a greater number or a greater number by a lesser number.

On Your Own • Independent Practice

For Exercises 6–13, remind students to write fractions that are greater than 1 as a whole number or a mixed number.

Problem Solving

Common Core MATHEMATICAL PRACTICES

UNLOCK THE PROBLEM For Exercise 14, students should recognize that the answer may include a fractional part. They should also understand that 3 friends will share 16 muffins equally.

Getting Ready Lessons and Resources, pp. GR37–GR38

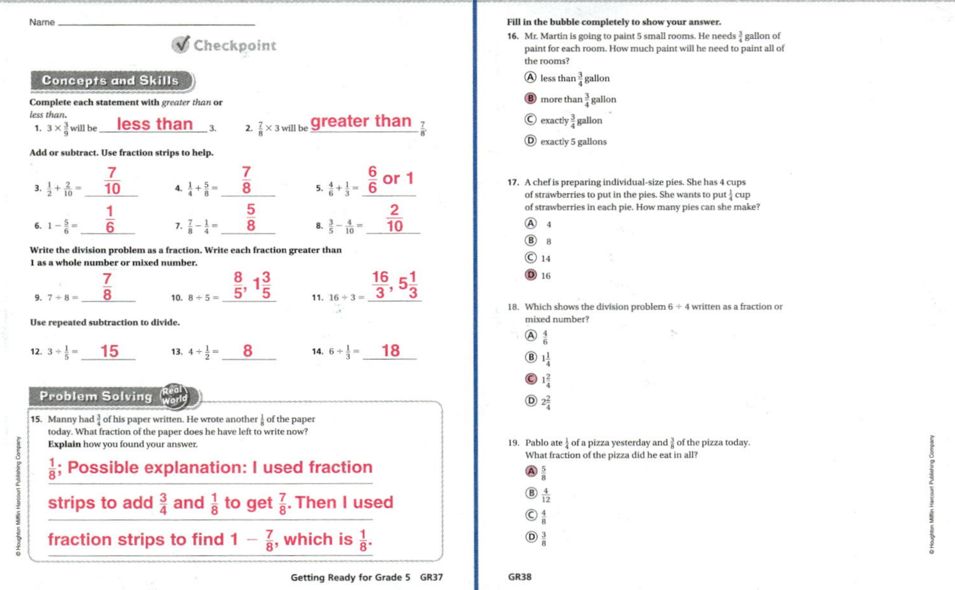

Name ____________

Checkpoint

Concepts and Skills

Complete each statement with *greater than* or *less than*.

1. $3 \times \frac{3}{9}$ will be **less than** 3.
2. $\frac{7}{8} \times 3$ will be **greater than** $\frac{7}{8}$.

Add or subtract. Use fraction strips to help.

3. $\frac{1}{2} + \frac{2}{10} =$ $\frac{7}{10}$
4. $\frac{1}{4} + \frac{5}{8} =$ $\frac{7}{8}$
5. $\frac{4}{6} + \frac{1}{3} =$ $\frac{6}{6}$ or 1
6. $1 - \frac{5}{6} =$ $\frac{1}{6}$
7. $\frac{7}{8} - \frac{1}{4} =$ $\frac{5}{8}$
8. $\frac{3}{5} - \frac{4}{10} =$ $\frac{2}{10}$

Write the division problem as a fraction. Write each fraction greater than 1 as a whole number or mixed number.

9. 7 ÷ 8 = $\frac{7}{8}$
10. 8 ÷ 5 = $\frac{8}{5}$, $1\frac{3}{5}$
11. 16 ÷ 3 = $\frac{16}{3}$, $5\frac{1}{3}$

Use repeated subtraction to divide.

12. $3 \div \frac{1}{5} =$ 15
13. $4 \div \frac{1}{2} =$ 8
14. $6 \div \frac{1}{3} =$ 18

Problem Solving Real World

15. Manny had $\frac{3}{4}$ of his paper written. He wrote another $\frac{1}{8}$ of the paper today. What fraction of the paper does he have left to write now? **Explain** how you found your answer.

$\frac{1}{8}$; Possible explanation: I used fraction strips to add $\frac{3}{4}$ and $\frac{1}{8}$ to get $\frac{7}{8}$. Then I used fraction strips to find $1 - \frac{7}{8}$, which is $\frac{1}{8}$.

© Houghton Mifflin Harcourt Publishing Company

Getting Ready for Grade 5 GR37

Fill in the bubble completely to show your answer.

16. Mr. Martin is going to paint 5 small rooms. He needs $\frac{3}{4}$ gallon of paint for each room. How much paint will he need to paint all of the rooms?
   - Ⓐ less than $\frac{3}{4}$ gallon
   - Ⓑ more than $\frac{3}{4}$ gallon
   - Ⓒ exactly $\frac{3}{4}$ gallon
   - Ⓓ exactly 5 gallons

17. A chef is preparing individual-size pies. She has 4 cups of strawberries to put in the pies. She wants to put $\frac{1}{4}$ cup of strawberries in each pie. How many pies can she make?
   - Ⓐ 4
   - Ⓑ 8
   - Ⓒ 14
   - Ⓓ 16

18. Which shows the division problem 6 ÷ 4 written as a fraction or mixed number?
   - Ⓐ $\frac{4}{6}$
   - Ⓑ $1\frac{1}{4}$
   - Ⓒ $1\frac{2}{4}$
   - Ⓓ $2\frac{2}{4}$

19. Pablo ate $\frac{1}{4}$ of a pizza yesterday and $\frac{3}{8}$ of the pizza today. What fraction of the pizza did he eat in all?
   - Ⓐ $\frac{5}{8}$
   - Ⓑ $\frac{4}{12}$
   - Ⓒ $\frac{4}{8}$
   - Ⓓ $\frac{3}{8}$

GR38

© Houghton Mifflin Harcourt Publishing Company

3 SUMMARIZE

Essential Question

How can you write division problems as fractions? Possible answer: write the dividend as the numerator and the divisor as the denominator. If the fraction is greater than 1, you can write the amount as a fraction greater than 1 or a mixed number.

Math Journal

WRITE Math

Write a word problem that can be solved by writing a division problem as a fraction. Include the division problem, the quotient written as a fraction, and the solution.

LESSON 17

Locate Points on a Grid

LESSON AT A GLANCE

Common Core Standards

Solve problems involving measurement and conversion of measurements from a larger unit to a smaller unit.

4.MD.A.1 Know relative sizes of measurement units within one system of units including km, m, cm; kg, g; lb, oz.; l, ml; hr, min, sec. Within a single system of measurement, express measurements in a larger unit in terms of a smaller unit. Record measurement equivalents in a two-column table.

Graph points on the coordinate plane to solve real-world and mathematical problems.

5.G.A.1 Use a pair of perpendicular number lines, called axes, to define a coordinate system, with the intersection of the lines (the origin) arranged to coincide with the 0 on each line and a given point in the plane located by using an ordered pair of numbers, called its coordinates. Understand that the first number indicates how far to travel from the origin in the direction of one axis, and the second number indicates how far to travel in the direction of the second axis, with the convention that the names of the two axes and the coordinates correspond (e.g., *x*-axis and *x*-coordinate, *y*-axis and *y*-coordinate).

Lesson Objective

Use ordered pairs to locate points on a grid.

Vocabulary

ordered pair

Materials

MathBoard

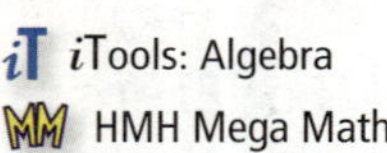
iTools: Algebra

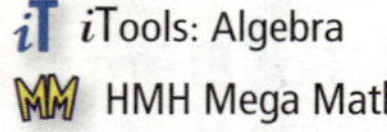
HMH Mega Math

1 TEACH and TALK

• iTools

▶ Unlock the Problem

MATHEMATICAL PRACTICES

Have students read the description of an ordered pair.

- **Why do you think the pairs of numbers are called "ordered pairs"?** Possible answer: to name the precise location of a point on a grid, the pair of numbers must be in a particular order.

Discuss the problem.

- **What do you need to find?** the ordered pair at which Terminal *A* is located

This lesson builds on measurement and data presented in Chapter 12, and prepares students for graphing ordered pairs taught in Grade 5.

Name ______________________

Locate Points on a Grid

Essential Question How can you use ordered pairs to locate points on a grid?

An ordered pair is a pair of numbers that names a point on a grid. The first number shows how many units to move horizontally. The second number shows how many units to move vertically.

(2 , 4)

↑ Move 2 units right from 0. ↑ Then move 4 units up.

Unlock the Problem Real World

At the airport, passengers travel from one terminal to another in shuttle buses. The shuttle buses travel in a route that begins at Terminal A. Where is Terminal A?

Count units on the grid to find out.

- Start at zero.
- Move right 5 units.
- From there, move up 9 units.

Terminal A is located at (5, 9).

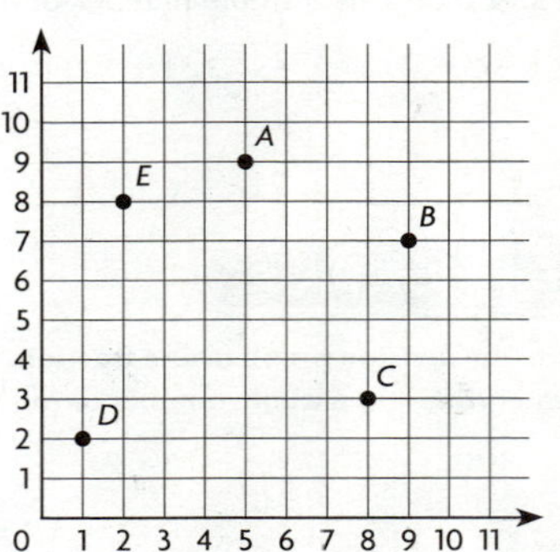

Try This!

What terminal is located at (8, 3)? Explain how you know.

Terminal *C*; possible explanation: I started at 0 and moved 8 units to the right. From there I moved 3 units up. Terminal *C* is located at (8, 3).

Possible explanation: the first ordered pair means right 3 and up 6. The next ordered pair means right 6 and up 3.

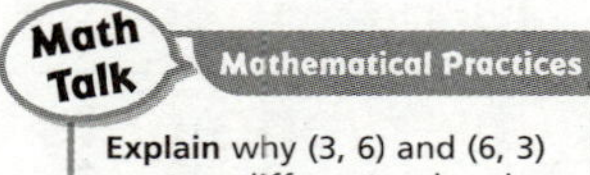

Explain why (3, 6) and (6, 3) are two different ordered pairs.

Getting Ready for Grade 5 GR39

GR: Practice, p. GRP17

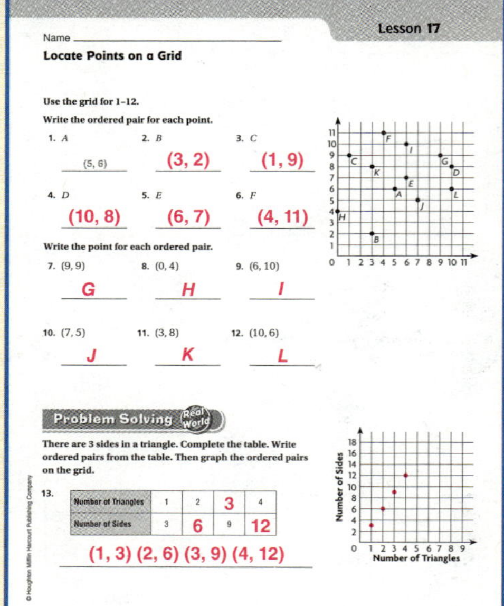

Lesson 17

Name ______________________

Locate Points on a Grid

Use the grid for 1–12.

Write the ordered pair for each point.

1. *A* (5, 6)
2. *B* (3, 2)
3. *C* (1, 9)
4. *D* (10, 8)
5. *E* (6, 7)
6. *F* (4, 11)

Write the point for each ordered pair.

7. (9, 9) G
8. (0, 4) H
9. (6, 10) I
10. (7, 5) J
11. (3, 8) K
12. (10, 6) L

Problem Solving Real World

There are 3 sides in a triangle. Complete the table. Write ordered pairs from the table. Then graph the ordered pairs on the grid.

13.

Number of Triangles	1	2	3	4
Number of Sides	3	6	9	12

(1, 3) (2, 6) (3, 9) (4, 12)

Number of Sides / Number of Triangles

Getting Ready for Grade 5 GRP17

GR: Reteach, p. GRR17

Lesson 17 Reteach

Name ______________________

Locate Points on a Grid

A map has horizontal and vertical lines that make a grid. You can name a point on the grid using an **ordered pair** of numbers.

The first number tells how many units to move right from zero. → (1, 5) ← The second number tells how many units to move up from zero.

Write the ordered pair for the location of the park.

Step 1 Start at zero. Move right. Count the number of units until you are directly below the park.

You move right 2 units.

Step 2 Move up. Count the number of units until you reach the park.

You move up 3 units.

Step 3 You move right 2 units and up 3 units, so the ordered pair is (2, 3).

So, the park is located at (2, 3) on the map.

N, S, E, W; Store, Library, Park, School, Ty's House

Use the grid. Write the ordered pair for each point.

1. *A* (4, 2)
2. *B* (0, 4)
3. *C* (10, 1)
4. *D* (3, 5)

Use the grid. Write the point for each ordered pair.

5. (8, 0) E
6. (9, 10) G
7. (6, 7) F
8. (2, 9) H

Reteach GRR17 Grade 4

*GR – Getting Ready Lessons and Resources (*www.thinkcentral.com*)

Share and Show

1. To graph the point (6, 3), where do you start? In which direction and how many units will you move first? What will you do next? Describe the steps and record them on the grid.
Start at 0. Move right 6 units. Then move up 3 units.

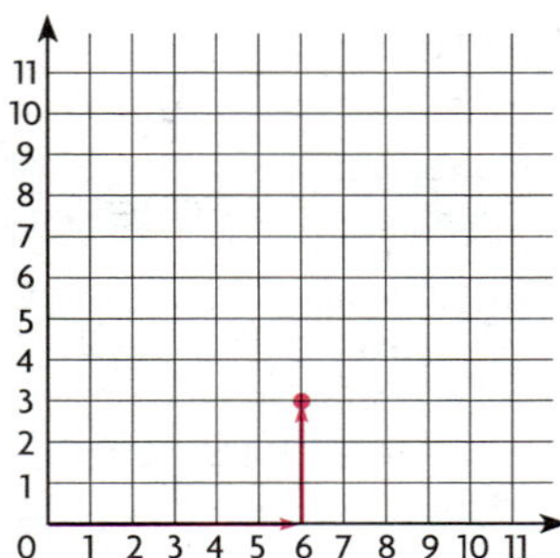

Use the grid for Exercises 2–5. Write the ordered pair for each point.

2. *A* **(2, 4)**
3. *B* **(4, 5)**
4. *C* **(9, 1)**
5. *D* **(3, 0)**

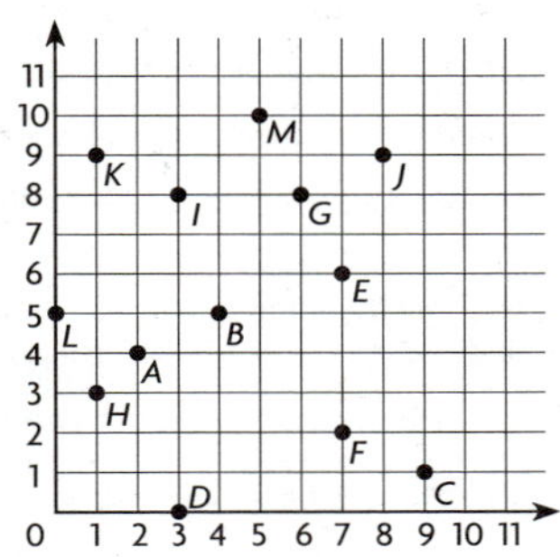

On Your Own

Use the grid for Exercises 6–13.
Write the ordered pair for each point.

6. *E* **(7, 6)**
7. *F* **(7, 2)**
8. *G* **(6, 8)**
9. *H* **(1, 3)**

Write the point for each ordered pair.

10. (3, 8) **I**
11. (8, 9) **J**
12. (1, 9) **K**
13. (0, 5) **L**

Problem Solving Real World

There are four photos on each page of a photo album. Complete the table. Write the data in the table as ordered pairs. Then graph the ordered pairs on the grid. Use the number of pages as the first number and the number of photos as the second number in the ordered pair.

14.

Number of Pages	1	**2**	3	4
Number of Photos	4	8	**12**	**16**

(1, 4) (2, 8) (3, 12) (4, 16)

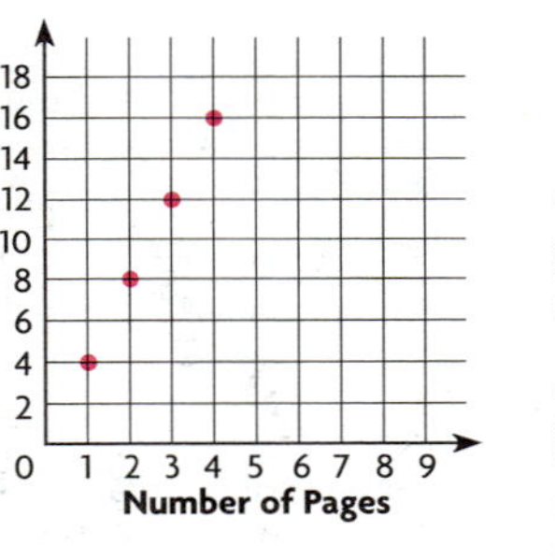

GR40

Try This!

- **Compare this problem to the previous problem.** Possible answer: in the previous problem, we were asked to find the ordered pair for a point on the grid; in this problem, we are asked to find the point for an ordered pair.

Use **Math Talk** to check students' understanding of ordered pairs.

2 PRACTICE

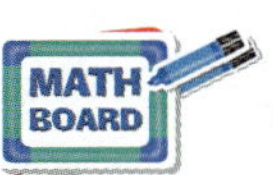

Share and Show • Guided Practice

For Exercise 1, be sure students understand that the first number in an ordered pair is the number of units to move horizontally from 0 and the second number is the number of units to move vertically. Discuss Exercises 2–5 with students.

On Your Own • Independent Practice

Point out that for Exercises 6–9, students must find the ordered pair for a given point, and for Exercises 10–13, they must find the point for the ordered pair.

Problem Solving MATHEMATICAL PRACTICES

UNLOCK THE PROBLEM For Exercise 14, students may benefit from drawing a picture of the photo album pages to understand the problem.

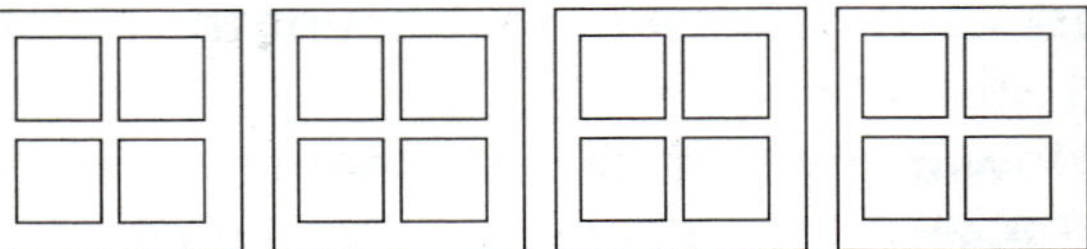

3 SUMMARIZE

MATHEMATICAL PRACTICES

Essential Question

How can you use ordered pairs to locate points on a grid? Possible answer: start at 0 and move right the number of units shown by the first number of the ordered pair. Then move up the number of units shown by the second number of the ordered pair.

Math Journal WRITE Math

Describe how to use an ordered pair to graph a point on a grid.

LESSON 18

Area and Tiling

LESSON AT A GLANCE

Common Core Standards

Solve problems involving measurement and conversion of measurements from a larger unit to a smaller unit.

4.MD.A.3 Apply the area and perimeter formulas for rectangles in real world and mathematical problems.

Apply and extend previous understandings of multiplication and division to multiply and divide fractions.

5.NF.B.4b Apply and extend previous understandings of multiplication to multiply a fraction or whole numberby a fraction.

Find the area of a rectangle with fractional side lengths by tiling it with unit squares of the appropriate unit fraction side lengths, and show that the area is the same as would be found by multiplying the side lengths. Multiply fractional side lengths to find areas of rectangles, and represent fraction products as rectangular areas.

Lesson Objective

Use tiling to find the area of a rectangle.

Materials

MathBoard

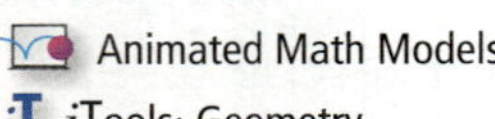

Animated Math Models

*i*Tools: Geometry

1 TEACH and TALK

Animated Math Models

Unlock the Problem

MATHEMATICAL PRACTICES

Read and discuss the problem. Have students mark each half tile as they count the number of half tiles.

- **How many half tiles are there?** 10
- **If each whole tile measures 4 square feet, how can you find the measure of each half tile?** Possible answer: divide 4 by 2.
- **What is the measure of each half tile?** 2 square feet
- **Why can you use the area formula for a rectangle to find the number of whole tiles?** Possible answer: the whole tiles form a rectangle, so you can count the number of whole tiles along the base and multiply it by the number whole tiles along the height.
- **Why do you have to multiply the number of whole tiles by 4 to find the area of the whole tiles?** Possible answer: because each whole tile measures 4 square feet

Use **Math Talk** to check students' understanding of how to find the area of half tiles when the area of a whole tile is an odd number of square units.

This lesson builds on finding the area of rectangles presented in Chapter 13 and prepares students for multiplying fractions taught in Grade 5.

Name ____________

Area and Tiling

Essential Question How can you use tiling to find the area of a rectangle?

Unlock the Problem (Real World)

Rhonda is tiling the floor of her new sunroom. The diagram shows the layout of the tiles. Each tile measures 4 square feet. What is the area of Rhonda's sunroom floor?

- Underline what you are asked to find.
- Circle the information you will use to solve the problem.

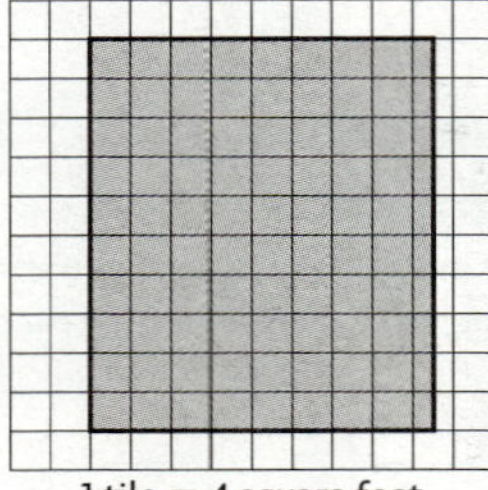

To find the area of the sunroom floor, you can combine the areas of the half tiles and the whole tiles.

Find the area of the sunroom floor.

STEP 1 Find the area of the half tiles.

Count the number of half tiles. 10

1 tile = 4 square feet, so 1 half tile = 4 ÷ 2 or 2 square feet.

Multiply the number of half tiles by 2 square feet to find the area of the half tiles:

10 × 2 = 20 square feet

STEP 2 Find the area of the whole tiles.

Find the number of whole tiles: $b \times h$ = 8 × 10 = 80 tiles

Since the area of 1 tile is 4 square feet, multiply the number of whole tiles by 4 to find the area of the whole tiles.

80 × 4 = 320 square feet

STEP 3 Find the total area.

Add the areas of the half tiles and whole tiles.

half tiles ↓ whole tiles ↓

20 + 320 = 340 square feet

So, the area of Rhonda's sunroom floor is 340 square feet.

Remember

The formula for the area of a rectangle is $A = b \times h$ or $l \times w$.

Math Talk — Mathematical Practices

Explain how to find the area of 6 half tiles if 1 whole tile is 9 square inches.

Possible answer: 6 half tiles ÷ 2 = 3 whole tiles, and 3 tiles × 9 square inches = 27 square inches.

Getting Ready for Grade 5 GR41

GR: Practice, p. GRP18

Name ____________ Lesson 18

Area and Tiling

Find the area of the shaded shape. Write the area in square units.

1. Area of the half squares: 6 half squares × 2 square inches = 12 square inches
Area of the whole squares: 18 whole squares × 4 square inches = 72 square inches
Total area: 12 + 72 = 84 square inches
1 square = 4 square inches

2. 1 square = 4 square meters — 60 square meters

3. 1 square = 4 square miles — 108 square miles

4. 1 square = 16 square feet — 704 square feet

5. 1 square = 25 square yards — 850 square yards

6. 1 square = 9 square inches — 216 square inches

7. 1 square = 16 square miles — 672 square miles

Problem Solving (Real World)

8. A deck is in the shape of a rectangle. What is the area of the deck if each square shown in the diagram is 9 square feet? Explain how you found the area.
1 square = 9 square feet
234 sq ft; possible answer: 24 whole squares + 4 half-squares is 24 + 2 = 26 whole squares; 26 × 9 = 234.

Getting Ready for Grade 5 GRP18

GR: Reteach, p. GRR18

Name ____________ Lesson 18 Reteach

Area and Tiling

In the model, whole tiles are shaded, and some half tiles are shaded. You can combine the areas of half tiles and whole tiles to find the total area.

Marta's Entryway — 1 square = 4 square feet

Find the area of the entryway. Write the area in square feet.

Step 1 Count the number of whole tiles. There are 42 whole tiles.

Step 2 Count the number of half tiles. There are 6 half tiles.
Think: 2 half tiles = 1 whole tile
6 half tiles = 3 whole tiles

Step 3 Use the total number of whole tiles to find the area.
42 + 3 = 45 whole tiles
Think: 1 tile = 4 square feet
Multiply the number of whole tiles by 4 to find the area.
45 × 4 = 180
So, the area of Marta's entryway is 180 square feet.

Find the area of each shaded shape. Write the area in square units.

1. 1 square = 4 square feet — 72 square feet
2. 1 square = 9 square meters — 135 square meters
3. 1 square = 16 square miles — 160 square miles

Reteach © Houghton Mifflin Harcourt Publishing Company GRR18 Grade 4

***GR** – Getting Ready Lessons and Resources (*www.thinkcentral.com*)

Share and Show

1. Find the area of the shaded shape.

STEP 1 Find the area of the half squares:

4 half squares × 8 square yards = 32 square yards

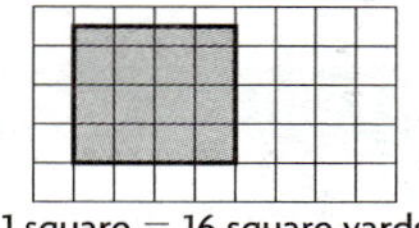

1 square = 16 square yards

STEP 2 Find the area of the whole squares:

4 × 3 = 12 squares

12 squares × 16 square yards = 192 square yards

STEP 3 Find the total area: 32 + 192 = 224 square yards

Find the area of each shaded shape. Write the area in square units.

2.

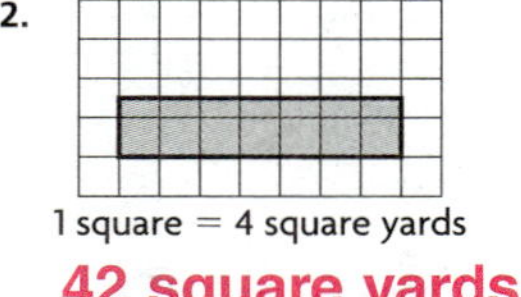

1 square = 4 square yards

42 square yards

3.

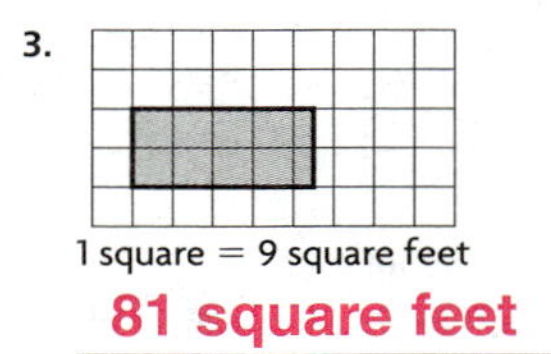

1 square = 9 square feet

81 square feet

4.

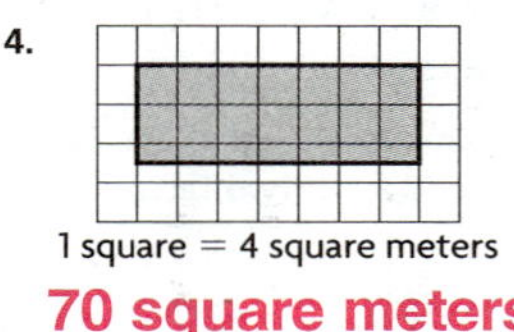

1 square = 4 square meters

70 square meters

On Your Own

Find the area of each shaded shape. Write the area in square units.

5.

1 square = 9 square miles

126 square miles

6.

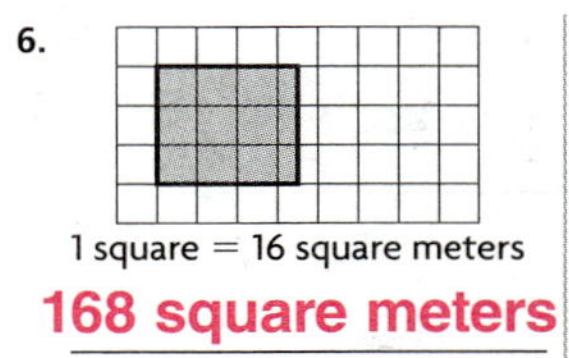

1 square = 16 square meters

168 square meters

7.

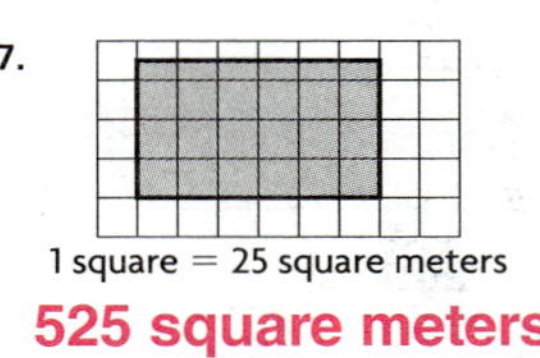

1 square = 25 square meters

525 square meters

Problem Solving

8. A mosaic table top is shown. Each square has an area of 5 square inches. What is the area of the table top? **Explain.**

90 square inches; 6 half squares = 15 square inches, and 15 whole squares = 75 square inches; 15 + 75 = 90.

Table Top

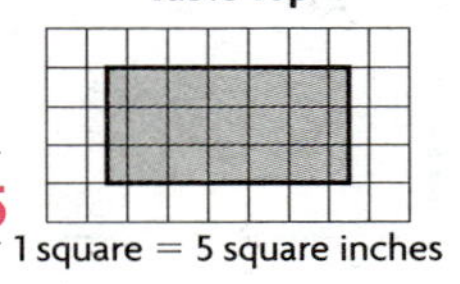

1 square = 5 square inches

GR42

2 PRACTICE

Share and Show • Guided Practice

Use Exercises 1–4 to check students' understanding of lesson concepts. Have students explain how they found the area of the half squares and the whole squares.

On Your Own • Independent Practice

For Exercises 5–7, remind students that area is expressed in square units. They should include the square units in their answers.

Problem Solving

Common Core MATHEMATICAL PRACTICES

UNLOCK THE PROBLEM For Exercise 8, a whole square is an odd number of square inches. Remind students that they can find the area of the half squares by finding one half the area of the same number of whole squares or they can combine two half squares into one whole square and count the number of whole squares formed.

3 SUMMARIZE

Essential Question

How can you use tiling to find the area of a rectangle? Possible answer: I can count the number of half squares and multiply by $\frac{1}{2}$ the area of a whole square. Then I can count the number of whole squares and multiply by the area of a square. Finally, I can add the areas of the half squares and the whole squares and express the answer in square units.

Math Journal WRITE Math

Use grid paper to draw a rectangle that contains whole squares and half squares. Explain how to find the area of the rectangle.

LESSON 19

Multiply Three Factors

LESSON AT A GLANCE

Common Core Standards
Use place value understanding and properties of operations to perform multi-digit arithmetic.
4.NBT.B.5 Multiply a whole number of up to four digits by a one-digit whole number, and multiply two two-digit numbers, using strategies based on place value and the properties of operations. Illustrate and explain the calculation by using equations, rectangular arrays, and/or area models.

Geometric measurement: understand concepts of volume and relate volume to multiplication and to addition.
5.MD.C.5b Relate volume to the operations of multiplication and addition and solve real world and mathematical problems involving volume. Apply the formulas $V = l \times w \times h$ and $V = b \times h$ for rectangular prisms to find volumes of right rectangular prisms with whole-number edge lengths in the context of solving real world and mathematical problems.

Materials
MathBoard

Lesson Objective
Find the product of three factors.

Animated Math Models

1 TEACH and TALK

• Animated Math Models

Unlock the Problem

MATHEMATICAL PRACTICES

Review the Associative and Commutative Properties. Read and discuss the problem.

- **Why can you use multiplication to solve the problem?** Possible answer: we are finding the total of same-size groups.

Example

- **How does using properties help you multiply 4 × (16 × 6)?** Possible answer: I can use the Commutative Property to write (16 × 6) as (6 × 16). Then I can use the Associative Property to write 4 × (6 × 16) as (4 × 6) × 16. The basic fact 4 × 6 is easy. Then I just need to multiply 24 × 16.

This lesson builds on multiplying whole numbers presented in Chapters 2 and 3 and prepares students for finding the volume of rectangular prisms taught in Grade 5.

Name ______

Multiply Three Factors

Essential Question How can you find the product of three factors?

Unlock the Problem Real World

You can use properties of multiplication to help make multiplication of three factors easier.

Sam ships 4 boxes of car model kits to Toy Mart. Each box contains 16 cartons, with 6 kits in each carton. How many car model kits does Sam ship?

- Underline what you are asked to find.
- Circle the numbers you will use to solve the problem.
- What operation can you use to solve the problem? **multiplication**

Example Find 4 × (16 × 6).

STEP 1

Simplify the problem. Rewrite 4 × (16 × 6) as a product of two factors.

4 × (16 × 6) = 4 × (**6** × 16) Commutative Property

= (4 × **6**) × 16 Associative Property

= **24** × 16

So, 4 × (16 × 6) = 24 × 16.

STEP 2

Multiply.

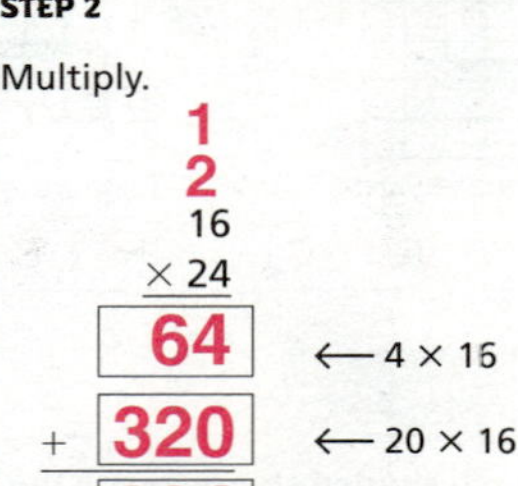

 1
 2
 16
× 24
64 ⟵ 4 × 16
+ **320** ⟵ 20 × 16
384 ⟵ Add.

So, Sam ships **384** car model kits.

Try This!

(18 × 8) × 3 = 18 × (**8** × **3**) Associative Property

= 18 × **24**

= **432**

Math Talk Mathematical Practices

Explain how using properties makes it easier to multiple three factors.

Possible explanation: the properties allow you to rearrange the factors, so it is possible to multiply the factors in fewer steps.

Getting Ready for Grade 5 GR43

GR: Practice, p. GRP19

Name ______ Lesson 19

Multiply Three Factors

Find each product.

1. 6 × (4 × 17)
 6 × (4 × 17) = (6 × 4) × 17
 = 24 × 17
 = 408
2. (28 × 8) × 3 = 672
3. (13 × 9) × 4 = 468
4. (6 × 26) × 3 = 468
5. 6 × (15 × 7) = 630
6. 2 × (8 × 18) = 288
7. (4 × 21) × 4 = 336
8. 8 × (4 × 33) = 1,056
9. 3 × (44 × 6) = 792
10. (36 × 9) × 5 = 1,620

Problem Solving Real World

11. There are 9 rows of 28 chairs set up for a play. A ticket to the play costs $4. How much money will be made on ticket sales if all the seats are sold for the play? **$1,008**
12. Three families are sharing the cost of renting a canoe for 7 days. The cost for each family is $14 per day. What is the total cost of renting the canoe for 7 days from the rental shop? **$294**

Getting Ready for Grade 5 GRP19

GR: Reteach, p. GRR19

Name ______ Lesson 19 Reteach

Multiply Three Factors

Step 1
Simplify the problem. Rewrite 2 × (14 × 6) as a product of two factors.
2 × (14 × 6) = 2 × (6 × 14) Commutative Property
= (2 × 6) × 14 Associative Property
= 12 × 14
So, 2 × (14 × 6) = 12 × 14.

Step 2
Multiply.
 12
× 14
 48 ⟵ 4 × 12
+ 120 ⟵ 10 × 12
 168 ⟵ Add.
So, 2 × (14 × 6) = 168.

Remember
Commutative Property of Multiplication
You can multiply factors in any order and still get the same product.
Example: 2 × 3 = 3 × 2
Associative Property of Multiplication
You can group factors in any order and still get the same product.
Example: 2 × (3 × 4) = (2 × 3) × 4

Find each product.

1. 3 × (16 × 4) = **192**
2. (4 × 14) × 6 = **336**
3. 5 × (13 × 5) = **325**
4. (16 × 7) × 3 = **336**
5. 7 × (18 × 6) = **756**
6. (12 × 8) × 6 = **576**

Reteach GRR19 Grade 4

*GR – Getting Ready Lessons and Resources (*www.thinkcentral.com*)

Share and Show 

1. Find the product of $7 \times (6 \times 13)$.

STEP 1 Simplify the problem.

Rewrite $7 \times (6 \times 13)$ as a product of two factors.

$7 \times (6 \times 13) = (\underline{7} \times \underline{6}) \times 13$

Associative Property

$= \underline{42} \times \underline{13}$

STEP 2 Multiply.

$$\begin{array}{r} 13 \\ \times\ 42 \\ \hline 546 \end{array}$$

Find each product.

2. $3 \times (14 \times 3) = \underline{126}$

3. $2 \times (4 \times 13) = \underline{104}$

4. $(16 \times 6) \times 3 = \underline{288}$

On Your Own

Find each product.

5. $7 \times (17 \times 4) = \underline{476}$

6. $(18 \times 4) \times 6 = \underline{432}$

7. $9 \times (17 \times 5) = \underline{765}$

8. $(5 \times 26) \times 3 = \underline{390}$

9. $9 \times (19 \times 2) = \underline{342}$

10. $(21 \times 4) \times 6 = \underline{504}$

Problem Solving 

11. There are 3 basketball leagues. Each league has 8 teams. Each team has 13 players. How many players are there in all 3 leagues?

312 players

12. There are 8 boxes of tennis balls. There are 24 cans of tennis balls in each box. There are 3 tennis balls in each can. How many tennis balls are there in all?

576 tennis balls

Try This!

Point out that it is not always necessary for students to use both the Associative and Commutative Properties when multiplying three factors.

Use Math Talk to check students' understanding of lesson concepts.

2 PRACTICE 

Share and Show • Guided Practice

Use Exercises 1–4 to check students' understanding of lesson concepts. Ask students to explain the steps they used to find each product.

On Your Own • Independent Practice

For Exercises 5–10, have students identify the properties they used to get each answer. Encourage students to try one property first before using both.

Problem Solving 

UNLOCK THE PROBLEM For Exercises 11 and 12, have students explain why they can use multiplication to solve each problem. Encourage students to write a multiplication expression for each problem.

3 SUMMARIZE

Essential Question

How can you find the product of three factors? Possible answer: I can use properties to rearrange the factors, so I can multiply two factors that form a basic fact first. Then I can use two factors to find the final product.

Math Journal WRITE Math

Write a word problem that can be solved by multiplying three factors. Include the solution.

LESSON 20

Find Area of the Base

LESSON AT A GLANCE

Common Core Standards

Solve problems involving measurement and conversion of measurements from a larger unit to a smaller unit.

4.MD.A.3 Apply the area and perimeter formulas for rectangles in real world and mathematical problems.

Geometric measurement: understand concepts of volume and relate volume to multiplication and to addition.

5.MD.C.5b Relate volume to the operations of multiplication and addition and solve real world and mathematical problems involving volume. Apply the formulas $V = l \times w \times h$ and $V = b \times h$ for rectangular prisms to find volumes of right rectangular prisms with whole-number edge lengths in the context of solving real world and mathematical problems.

Lesson Objective

Find the area of the base of a rectangular prism.

Vocabulary

rectangular prism, base

Materials

MathBoard

*i*Tools: Geometry

1 TEACH and TALK

• *i*Tools

▶ Unlock the Problem

MATHEMATICAL PRACTICES

Be sure students understand the definitions of rectangular prism and base.

▶ Example

Read and discuss the problem.

- **What do you need to find?** the area of the base of the box
- **Why can you use the area formula of a rectangle to find the area of the base?** The base shape is a rectangle.
- **How can you find the base and the height of the base?** Possible answer: I can use the labels on the rectangular prism to find the base and height.

This lesson builds on finding the area of rectangles presented in Chapter 13 and prepares students for finding volume of a rectangular prism taught in Grade 5.

Name ______________________

Find Area of the Base

Essential Question How can you find the area of the base of a rectangular prism?

Connect The base of a rectangle is different than the base of a rectangular prism. The base of a rectangle is a side, but the base of a rectangular prism is a rectangle. To find the area of a rectangle, use the formula $A = b \times h$ or $l \times w$.

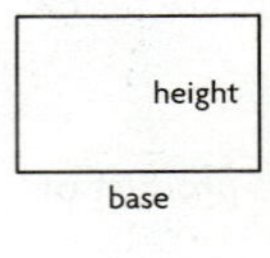

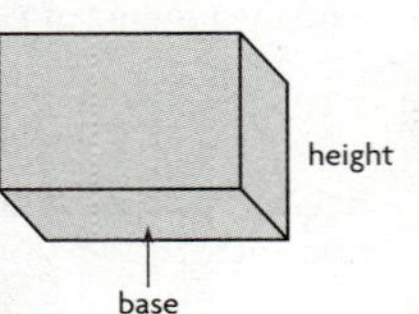

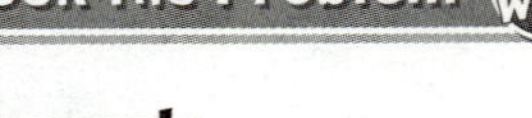

Example

Ana is making a diorama for a class project. The diorama is in the shape of a rectangular prism. She wants to paint the bottom of the diorama. What is the area of the base?

The base shape is a rectangle.

Use a formula to find the area.

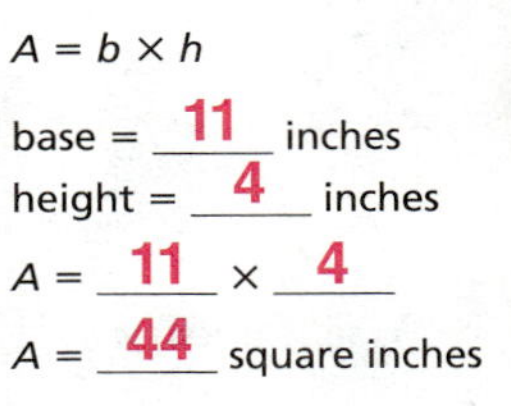

$A = b \times h$

base = __11__ inches

height = __4__ inches

$A =$ __11__ $\times$ __4__

$A =$ __44__ square inches

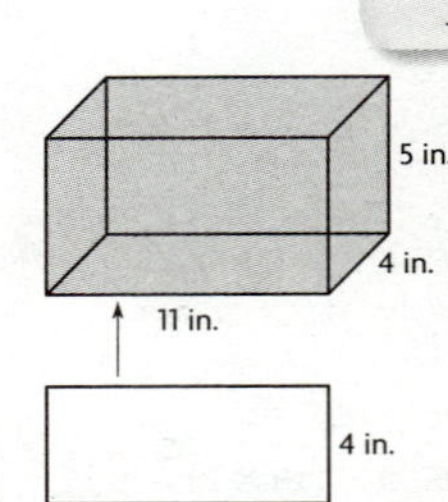

So, the area of the base of the diorama is __44__ square inches.

Remember

Area of a rectangle: $A = b \times h$ or $l \times w$

Area of a square: $A = s \times s$

- What shape is the base of the diorama? rectangle
- What are the base and height of the base of the diorama? base is 11 inches; height is 4 inches

Math Talk — Mathematical Practices

Why would multiplying 11 by 5 give an incorrect answer for the area of the base?

Possible explanation: The diorama is 5 inches tall. The bottom of the box is 11 inches long and 4 inches wide.

Getting Ready for Grade 5 GR45

GR: Practice, p. GRP20

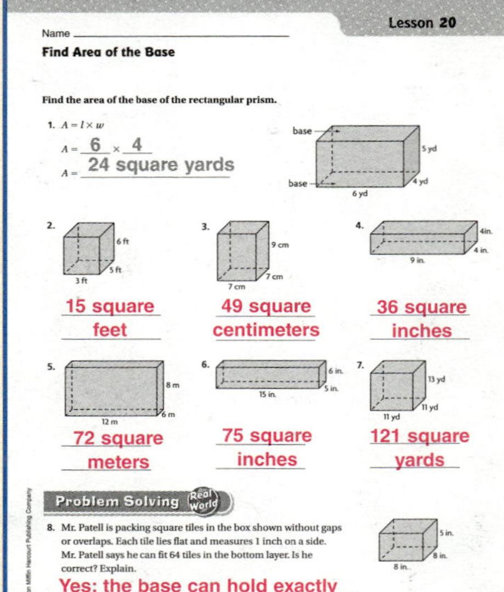

Name ______ Lesson 20

Find Area of the Base

Find the area of the base of the rectangular prism.

1. $A = l \times w$
   $A =$ 6 $\times$ 4
   $A =$ 24 square yards
2. 15 square feet
3. 49 square centimeters
4. 36 square inches
5. 72 square meters
6. 75 square inches
7. 121 square yards

Problem Solving Real World

8. Mr. Patell is packing square tiles in the box shown without gaps or overlaps. Each tile lies flat and measures 1 inch on a side. Mr. Patell says he can fit 64 tiles in the bottom layer. Is he correct? Explain.
   Yes; the base can hold exactly $8 \times 8 = 64$ square inches.

Getting Ready for Grade 5 GRP20

GR: Reteach, p. GRR20

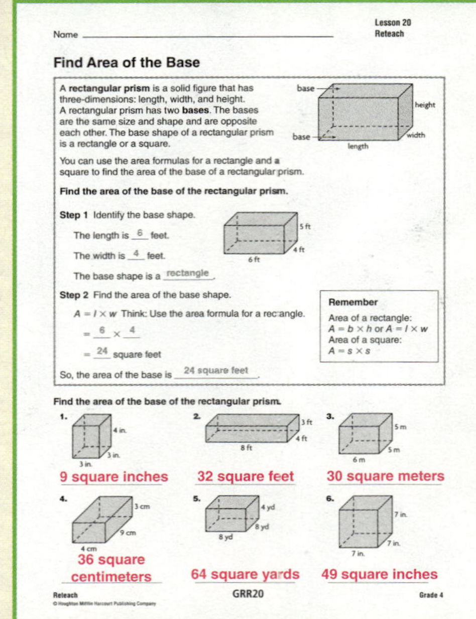

Name ______ Lesson 20 Reteach

Find Area of the Base

A **rectangular prism** is a solid figure that has three-dimensions: length, width, and height. A rectangular prism has two **bases**. The bases are the same size and shape and are opposite each other. The base shape of a rectangular prism is a rectangle or a square.

You can use the area formulas for a rectangle and a square to find the area of the base of a rectangular prism.

Find the area of the base of the rectangular prism.

Step 1 Identify the base shape.
The length is 6 feet.
The width is 4 feet.
The base shape is a rectangle.

Step 2 Find the area of the base shape.
$A = l \times w$ Think: Use the area formula for a rectangle.
= 6 $\times$ 4
= 24 square feet

So, the area of the base is 24 square feet.

Remember
Area of a rectangle: $A = b \times h$ or $A = l \times w$
Area of a square: $A = s \times s$

Find the area of the base of the rectangular prism.

1. 9 square inches
2. 32 square feet
3. 30 square meters
4. 36 square centimeters
5. 64 square yards
6. 49 square inches

Reteach GRR20 Grade 4

*GR – Getting Ready Lessons and Resources (*www.thinkcentral.com*)

Share and Show

1. Find the area of the base of the rectangular prism.

The base shape is a **rectangle**.

length = **5** yards, width = **2** yards

A = **5** × **2** = **10** square yards

So, the area of the base is **10** square yards.

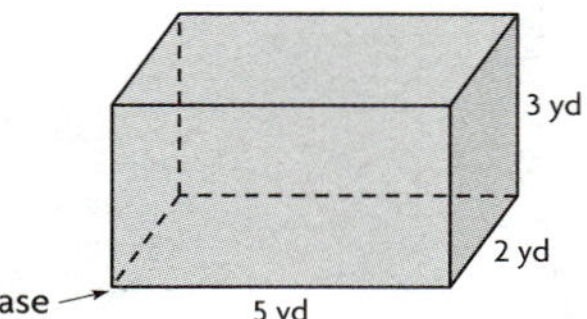

Find the area of the base of the rectangular prism.

2. 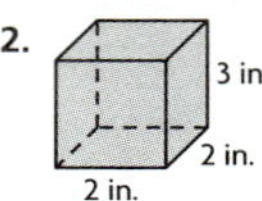

4 square inches

3. 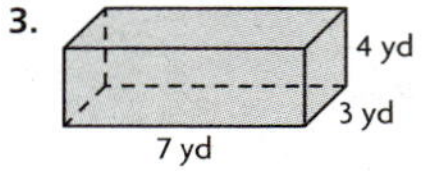

21 square yards

4. 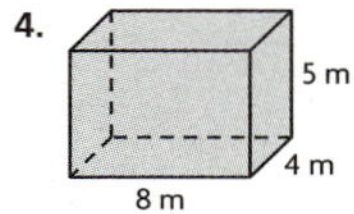

32 square meters

On Your Own

Find the area of the base of the rectangular prism.

5. 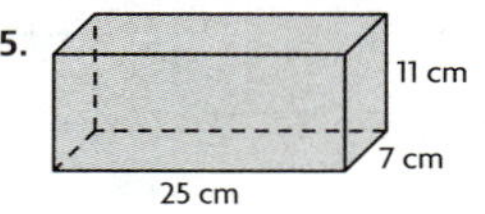

175 square cm

6. 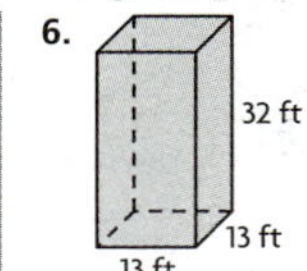

169 square feet

7. 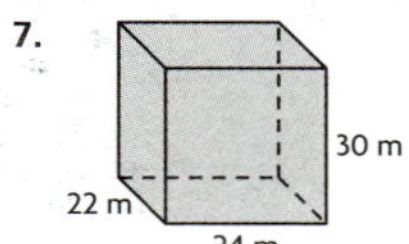

528 square meters

Problem Solving Real World

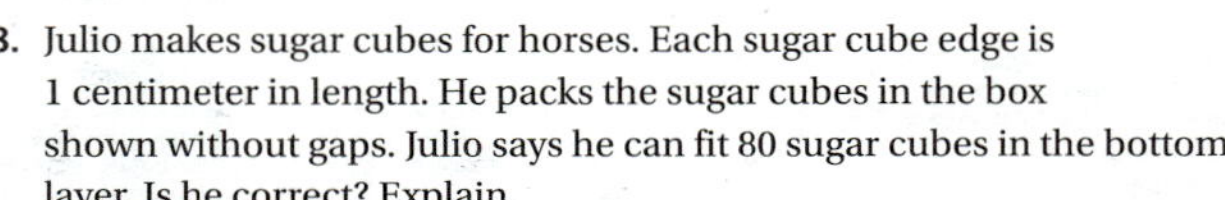

8. Julio makes sugar cubes for horses. Each sugar cube edge is 1 centimeter in length. He packs the sugar cubes in the box shown without gaps. Julio says he can fit 80 sugar cubes in the bottom layer. Is he correct? Explain.

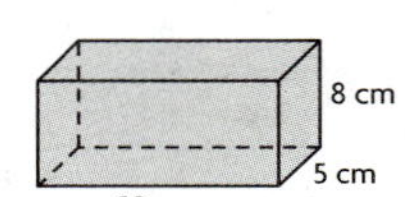

No. Possible explanation: the base of the box is a 10 cm by 5 cm rectangle. The area is 10 × 5 = 50 square centimeters, so only 50 sugar cubes will fit.

GR46

Getting Ready Lessons and Resources, pp. GR47–GR48

Checkpoint

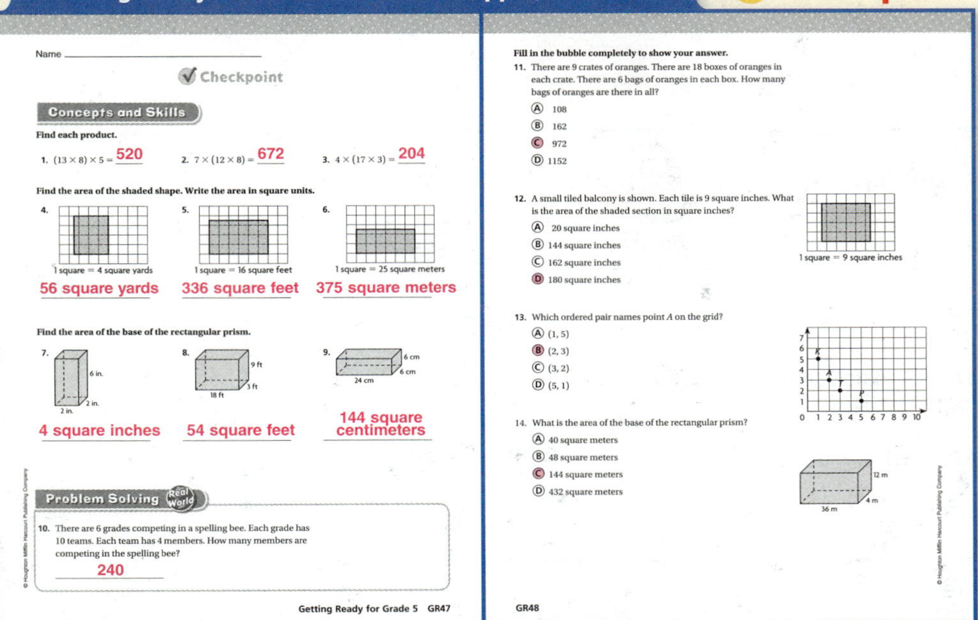

Name

Checkpoint

Concepts and Skills

Find each product.

1. $(13 \times 8) \times 5 =$ **520**
2. $7 \times (12 \times 8) =$ **672**
3. $4 \times (17 \times 3) =$ **204**

Find the area of the shaded shape. Write the area in square units.

4. 1 square = 4 square yards — **56 square yards**
5. 1 square = 16 square feet — **336 square feet**
6. 1 square = 25 square meters — **375 square meters**

Find the area of the base of the rectangular prism.

7. 6 in., 2 in., 2 in. — **4 square inches**
8. 9 ft, 18 ft, 3 ft — **54 square feet**
9. 6 cm, 6 cm, 24 cm — **144 square centimeters**

Problem Solving Real World

10. There are 6 grades competing in a spelling bee. Each grade has 10 teams. Each team has 4 members. How many members are competing in the spelling bee?

240

Getting Ready for Grade 5 GR47

Fill in the bubble completely to show your answer.

11. There are 9 crates of oranges. There are 18 boxes of oranges in each crate. There are 6 bags of oranges in each box. How many bags of oranges are there in all?

Ⓐ 108
Ⓑ 162
Ⓒ 972
Ⓓ 1152

12. A small tiled balcony is shown. Each tile is 9 square inches. What is the area of the shaded section in square inches?

Ⓐ 20 square inches
Ⓑ 144 square inches
Ⓒ 162 square inches
Ⓓ 180 square inches

1 square = 9 square inches

13. Which ordered pair names point A on the grid?

Ⓐ (1, 5)
Ⓑ (2, 3)
Ⓒ (3, 2)
Ⓓ (5, 1)

14. What is the area of the base of the rectangular prism?

Ⓐ 40 square meters
Ⓑ 48 square meters
Ⓒ 144 square meters
Ⓓ 432 square meters

12 m, 4 m, 36 m

GR48

Use **Math Talk** to check students' understanding of lesson concepts.

Read the Remember box with students to help them recognize that the base and height of a rectangle can also be referred to as the length and width.

2 PRACTICE

▶ Share and Show • Guided Practice

Use Exercises 1–4 to check students' understanding of lesson concepts. Have students identify the base of each rectangular prism and explain how they found the area.

▶ On Your Own • Independent Practice

For Exercises 5–7, remind students that area is given in square units. Students should write their answers in square units. Encourage students to circle the length and the width of the base as a reminder of what numbers to use to find each area.

▶ Problem Solving

Common Core MATHEMATICAL PRACTICES

UNLOCK THE PROBLEM For Exercise 8, students must find the area of the base of the box to determine whether the 80 sugar cubes will fit in the bottom layer.

3 SUMMARIZE

Common Core MATHEMATICAL PRACTICES

Essential Question

How can you find the area of the base of a rectangular prism? Possible answer: for the base of a rectangular prism, I can identify the measures of the base and height. Then I can use the formula $A = b \times h$ to find the area of the base in square units.

Math Journal

WRITE Math

Explain how to find the area of the base of a rectangular prism with a length of 5 ft, a width of 4 ft, and a height of 3 ft.

Getting Ready for Grade 5

Test

LESSONS 12 TO 20

Summative Assessment

Use the **Getting Ready Test** to assess students' progress in Getting Ready for Grade 5 Lessons 12–20.

Getting Ready Tests are provided in multiple-choice and mixed-response format in the *Getting Ready Lessons and Resources.*

Getting Ready Test is available online.

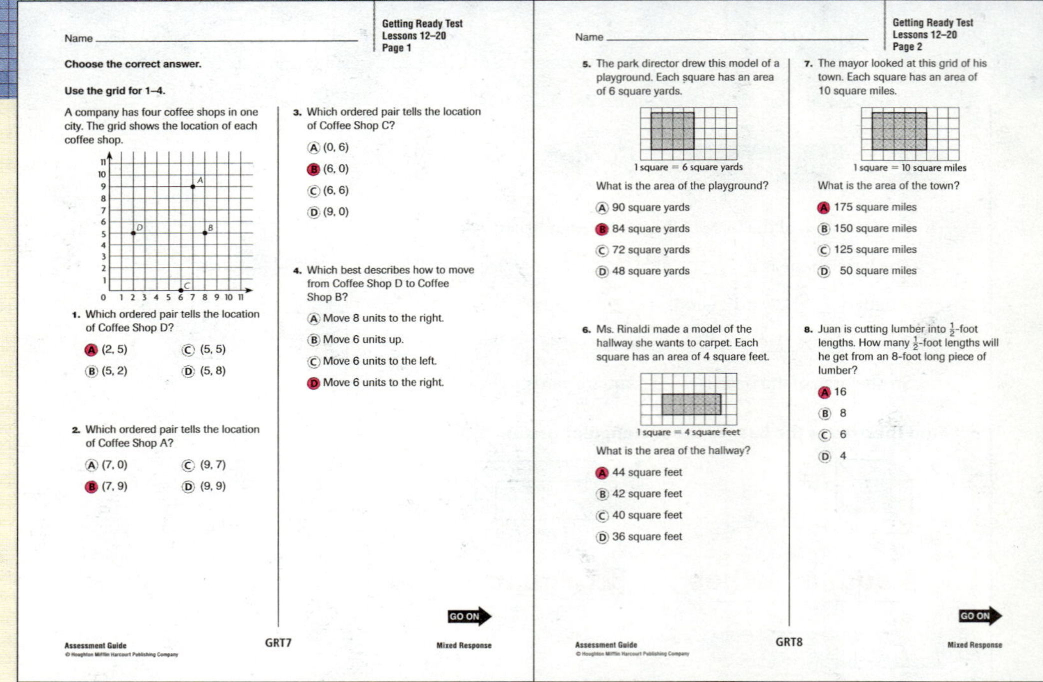

Name ______________ **Getting Ready Test Lessons 12–20 Page 1**

Choose the correct answer.

Use the grid for 1–4.

A company has four coffee shops in one city. The grid shows the location of each coffee shop.

1. Which ordered pair tells the location of Coffee Shop D?
   - (A) (2, 5)
   - (B) (5, 2)
   - (C) (5, 5)
   - (D) (5, 8)

2. Which ordered pair tells the location of Coffee Shop A?
   - (A) (7, 0)
   - (B) (7, 9)
   - (C) (9, 7)
   - (D) (9, 9)

3. Which ordered pair tells the location of Coffee Shop C?
   - (A) (0, 6)
   - (B) (6, 0)
   - (C) (6, 6)
   - (D) (9, 0)

4. Which best describes how to move from Coffee Shop D to Coffee Shop B?
   - (A) Move 8 units to the right.
   - (B) Move 6 units up.
   - (C) Move 6 units to the left.
   - (D) Move 6 units to the right.

GO ON

Assessment Guide GRT7 Mixed Response
© Houghton Mifflin Harcourt Publishing Company

Name ______________ **Getting Ready Test Lessons 12–20 Page 2**

5. The park director drew this model of a playground. Each square has an area of 6 square yards.

   1 square = 6 square yards

   What is the area of the playground?
   - (A) 90 square yards
   - (B) 84 square yards
   - (C) 72 square yards
   - (D) 48 square yards

6. Ms. Rinaldi made a model of the hallway she wants to carpet. Each square has an area of 4 square feet.

   1 square = 4 square feet

   What is the area of the hallway?
   - (A) 44 square feet
   - (B) 42 square feet
   - (C) 40 square feet
   - (D) 36 square feet

7. The mayor looked at this grid of his town. Each square has an area of 10 square miles.

   1 square = 10 square miles

   What is the area of the town?
   - (A) 175 square miles
   - (B) 150 square miles
   - (C) 125 square miles
   - (D) 50 square miles

8. Juan is cutting lumber into $\frac{1}{2}$-foot lengths. How many $\frac{1}{2}$-foot lengths will he get from an 8-foot long piece of lumber?
   - (A) 16
   - (B) 8
   - (C) 6
   - (D) 4

GO ON

Assessment Guide GRT8 Mixed Response
© Houghton Mifflin Harcourt Publishing Company

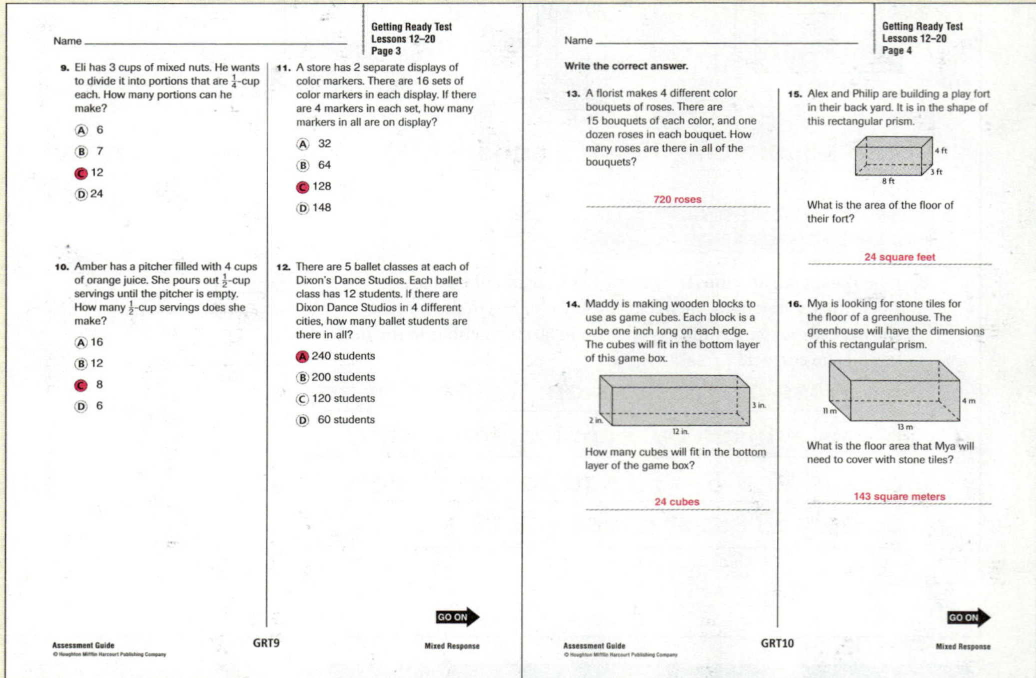

Name ______________ **Getting Ready Test Lessons 12–20 Page 3**

9. Eli has 3 cups of mixed nuts. He wants to divide it into portions that are $\frac{1}{4}$-cup each. How many portions can he make?
   - (A) 6
   - (B) 7
   - (C) 12
   - (D) 24

10. Amber has a pitcher filled with 4 cups of orange juice. She pours out $\frac{1}{2}$-cup servings until the pitcher is empty. How many $\frac{1}{2}$-cup servings does she make?
    - (A) 16
    - (B) 12
    - (C) 8
    - (D) 6

11. A store has 2 separate displays of color markers. There are 16 sets of color markers in each display. If there are 4 markers in each set, how many markers in all are on display?
    - (A) 32
    - (B) 64
    - (C) 128
    - (D) 148

12. There are 5 ballet classes at each of Dixon's Dance Studios. Each ballet class has 12 students. If there are Dixon Dance Studios in 4 different cities, how many ballet students are there in all?
    - (A) 240 students
    - (B) 200 students
    - (C) 120 students
    - (D) 60 students

GO ON

Assessment Guide GRT9 Mixed Response
© Houghton Mifflin Harcourt Publishing Company

Name ______________ **Getting Ready Test Lessons 12–20 Page 4**

Write the correct answer.

13. A florist makes 4 different color bouquets of roses. There are 15 bouquets of each color, and one dozen roses in each bouquet. How many roses are there in all of the bouquets?

    720 roses

14. Maddy is making wooden blocks to use as game cubes. Each block is a cube one inch long on each edge. The cubes will fit in the bottom layer of this game box.

    How many cubes will fit in the bottom layer of the game box?

    24 cubes

15. Alex and Philip are building a play fort in their back yard. It is in the shape of this rectangular prism.

    What is the area of the floor of their fort?

    24 square feet

16. Mya is looking for stone tiles for the floor of a greenhouse. The greenhouse will have the dimensions of this rectangular prism.

    What is the floor area that Mya will need to cover with stone tiles?

    143 square meters

GO ON

Assessment Guide GRT10 Mixed Response
© Houghton Mifflin Harcourt Publishing Company

Data-Driven Decision Making RtI

Item	Lesson	Common Error	Intervene With
1–4	17	May not understand how to use ordered pairs to locate points on a grid	**R**—GRR17
5–7	18	May not understand how to use tiling to find the area of a rectangle	**R**—GRR18
8–10	15	May not understand how to use repeated subtraction to solve problems involving division with fractions	**R**—GRR15
11–13	19	May not understand how to find the product of three factors	**R**—GRR19
14–16	20	May not understand how to find the area of the base of a rectangular prism	**R**—GRR20

Key: R—Getting Ready Lessons and Resources: Reteach

Name ______________

Getting Ready Test
Lessons 12–20
Page 5

17. Mr. Martin cooked some chili. His family ate $\frac{1}{3}$ of the chili for dinner. Later, as a snack, the family ate $\frac{1}{6}$ more of the chili. What part of the chili was eaten in all?

$\frac{3}{6}$

18. In January of one winter, $\frac{3}{10}$ of a wood pile was used in a wood stove. In February, $\frac{2}{5}$ of the wood pile was used. What part of the wood pile was used up at the end of February?

$\frac{7}{10}$

19. Josh needs $\frac{2}{3}$ hour to weed a garden and $\frac{1}{12}$ hour to water the garden. What part of an hour do these two jobs take?

$\frac{9}{12}$

20. It is $\frac{3}{5}$ mile from Elaine's home to her school. It is $\frac{1}{10}$ mile from her home to the library. How much farther is Elaine's home from her school than it is from the library?

$\frac{5}{10}$ mile

GO ON

Assessment Guide
© Houghton Mifflin Harcourt Publishing Company

GRT11

Mixed Response

Name ______________

Getting Ready Test
Lessons 12–20
Page 6

21. Jacob had $\frac{3}{4}$ of his book report left to do. He completed $\frac{3}{8}$ more of the report today. What fraction of the book report does Jacob still need to do?

$\frac{3}{8}$

22. Luis played soccer for $\frac{1}{2}$ hour. Gabriella played soccer for $\frac{5}{6}$ hour. What part of an hour more did Gabriella play than Luis?

$\frac{2}{6}$

23. Write the division problem $1 \div 9$ as a fraction or a mixed number.

$\frac{1}{9}$

24. A group of people buys 5 pounds of corn meal to divide equally among 6 families. Write a fraction or mixed number that shows how many pounds of corn meal each family gets.

$\frac{5}{6}$

25. Vanessa uses $\frac{3}{4}$ pound of flour to make a loaf of bread. To make 6 loaves, will she use more than 6 pounds of flour or less than 6 pounds of flour?

less than 6 pounds of flour

STOP

Assessment Guide
© Houghton Mifflin Harcourt Publishing Company

GRT12

Mixed Response

Portfolio Suggestions The portfolio represents the growth, talents, achievements, and reflections of the mathematics learner. Students might spend a short time selecting work samples for their portfolios.

You may want to have students respond to the following questions:

- What new understanding of math have I developed in the past several weeks?
- What growth in understanding or skills can I see in my work?
- What can I do to improve my understanding of math ideas?
- What would I like to learn more about?

For information about how to organize, share, and evaluate portfolios, see the *Chapter Resources*.

Data-Driven Decision Making

Item	Lesson	Common Error	Intervene With
17–19	12	May not know how to add fractions when one denominator is a multiple of the other	**R**—GRR12
20–22	13	May not know how to add fractions when one denominator is a multiple of the other	**R**—GRR13
23, 24	16	May not understand how to write division problems as fractions	**R**—GRR16
25	14	May not understand how to compare the size of the product to the size of each factor when multiplying fractions	**R**—GRR14

Key: R—Getting Ready Lessons and Resources: Reteach

Grab-and-Go!™

Differentiated Centers Kit

The Grab-and-Go!™ Differentiated Centers Kit contains ready-to-use readers, games, and math center activities that are designed for flexible usage.

- Readers that integrate math skills with cross-curricular content.
- Games that engage students to practice math skills.
- Math Center Activities that focus on computation, mental math, geometry, measurement, and challenge activities.

See the Grab-and-Go!™ Teacher Guide and Activity Resources for more information.

<table>
<tr><th>Chapter</th><th colspan="3">Grade 4</th></tr>
<tr><td rowspan="4">1 Place Value, Addition, and Subtraction to One Million</td><td>Readers</td><td colspan="2">Summing Up a Pet's Needs
The World's Tallest Buildings</td></tr>
<tr><td>Games</td><td colspan="2">Tree Climb
Who's the Closest?</td></tr>
<tr><td rowspan="2">Activity Cards</td><td>Card 1</td><td>Round Up!
It's in the Area</td></tr>
<tr><td>Card 4</td><td>Ask Me About Area
Tile Tabulations</td></tr>
<tr><td rowspan="4">2 Multiply by 1-Digit Numbers</td><td>Readers</td><td colspan="2">Multiplying a Good Deed
Putting the World on a Page
Tickle My Memory</td></tr>
<tr><td>Games</td><td colspan="2">Multiplication Marathon
Triangle Products</td></tr>
<tr><td rowspan="2">Activity Cards</td><td>Card 3</td><td>Know Your Nines
What's My Fact?</td></tr>
<tr><td>Card 5</td><td>First One Out
Roll to Measure
Product Power</td></tr>
<tr><td rowspan="4">3 Multiply 2-Digit Numbers</td><td>Readers</td><td colspan="2">Multiplying a Good Deed
Putting the World on a Page</td></tr>
<tr><td>Games</td><td colspan="2">Multiplication Marathon
Triangle Products</td></tr>
<tr><td rowspan="2">Activity Cards</td><td>Card 3</td><td>Roomy Dimensions</td></tr>
<tr><td>Card 5</td><td>First One Out
Product Power</td></tr>
</table>

Chapter	Grade 4		
4 Divide by 1-Digit Numbers	Readers	The Division Champs The Thirst Quencher	
	Games	Divide All Five Divide to Win Remainder or Not?	
	Activity Cards	Card 3	What's My Fact?
		Card 7	Divide and Conquer! Moon Weight Estimate It
		Card 9	Remainders Rule! Bits and Pieces Dividend Rolls!
5 Factors, Multiples, and Patterns	Reader	Eratosthenes and His Sieve	
	Game	Factor Farm	
	Activity Cards	Card 3	What's My Fact?
		Card 5	First One Out
		Card 15	Follow the Leader
		Card 17	Flowering Factors Prime Time
6 Fraction Equivalence and Comparison	Readers	Fundraising Fair A Melody in Fractions Sleeping Half the Day Away	
	Game	Fraction Action	
	Activity Cards	Card 6	Fraction Swap Ruler Challenge Fraction Bingo!
		Card 8	What's Your Order?

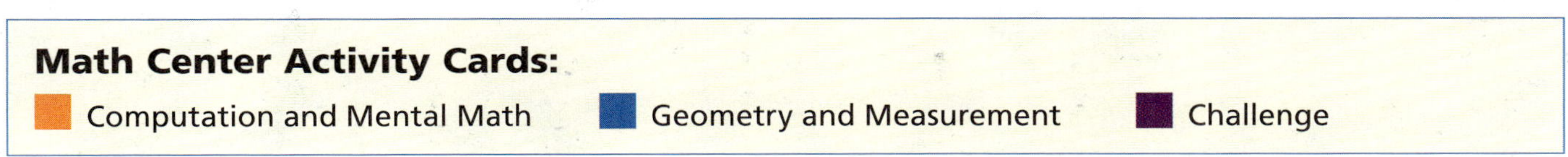
Math Center Activity Cards:
Computation and Mental Math — Geometry and Measurement — Challenge

Chapter	Grade 4		
7 Add and Subtract Fractions	Reader	Sleeping Half the Day Away	
	Games	Fraction Action Fraction Concentration	
	Activity Cards	Card 6	Ruler Challenge Fraction Bingo!
		Card 8	Fantastic Fractions Pencil Me In
8 Multiply Fractions by Whole Numbers	Reader	A Melody in Fractions	
	Activity Card	Card 6	Ruler Challenge Fraction Bingo!
9 Relate Fractions and Decimals	Readers	And the Total Is Decimals on a Diamond Elizabeth's Groovy Green Racing Machine A Melody in Fractions	
	Games	Fraction Action Order, Please!	
	Activity Card	Card 10	What's My Place? Where is the Decimal?
10 Two-Dimensional Figures	Readers	A Mirror Image A New Angle on Trains and Train Stations Skateboarding Takes Shape	
	Activity Card	Card 13	Concentrate! Picture Perfect! Connecting Vertices
11 Angles	Reader	Skateboarding Takes Shape	
	Activity Card	Card 13	Concentrate! Picture Perfect!

Chapter	Grade 4		
12 Relative Sizes of Measurement Units	Readers	Measuring the Mississippi A Trip to the Pond	
	Game	Time to Go	
	Activity Cards	Card 1	Measure Up
		Card 14	Mass Match-Up Balancing Act Challenging Changes
		Card 16	Capacity Overload! Ultimate Units Capacity Challenge
13 Algebra: Perimeter and Area	Readers	Designing a Skatepark Fighting Fire with Fire Paint By Numbers	
	Activity Cards	Card 3	Roomy Dimensions
		Card 4	Meter Math
		Card 20	Perimeter Pairs 36 Is My Area Spinning Rectangles

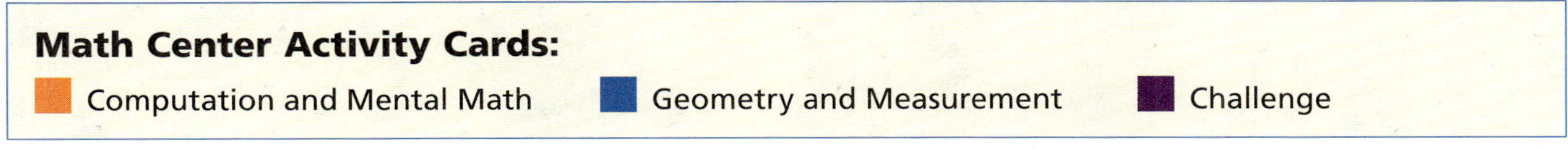

Sequence Options

***Go Math!* provides the flexibility to teach the program in a different sequence. For chapters that need student background knowledge, use the list of prerequisites.**

Chapter	Objectives	Prerequisites
1 Place Value, Addition, and Subtraction to One Million COMMON CORE STATE STANDARDS 4.NBT.A.1, 4.NBT.A.2, 4.NBT.A.3, 4.NBT.B.4	• Use models to show place value of numbers through 1,000,000. • Read and write whole numbers through 999,999. • Compare and order whole numbers. • Round whole numbers. • Add and subtract whole numbers. • Use the strategy *draw a diagram* to solve comparison problems.	
2 Multiply by 1-Digit Numbers COMMON CORE STATE STANDARDS 4.OA.A.1, 4.OA.A.2, 4.NBT.B.5, 4.OA.A.3	• Multiply tens, hundreds, and thousands by whole numbers through 10. • Estimate products by rounding. • Use a variety of strategies and models to multiply by 1-digit numbers. • Solve multiplication comparison and multistep problems.	Chapter 1
3 Multiply 2-Digit Numbers COMMON CORE STATE STANDARDS 4.NBT.B.5, 4.OA.A.3	• Use place value and multiplication properties to multiply by tens. • Estimate products by rounding or by using compatible numbers. • Use a variety of strategies and models to multiply 2-digit numbers. • Use the strategy *draw a diagram* to solve multistep problems.	Chapter 2
4 Divide by 1-Digit Numbers COMMON CORE STATE STANDARDS 4.NBT.B.6, 4.OA.A.3	• Use multiples and compatible numbers to estimate quotients. • Divide tens, hundreds, and thousands by whole numbers through 10. • Use a variety of strategies and models to divide with and without remainders. • Interpret remainders. • Use the strategy *draw a diagram* to solve multistep problems.	Chapter 2
5 Factors, Multiples, and Patterns COMMON CORE STATE STANDARDS 4.OA.B.4, 4.OA.C.5	• Find all the factors of a number. • Determine whether a number is a multiple of a given number. • Determine whether a number is prime or composite. • Generate a number pattern and describe features of the pattern. • Use models and the strategy *make a list* to solve problems.	Chapters 2, 4
6 Fraction Equivalence and Comparison COMMON CORE STATE STANDARDS 4.NF.A.1, 4.NF.A.2	• Use a variety of strategies and models to generate equivalent fractions. • Write equivalent fractions in simplest form. • Use equivalent fractions to write fractions with a common denominator. • Compare and order fractions.	Chapter 5

Chapter	Objectives	Prerequisites
7 Add and Subtract Fractions COMMON CORE STATE STANDARDS 4.NF.B.3a, 4.NF.B.3b, 4.NF.B.3d, 4.NF.B.3c	• Decompose a fraction by writing it as a sum. • Use a variety of strategies and models to add and subtract fractions and mixed numbers. • Write fractions greater than 1 as mixed numbers and write mixed numbers as fractions greater than 1.	Chapter 6
8 Multiply Fractions by Whole Numbers COMMON CORE STATE STANDARDS 4.NF.B.4a, 4.NF.B.4b, 4.NF.B.4c	• Find multiples of a unit fraction. • Find multiples of a fraction. • Multiply a fraction or mixed number by a whole number. • Use the strategy *draw a diagram* to solve comparison problems with fractions.	Chapters 5, 7
9 Relate Fractions and Decimals COMMON CORE STATE STANDARDS 4.NF.C.6, 4.NF.C.5, 4.MD.A.2, 4.NF.C.7	• Record tenths and hundredths as fractions and as decimals. • Relate fractions, decimals, and money. • Add fractions with denominators of 10 and 100. • Compare decimals to hundredths. • Use the strategy *act it out* to solve problems.	Chapters 1, 6, 7
10 Two-Dimensional Figures COMMON CORE STATE STANDARDS 4.G.A.1, 4.G.A.2, 4.G.A.3, 4.OA.C.5	• Identify and draw points, lines, line segments, rays, angles, parallel lines, and perpendicular lines. • Classify triangles by the size of their angles. • Sort and classify quadrilaterals. • Identify and draw lines of symmetry in two-dimensional figures. • Use the strategy *act it out* to solve pattern problems.	
11 Angles COMMON CORE STATE STANDARDS 4.MD.C.5a, 4.MD.C.5b, 4.MD.C.6, 4.MD.C.7	• Relate angles and degrees to fractional parts of a circle. • Use a protractor to measure and draw angles. • Determine the measure of an angle separated into parts.	Chapter 10
12 Relative Sizes of Measurement Units COMMON CORE STATE STANDARDS 4.MD.A.1, 4.MD.A.2	• Use benchmarks to understand the relative sizes of measurement units. • Use models to compare customary units of length, weight, and liquid volume. • Make and interpret line plots. • Use models to compare metric units of length, mass, and liquid volume. • Use models to compare units of time and solve elapsed time problems. • Solve problems involving mixed measures.	Chapter 9
13 Algebra: Perimeter and Area COMMON CORE STATE STANDARDS 4.MD.A.3	• Use formulas to find the perimeter and area of a rectangle. • Find the area of combined rectangles. • Find the unknown measure of a side of a rectangle, given perimeter or area. • Use the strategy *solve a simpler problem* to solve area problems.	Chapter 12

Common Core

COMMON CORE STATE STANDARDS FOR MATHEMATICS

Correlations

Standards for Mathematical Practices		Student Edition and Teacher Edition Pages
MP1	Make sense of problems and persevere in solving them.	In most Student Edition lessons. Some examples are: 23, 37, 43, 45, 83, 107, 133, 183, 200, 221, 250, 294, 311, 359, 417, 441, 444, 481, 519, 581, 607, 644, 653, 717, 746 In most Teacher Edition lessons. Some examples are: *14, 23A, 37A, 45, 49, 125, 197, 238, 469, 472, 481, 573, 644, 726*
MP2	Reason abstractly and quantitatively.	In most Student Edition lessons. Some examples are: 11, 17, 39, 65, 72, 122, 151, 165, 183, 209, 222, 285, 339, 361, 391, 423, 469, 481, 507, 527, 535, 575, 621, 647, 697,725, 737 In most Teacher Edition lessons. Some examples are: *17A, 23A, 34, 39, 45, 51, 125, 229, 235, 247, 259A, 335, 339, 361, 373, 391A, 461A, 469, 641, 660, 703A, 725*
MP3	Construct viable arguments and critique the reasoning of others.	In most Student Edition lessons. Some examples are: 46, 49, 69, 128, 177, 212, 235, 288, 351, 359, 393, 397, 429, 495, 555, 575, 584, 601, 650, 659, 662, 681, 691, 706, 723 In most Teacher Edition lessons. Some examples are: *46, 49A, 125, 204, 330, 372, 470, 584, 662, 706, 744*
MP4	Model with mathematics.	In most Student Edition lessons. Some examples are: 5, 13, 17, 31, 52, 63, 93, 95, 145, 148, 203, 227, 279, 305, 339, 351, 399, 403, 461, 469, 495, 519, 549, 552, 567, 613, 621, 655, 665, 703, 737 In most Teacher Edition lessons. Some examples are: *5A, 13, 17A, 17, 20, 23, 49A, 52, 63A, 88, 113, 227, 247, 328, 351A, 371, 441A, 456, 478, 550, 661, 687*
MP5	Use appropriate tools strategically.	In most Student Edition lessons. Some examples are: 17, 49, 75, 151, 183, 197, 221, 237, 254, 291, 311, 313, 336, 385, 397, 455, 519, 561, 575, 590, 601, 613, 621, 641, 665, 685, 688, 729 In most Teacher Edition lessons. Some examples are: *17A, 23A, 31, 37A, 49A, 329, 336, 359, 582, 590, 613A, 688, 737A*
MP6	Attend to precision.	In most Student Edition lessons. Some examples are: 5, 40, 81, 159, 205, 215, 235, 247, 281, 299, 308, 339, 365, 371, 411, 457, 513, 527, 549, 558, 567, 610, 613, 653, 723, 731, 743 In most Teacher Edition lessons. Some examples are: *5A, 6, 40, 87, 93, 99, 115, 205, 233, 265, 340, 360, 455, 457, 481, 549A, 549, 561, 587A, 659, 686*
MP7	Look for and make use of structure.	In most Student Edition lessons. Some examples are: 5, 23, 31, 63, 75, 109, 120, 145, 171, 173, 197, 209, 299, 302, 327, 342, 435, 441, 477, 501, 555, 581, 653, 665, 673, 717, 737, 740 In most Teacher Edition lessons. Some examples are: *5A, 11, 23A, 31, 95, 327, 333, 342, 359, 455, 471, 476, 501A, 563, 588, 642, 686*
MP8	Look for and express regularity in repeated reasoning.	In most Student Edition lessons. Some examples are: 37, 49, 75, 125, 157, 171, 235, 301, 391, 419, 463, 507, 527, 587, 659, 691, 717 In most Teacher Edition lessons. Some examples are: *37A, 37, 43, 49A, 171A, 198, 248, 334, 475, 568, 581*

Domain: Operations and Algebraic Thinking

		Student Edition and Teacher Edition Pages
Use the four operations with whole numbers to solve problems.		
4.OA.A.1	Interpret a multiplication equation as a comparison, e.g., interpret 35 = 5 × 7 as a statement that 35 is 5 times as many as 7 and 7 times as many as 5. Represent verbal statements of multiplicative comparisons as multiplication equations.	***63A–63B,*** **63–66**
4.OA.A.2	Multiply or divide to solve word problems involving multiplicative comparison, e.g., by using drawings and equations with a symbol for the unknown number to represent the problem, distinguishing multiplicative comparison from additive comparison.	***69A–69B,*** **69–72**
4.OA.A.3	Solve multistep word problems posed with whole numbers and having whole-number answers using the four operations, including problems in which remainders must be interpreted. Represent these problems using equations with a letter standing for the unknown quantity. Assess the reasonableness of answers using mental computation and estimation strategies including rounding.	***113A–113B,*** **113–116,** ***131A–131B,*** **131–134,** ***183A–183B,*** **183–186,** ***209A–209B,*** **209–212** See Also: *37A–37B*, 37–40, *43A–43B*, 43–46, *119A–119B*, 119–122, *171A–171B*, 171–174, *265A–265B*, 265–268
Gain familiarity with factors and multiples.		
4.OA.B.4	Find all factor pairs for a whole number in the range 1–100. Recognize that a whole number is a multiple of each of its factors. Determine whether a given whole number in the range 1–100 is a multiple of a given one-digit number. Determine whether a given whole number in the range 1–100 is prime or composite.	***279A–279B,*** **279–282,** ***285A–285B,*** **285–288,** ***291A–291B,*** **291–294,** ***299A–299B,*** **299–302** ***305A–305B,*** **305–308**
Generate and analyze patterns.		
4.OA.C.5	Generate a number or shape pattern that follows a given rule. Identify apparent features of the pattern that were not explicit in the rule itself.	***311A–311B,*** **311–314,** ***587A–587B,*** **587–590**

Pages only in Teacher Edition are shown in italics.

Domain: Number and Operations in Base Ten

		Student Edition and Teacher Edition Pages
Generalize place value understanding for multi-digit whole numbers.		
4.NBT.A.1	Recognize that in a multi-digit whole number, a digit in one place represents ten times what it represents in the place to its right.	***5A–5B*, 5–8, 31–34** See Also: *75A–75B*, 75–78, *145A–145B*, 145–148, *215A–215B*, 215–218
4.NBT.A.2	Read and write multi-digit whole numbers using base-ten numerals, number names, and expanded form. Compare two multi-digit numbers based on meanings of the digits in each place, using >, =, and < symbols to record the results of comparisons.	***11A–11B*, 11–14, *17A–17B*, 17–20** See Also: *31A–31B*, 21–34
4.NBT.A.3	Use place value understanding to round multi-digit whole numbers to any place.	***23A–23B*, 23–26** See Also: *37A–37B*, 37–40, *43A–43B*, 43–46, *81A–81B*, 81–84, *151A–151B*, 151–154
Use place value understanding and properties of operations to perform multi-digit arithmetic.		
4.NBT.B.4	Fluently add and subtract multi-digit whole numbers using the standard algorithm.	***37A–37B*, 37–40, *43A–43B*, 43–46, *49A–49B*, 49–52**
4.NBT.B.5	Multiply a whole number of up to four digits by a one-digit whole number, and multiply two two-digit numbers, using strategies based on place value and the properties of operations. Illustrate and explain the calculation by using equations, rectangular arrays, and/or area models.	***75A–75B*, 75–78, *81A–81B*, 81–84, *87A–87B*, 87–90, *93A–93B*, 93–96, *99A–99B*, 99–102, *107A–107B*, 107–110, *119A–119B*, 119–122, *125A–125B*, 125–128, *145A–145B*, 145–148, *151A–151B*, 151–154, *157A–157B*, 157–160, *163A–163B*, 163–166, *171A–171B*, 171–174, *177A–177B*, 177–180** See Also: *81A–81B*, 81–84, *183A–183B*, 183–186
4.NBT.B.6	Find whole-number quotients and remainders with up to four-digit dividends and one-digit divisors, using strategies based on place value, the properties of operations, and/or the relationship between multiplication and division. Illustrate and explain the calculation by using equations, rectangular arrays, and/or area models.	***197A–197B*, 197–200, *203A–203B*, 203–206, *215A–215B*, 215–218, *221A–221B*, 221–224, *227A–227B*, 227–230, *235A–235B*, 235–238, *241A–241B*, 241–244, *247A–247B*, 247–250, *253A–253B*, 253–256, *259A–259B*, 259–262** See Also: *209A–209B*, 209–212, *265A–265B*, 265–268

Domain: Number and Operations—Fractions

Standard	Description	Student Edition and Teacher Edition Pages
Extend understanding of fraction equivalence and ordering.		
4.NF.A.1	Explain why a fraction *a*/*b* is equivalent to a fraction ($n \times a$)/($n \times b$) by using visual fraction models, with attention to how the number and size of the parts differ even though the two fractions themselves are the same size. Use this principle to recognize and generate equivalent fractions.	***327A–327B,*** **327–330,** ***333A–333B,*** **333–336,** ***339A–339B,*** **339–342,** ***345A–345B,*** **345–348,** ***351A–351B,*** **351–354**
4.NF.A.2	Compare two fractions with different numerators and different denominators, e.g., by creating common denominators or numerators, or by comparing to a benchmark fraction such as 1/2. Recognize that comparisons are valid only when the two fractions refer to the same whole. Record the results of comparisons with symbols $>$, $=$, or $<$, and justify the conclusions, e.g., by using a visual fraction model.	***359A–359B,*** **359–362,** ***365A–365B,*** **365–368,** ***371A–371B,*** **371–374**
Build fractions from unit fractions.		
4.NF.B.3	Understand a fraction *a*/*b* with $a > 1$ as a sum of fractions 1/*b*.	
	a. Understand addition and subtraction of fractions as joining and separating parts referring to the same whole.	***385A–385B,*** **385–388**
	b. Decompose a fraction into a sum of fractions with the same denominator in more than one way, recording each decomposition by an equation. Justify decompositions, e.g., by using a visual fraction model.	***391A–391B,*** **391–394,** ***417A–417B,*** **417–420**
	c. Add and subtract mixed numbers with like denominators, e.g., by replacing each mixed number with an equivalent fraction, and/or by using properties of operations and the relationship between addition and subtraction.	***423A–423B,*** **423–426,** ***429A–429B,*** **429–432,** ***313A-313B,*** **313–316**
	d. Solve word problems involving addition and subtraction of fractions referring to the same whole and having like denominators, e.g., by using visual fraction models and equations to represent the problem.	***397A–397B,*** **397–400,** ***403A–403B,*** **403–406,** ***409A–409B,*** **409-412,** ***441A–441B,*** **441–444**
4.NF.B.4	Apply and extend previous understandings of multiplication to multiply a fraction by a whole number.	
	a. Understand a fraction *a*/*b* as a multiple of 1/*b*.	***455A–455B,*** **455–458**
	b. Understand a multiple of *a*/*b* as a multiple of 1/*b*, and use this understanding to multiply a fraction by a whole number.	***461A–461B,*** **461–464,** ***469A–469B,*** **469–472**
	c. Solve word problems involving multiplication of a fraction by a whole number, e.g., by using visual fraction models and equations to represent the problem.	***475A–475B,*** **475–478,** ***481A–481B,*** **481–484** See Also: *461A–461B*, 461–464, *469A–469B*, 469–472

Pages only in Teacher Edition are shown in italics.

Domain continued on next page ►

Domain: Number and Operations—Fractions *(continued)*

Understand decimal notation for fractions, and compare decimal fractions.		Student Edition and Teacher Edition Pages
4.NF.C.5	Express a fraction with denominator 10 as an equivalent fraction with denominator 100, and use this technique to add two fractions with respective denominators 10 and 100.	***507A-507B*, 507–510, *527A-527B*, 527–530**
4.NF.C.6	Use decimal notation for fractions with denominators 10 or 100.	***495A-495B*, 495–498, *501A-501B*, 501–504, *513A-513B*, 513–516** See Also: *507A–507B*, 507–510
4.NF.C.7	Compare two decimals to hundredths by reasoning about their size. Recognize that comparisons are valid only when the two decimals refer to the same whole. Record the results of comparisons with the symbols >, =, or <, and justify the conclusions, e.g., by using a visual model.	***533A-533B*, 533–536**

Domain: Measurement and Data

Solve problems involving measurement and conversion of measurements.		Student Edition and Teacher Edition Pages
4.MD.A.1	Know relative sizes of measurement units within one system of units including km, m, cm; kg, g; lb, oz.; l, ml; hr, min, sec. Within a single system of measurement, express measurements in a larger unit in terms of a smaller unit. Record measurement equivalents in a two-column table.	***641A-641B*, 641–644, *647A-647B*, 647–650, *653A-653B*, 653–656, *659A-659B*, 659–662, *673A-673B*, 673–676, *679A-679B*, 679–682, *685A-685B*, 685–688, *703A-703B*, 703–706** See Also: *691A–691B*, 691–694, *697A–697B*, 697–700
4.MD.A.2	Use the four operations to solve word problems involving distances, intervals of time, liquid volumes, masses of objects, and money, including problems involving simple fractions or decimals, and problems that require expressing measurements given in a larger unit in terms of a smaller unit. Represent measurement quantities using diagrams such as number line diagrams that feature a measurement scale.	***519A-519B*, 519–522, *685A-685B*, 685–688, *691A-691B*, 691–694, *697A-697B*, 697–700** See Also: *647A-647B*, 647–650, *653A-653B*, 653–656, *659A-659B*, 659–662, *665A-665B*, 665–668, *673A-673B*, 673–676, *679A-679B*, 679–682, *685A-685B*, 685–688
4.MD.A.3	Apply the area and perimeter formulas for rectangles in real world and mathematical problems.	***717A-717B*, 717–720, *723A-723B*, 723–726, *729A-729B*, 729–732, *737A-737B*, 737–740, *743A-743B*, 743–746**
Represent and interpret data.		
4.MD.B.4	Make a line plot to display a data set of measurements in fractions of a unit (1/2, 1/4, 1/8). Solve problems involving addition and subtraction of fractions by using information presented in line plots.	***665A-665B*, 665–668**

Domain continued on next page ►

Domain: Measurement and Data *(continued)*

		Student Edition and Teacher Edition Pages
Geometric measurement: understand concepts of angle and measure angles.		
4.MD.C.5	Recognize angles as geometric shapes that are formed wherever two rays share a common endpoint, and understand concepts of angle measurement:	
	a. An angle is measured with reference to a circle with its center at the common endpoint of the rays, by considering the fraction of the circular arc between the points where the two rays intersect the circle. An angle that turns through 1/360 of a circle is called a "one-degree angle," and can be used to measure angles.	***601A–601B*, 601–604, *607A–607B*, 607–610**
	b. An angle that turns through *n* one-degree angles is said to have an angle measure of *n* degrees.	***607A–607B*, 607–624**
4.MD.C.6	Measure angles in whole-number degrees using a protractor. Sketch angles of specified measure.	***613A–613B*, 613–616**
4.MD.C.7	Recognize angle measure as additive. When an angle is decomposed into non-overlapping parts, the angle measure of the whole is the sum of the angle measures of the parts. Solve addition and subtraction problems to find unknown angles on a diagram in real world and mathematical problems, e.g., by using an equation with a symbol for the unknown angle measure.	***621A–621B*, 621–624, *627A–627B*, 627–630**

Domain: Geometry

		Student Edition and Teacher Edition Pages
Draw and identify lines and angles, and classify shapes by properties of their lines and angles.		
4.G.A.1	Draw points, lines, line segments, rays, angles (right, acute, obtuse), and perpendicular and parallel lines. Identify these in two-dimensional figures.	***549A–549B*, 549–552, *561A–561B*, 561–564** See Also: *555A–555B*, 555–558
4.G.A.2	Classify two-dimensional figures based on the presence or absence of parallel or perpendicular lines, or the presence or absence of angles of a specified size. Recognize right triangles as a category, and identify right triangles.	***555A–555B*, 555–558, *567A–567B*, 567–570**
4.G.A.3	Recognize a line of symmetry for a two-dimensional figure as a line across the figure such that the figure can be folded along the line into matching parts. Identify line-symmetric figures and draw lines of symmetry.	***575A–575B*, 575–578, *581A–581B*, 581–584**

Pages only in Teacher Edition are shown in italics.

Student Edition Glossary

Glossary

Pronunciation Key

a	add, map	ē	equal, tree	m	move, seem	o͞o	pool, food	u̇	pull, book
ā	ace, rate	f	fit, half	n	nice, tin	p	pit, stop	û(r)	burn, term
â(r)	care, air	g	go, log	ng	ring, song	r	run, poor	yo͞o	fuse, few
ä	palm, father	h	hope, hate	o	odd, hot	s	see, pass	v	vain, eve
b	bat, rub	i	it, give	ō	open, so	sh	sure, rush	w	win, away
ch	check, catch	ī	ice, write	ô	order, jaw	t	talk, sit	y	yet, yearn
d	dog, rod	j	joy, ledge	oi	oil, boy	th	thin, both	z	zest, muse
e	end, pet	k	cool, take	ou	pout, now	t͟h	this, bathe	zh	vision, pleasure
		l	look, rule	o͝o	took, full	u	up, done		

ə the schwa, an unstressed vowel representing the sound spelled *a* in *above*, *e* in *sicken*, *i* in *possible*, *o* in *melon*, *u* in *circus*

Other symbols:
- • separates words into syllables
- ′ indicates stress on a syllable

A

acute angle [ə•kyo͞ot′ ang′gəl] **ángulo agudo** An angle that measures greater than 0° and less than 90°
Example:

acute triangle [ə•kyo͞ot′ trī′ang•gəl] **triángulo acutángulo** A triangle with three acute angles
Example:

addend [a′dend] **sumando** A number that is added to another in an addition problem
Example: 2 + 4 = 6;
2 and 4 are addends.

addition [ə•di′shən] **suma** The process of finding the total number of items when two or more groups of items are joined; the opposite operation of subtraction

A.M. [ā•em′] **a.m.** The times after midnight and before noon

analog clock [anəl• ôg kläk] **reloj analógico** A tool for measuring time, in which hands move around a circle to show hours, minutes, and sometimes seconds
Example:

angle [ang′gəl] **ángulo** A shape formed by two line segments or rays that share the same endpoint
Example:

area [âr′ē•ə] **área** The number of square units needed to cover a flat surface
Example:

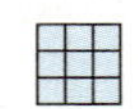

area = 9 square units

array [ə•rā′] **matriz** An arrangement of objects in rows and columns
Example:

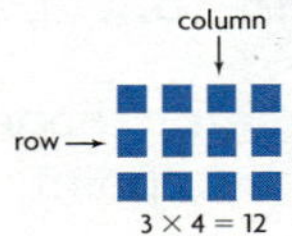

Associative Property of Addition [ə•sō′shē•āt•iv präp′ər•tē əv ə•dish′ən] **propiedad asociativa de la suma** The property that states that you can group addends in different ways and still get the same sum
Example: 3 + (8 + 5) = (3 + 8) + 5

Associative Property of Multiplication [ə•sō′shē•ə•tiv präp′ər•tē əv mul•tə•pli•kā′shən] **propiedad asociativa de la multiplicación** The property that states that you can group factors in different ways and still get the same product
Example: 3 × (4 × 2) = (3 × 4) × 2

bar graph [bär graf] **gráfica de barras** A graph that uses bars to show data
Example:

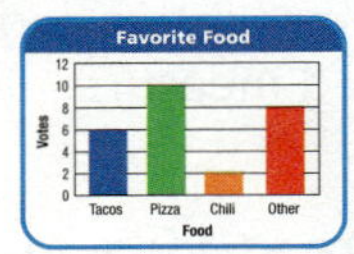

base [bās] **base** A polygon's side or a two-dimensional shape, usually a polygon or circle, by which a three-dimensional shape is measured or named
Examples:

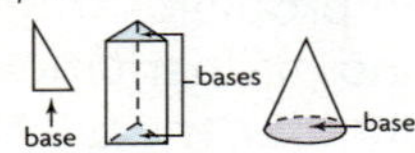

benchmark [bench′märk] **punto de referencia** A known size or amount that helps you understand a different size or amount

calendar [kal′ən•dər] **calendario** A table that shows the days, weeks, and months of a year

capacity [kə•pas′i•tē] **capacidad** The amount a container can hold when filled

Celsius (°C) [sel′sē•əs] **Celsius** A metric scale for measuring temperature

centimeter (cm) [sen′tə•mēt•ər] **centímetro (cm)** A metric unit for measuring length or distance
1 meter = 100 centimeters
Example:

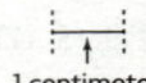

1 centimeter

cent sign (¢) [sent sīn] **símbolo de centavo** A symbol that stands for *cent* or *cents*
Example: 53¢

clockwise [kläk′wīz] **en el sentido de las manecillas del reloj** In the same direction in which the hands of a clock move

closed shape [klōzd shāp] **figura cerrada** A two-dimensional shape that begins and ends at the same point
Examples:

common denominator [käm′ən dē•näm′ə•nāt•ər] **denominador común** A common multiple of two or more denominators
Example: Some common denominators for $\frac{1}{4}$ and $\frac{5}{6}$ are 12, 24, and 36.

common factor [käm′ən fak′tər] **factor común** A number that is a factor of two or more numbers

common multiple [käm′ən mul′tə•pəl] **múltiplo común** A number that is a multiple of two or more numbers

Commutative Property of Addition [kə•myo͞ot′ə•tiv präp′ər•tē əv ə•dish′ən] **propiedad conmutativa de la suma** The property that states that when the order of two addends is changed, the sum is the same
Example: 4 + 5 = 5 + 4

Commutative Property of Multiplication [kə•myo͞ot′ə•tiv präp′ər•tē əv mul•tə•pli•kā′shən] **propiedad conmutativa de la multiplicación** The property that states that when the order of two factors is changed, the product is the same
Example: 4 × 5 = 5 × 4

compare [kəm•pâr′] **comparar** To describe whether numbers are equal to, less than, or greater than each other

compatible numbers [kəm•pat′ə•bəl num′bərz] **números compatibles** Numbers that are easy to compute mentally

composite number [kəm•päz′it num′bər] **número compuesto** A number having more than two factors
Example: 6 is a composite number, since its factors are 1, 2, 3, and 6.

corner [kôr′nər] **esquina** See *vertex*.

counterclockwise [kount•ər•kläk′wīz] **en sentido contrario a las manecillas del reloj** In the opposite direction in which the hands of a clock move

counting number [kount′ing num′bər] **número natural** A whole number that can be used to count a set of objects (1, 2, 3, 4, . . .)

cube [kyo͞ob] **cubo** A three-dimensional shape with six square faces of the same size
Example:

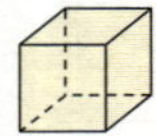

cup (c) [kup] **taza (tz)** A customary unit used to measure capacity and liquid volume
1 cup = 8 ounces

data [dāt′ə] **datos** Information collected about people or things

decagon [dek′ə•gän] **decágono** A polygon with ten sides and ten angles

decimal [des′ə•məl] **decimal** A number with one or more digits to the right of the decimal point

decimal point [des′ə•məl point] **punto decimal** A symbol used to separate dollars from cents in money amounts, and to separate the ones and the tenths places in a decimal
Example: 6.4
↑ decimal point

decimeter (dm) [des′i•mēt•ər] **decímetro (dm)** A metric unit for measuring length or distance
1 meter = 10 decimeters

degree (°) [di•grē′] **grado (°)** The unit used for measuring angles and temperatures

denominator [dē•näm′ə•nāt•ər] **denominador** The number below the bar in a fraction that tells how many equal parts are in the whole or in the group
Example: $\frac{3}{4}$ ← denominator

diagonal [dī•ag′ə•nəl] **diagonal** A line segment that connects two vertices of a polygon that are not next to each other
Example:

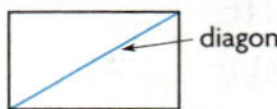

difference [dif′ər•əns] **diferencia** The answer to a subtraction problem

digit [dij′it] **dígito** Any one of the ten symbols 0, 1, 2, 3, 4, 5, 6, 7, 8, or 9 used to write numbers

digital clock [dij′i•təl kläk] **reloj digital** A clock that shows time to the minute, using digits
Example:

dime [dīm] **moneda de 10¢** A coin worth 10 cents and with a value equal to that of 10 pennies; 10¢
Example:

dimension [də•men′shən] **dimensión** A measure in one direction

Distributive Property [di•strib′yo͞o•tiv präp′ər•tē] **propiedad distributiva** The property that states that multiplying a sum by a number is the same as multiplying each addend by the number and then adding the products
Example: 5 × (10 + 6) = (5 × 10) + (5 × 6)

divide [də•vīd′] **dividir** To separate into equal groups; the opposite operation of multiplication

dividend [dav′ə•dend] **dividendo** The number that is to be divided in a division problem
Example: 36 ÷ 6; $6\overline{)36}$; the dividend is 36.

divisible [də•viz′ə•bəl] **divisible** A number is divisible by another number if the quotient is a counting number and the remainder is zero
Example: 18 is divisible by 3.

division [də•vi′zhən] **división** The process of sharing a number of items to find how many equal groups can be made or how many items will be in each equal group; the opposite operation of multiplication

divisor [də•vī′zər] **divisor** The number that divides the dividend
Example: 15 ÷ 3; $3\overline{)15}$; the divisor is 3.

dollar [däl′ər] **dólar** Paper money worth 100 cents and equal to 100 pennies; $1.00
Example:

elapsed time [ē•lapst′ tīm] **tiempo transcurrido** The time that passes from the start of an activity to the end of that activity

endpoint [end′point] **extremo** The point at either end of a line segment or the starting point of a ray

equal groups [ē′kwəl gro͞opz] **grupos iguales** Groups that have the same number of objects

equal parts [ē′kwəl pärts] **partes iguales** Parts that are exactly the same size

equal sign (=) [ē′kwəl sīn] **signo de igualdad** A symbol used to show that two numbers have the same value
Example: 384 = 384

equal to [ē′kwəl to͞o] **igual a** Having the same value
Example: 4 + 4 is equal to 3 + 5.

equation [ē•kwā′zhən] **ecuación** A number sentence which shows that two quantities are equal
Example: 4 + 5 = 9

equivalent [ē•kwiv′ə•lənt] **equivalente** Having the same value or naming the same amount

equivalent decimals [ē•kwiv′ə•lənt des′ə•məlz] **decimales equivalentes** Two or more decimals that name the same amount

equivalent fractions [ē•kwiv′ə•lənt frak′shənz] **fracciones equivalentes** Two or more fractions that name the same amount
Example: $\frac{3}{4}$ and $\frac{6}{8}$ name the same amount.

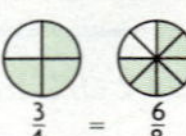

estimate [es′tə•māt] *verb* **estimar** To find an answer that is close to the exact amount

estimate [es′tə•mit] *noun* **estimación** A number that is close to the exact amount

even [ē′vən] **par** A whole number that has a 0, 2, 4, 6, or 8 in the ones place

expanded form [ek•span′did fôrm] **forma desarrollada** A way to write numbers by showing the value of each digit
Example: 253 = 200 + 50 + 3

expression [ek•spresh′ən] **expresión** A part of a number sentence that has numbers and operation signs but does not have an equal sign

F

fact family [fakt fam′ə•lē] **familia de operaciones** A set of related multiplication and division equations, or addition and subtraction equations
Example: 7 × 8 = 56   8 × 7 = 56
56 ÷ 7 = 8   56 ÷ 8 = 7

factor [fak′tər] **factor** A number that is multiplied by another number to find a product

Fahrenheit (°F) [fâr′ən•hīt] **Fahrenheit** A customary scale for measuring temperature

fluid ounce (fl oz) [flo͞o′id ouns] **onza fluida (fl oz)** A customary unit used to measure liquid capacity and liquid volume
1 cup = 8 fluid ounces

foot (ft) [fo͝ot] **pie (ft)** A customary unit used for measuring length or distance
1 foot = 12 inches

formula [fôr′myo͞o•lə] **fórmula** A set of symbols that expresses a mathematical rule
Example: Area = base × height, or $A = b \times h$

fraction [frak′shən] **fracción** A number that names a part of a whole or part of a group
Example:

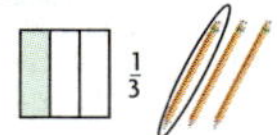

fraction greater than 1 [frak′shən grāt′ər t͟hən wun] **fracción mayor que 1** A number which has a numerator that is greater than its denominator

frequency table [frē′kwən•sē tā′bəl] **tabla de frecuencia** A table that uses numbers to record data about how often something happens
Example:

Favorite Color

Color	Frequency
Blue	10
Red	7
Green	5
Other	3

G

gallon (gal) [gal′ən] **galón (gal)** A customary unit for measuring capacity and liquid volume
1 gallon = 4 quarts

gram (g) [gram] **gramo (g)** A metric unit for measuring mass
1 kilogram = 1,000 grams

greater than sign (>) [grāt′ər t͟hən sīn] **signo de mayor que** A symbol used to compare two quantities, with the greater quantity given first
Example: 6 > 4

grid [grid] **cuadrícula** Evenly divided and equally spaced squares on a shape or flat surface

H

half gallon [haf gal′ən] **medio galón** A customary unit for measuring capacity and liquid volume
1 half gallon = 2 quarts

half hour [haf our] **media hora** 30 minutes
Example: 4:00 to 4:30 is one half hour.

half-square unit [haf skwâr yo͞o′nit] **media unidad cuadrada** Half of a unit of area with dimensions of 1 unit × 1 unit

height [hīt] **altura** The measure of a perpendicular from the base to the top of a two-dimensional shape

hexagon [hek′sə•gän] **hexágono** A polygon with six sides and six angles
Examples:

horizontal [hôr•i•zänt′l] **horizontal** In the direction from left to right

hour (hr) [our] **hora (hr)** A unit used to measure time
1 hour = 60 minutes

hundredth [hun′drədth] **centésimo** One of one hundred equal parts
Example:

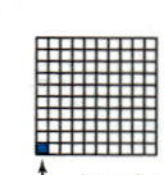

I

Identity Property of Addition [ī•den′tə•tē präp′ər•tē əv ə•dish′ən] **propiedad de identidad de la suma** The property that states that when you add zero to any number, the sum is that number
Example: 16 + 0 = 16

Identity Property of Multiplication [ī•den′tə•tē präp′ər•tē əv mul•tə•pli•kā′shən] **propiedad de identidad de la multiplicación** The property that states that the product of any number and 1 is that number
Example: 9 × 1 = 9

inch (in.) [inch] **pulgada (pulg)** A customary unit used for measuring length or distance
Example:

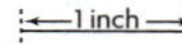

intersecting lines [in•tər•sekt′ing līnz] **líneas secantes** Lines that cross each other at exactly one point
Example:

inverse operations [in′vûrs äp•ə•rā′shənz] **operaciones inversas** Operations that undo each other, such as addition and subtraction or multiplication and division
Example: 6 × 8 = 48 and 48 ÷ 6 = 8

K

key [kē] **clave** The part of a map or graph that explains the symbols

kilogram (kg) [kil′ō•gram] **kilogramo (kg)** A metric unit for measuring mass
1 kilogram = 1,000 grams

kilometer (km) [kə•läm′ət•ər] **kilómetro (km)** A metric unit for measuring length or distance
1 kilometer = 1,000 meters

L

length [lengkth] **longitud** The measurement of the distance between two points

less than sign (<) [les t͟hən sīn] **signo de menor que** A symbol used to compare two quantities, with the lesser quantity given first
Example: 3 < 7

line [līn] **línea** A straight path of points in a plane that continues without end in both directions with no endpoints
Example:

line graph [līn graf] **gráfica lineal** A graph that uses line segments to show how data change over time

line of symmetry [līn əv sim′ə•trē] **eje de simetría** An imaginary line on a shape about which the shape can be folded so that its two parts match exactly
Example:

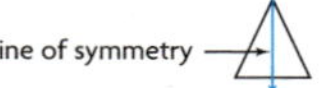

line plot [līn plöt] **diagrama de puntos** A graph that records each piece of data on a number line
Example:

line segment [līn seg′mənt] **segmento** A part of a line that includes two points called endpoints and all the points between them
Example:

line symmetry [līn sim′ə•trē] **simetría axial** What a shape has if it can be folded about a line so that its two parts match exactly

linear units [lin′ē•ər yo͞o′nits] **unidades lineales** Units that measure length, width, height, or distance

liquid volume [lik′wid väl′yo͞om] **volumen de un líquido** The measure of the space a liquid occupies

liter (L) [lēt′ər] **litro (L)** A metric unit for measuring capacity and liquid volume
1 liter = 1,000 milliliters

M

mass [mas] **masa** The amount of matter in an object

meter (m) [mēt′ər] **metro (m)** A metric unit for measuring length or distance
1 meter = 100 centimeters

midnight [mid′nīt] **medianoche** 12:00 at night

mile (mi) [mīl] **milla (mi)** A customary unit for measuring length or distance
1 mile = 5,280 feet

milliliter (mL) [mil′i•lēt•ər] **mililitro (mL)** A metric unit for measuring capacity and liquid volume
1 liter = 1,000 milliliters

millimeter (mm) [mil′i•mēt•ər] **milímetro (mm)** A metric unit for measuring length or distance
1 centimeter = 10 millimeters

million [mil′yən] **millón** The counting number after 999,999; 1,000 thousands; written as 1,000,000

millions [mil′yənz] **millones** The period after thousands

minute (min) [min′it] **minuto (min)** A unit used to measure short amounts of time
1 minute = 60 seconds

mixed number [mikst num′bər] **número mixto** An amount given as a whole number and a fraction

multiple [mul′tə•pəl] **múltiplo** The product of a number and a counting number is called a multiple of the number
Example:

```
  3     3     3     3
× 1   × 2   × 3   × 4  ← counting numbers
  3     6     9    12  ← multiples of 3
```

multiplication [mul•tə•pli•kā′shən] **multiplicación** A process to find the total number of items in equal-sized groups, or to find the total number of items in a given number of groups when each group contains the same number of items; multiplication is the inverse of division

multiply [mul′tə•plī] **multiplicar** To combine equal groups to find how many in all; the opposite operation of division

N

nickel [nik′əl] **moneda de 5¢** A coin worth 5 cents and with a value equal to that of 5 pennies; 5¢
Example:

noon [no͞on] **mediodía** 12:00 in the day

not equal to sign (≠) [not ē′kwəl to͞o sīn] **signo de no igual a** A symbol that indicates one quantity is not equal to another
Example: 12 × 3 ≠ 38

number line [num′bər līn] **recta numérica** A line on which numbers can be located
Example:

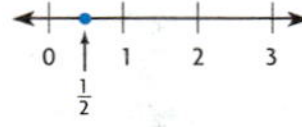

number sentence [num′bər sent′ns] **enunciado numérico** A sentence that includes numbers, operation symbols, and a greater than or less than symbol or an equal sign
Example: 5 + 3 = 8

numerator [no͞o′mər•āt•ər] **numerador** The number above the bar in a fraction that tells how many parts of the whole or group are being considered

Example: $\frac{2}{3}$ ← numerator

O

obtuse angle [äb•to͞os′ ang′gəl] **ángulo obtuso** An angle that measures greater than 90° and less than 180°
Example:

Word History

The Latin prefix ***ob-*** means "against." When combined with ***-tusus***, meaning "beaten," the Latin word ***obtusus***, from which we get ***obtuse***, means "beaten against." This makes sense when you look at an obtuse angle, because the angle is not sharp or acute. The angle looks as if it has been beaten against and become blunt and rounded.

obtuse triangle [äb•to͞os′ trī′ang•gəl] **triángulo obtusángulo** A triangle with one obtuse angle

Example:

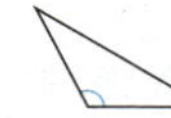

octagon [äk′tə•gän] **octágono** A polygon with eight sides and eight angles
Examples:

odd [od] **impar** A whole number that has a 1, 3, 5, 7, or 9 in the ones place

one-dimensional [wun də•men′shə•nəl] **unidimensional** Measured in only one direction, such as length
Examples:

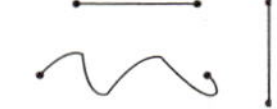

open shape [ō′pən shāp] **figura abierta** A shape that does not begin and end at the same point
Examples:

order [ôr′dər] **orden** A particular arrangement or placement of things one after the other

order of operations [ôr′dər əv äp•ə•rā′shənz] **orden de las operaciones** A special set of rules which gives the order in which calculations are done

ounce (oz) [ouns] **onza (oz)** A customary unit for measuring weight
1 pound = 16 ounces

P

parallel lines [pâr′ə•lel līnz] **líneas paralelas** Lines in the same plane that never intersect and are always the same distance apart
Example:

Word History

Euclid, an early Greek mathematician, was one of the first to explore the idea of parallel lines. The prefix ***para-*** means "beside or alongside." This prefix helps you understand the meaning of the word ***parallel***.

Student Edition Glossary *continued*

parallelogram [pâr•ə•lel′ə•gram] **paralelogramo** A quadrilateral whose opposite sides are parallel and of equal length
Example:

parentheses [pə•ren′thə•sēz] **paréntesis** The symbols used to show which operation or operations in an expression should be done first

partial product [pär′shəl präd′əkt] **producto parcial** A method of multiplying in which the ones, tens, hundreds, and so on are multiplied separately and then the products are added together

partial quotient [pär′shəl kwō′shənt] **cociente parcial** A method of dividing in which multiples of the divisor are subtracted from the dividend and then the quotients are added together

pattern [pat′ərn] **patrón** An ordered set of numbers or objects; the order helps you predict what will come next
Examples: 2, 4, 6, 8, 10

pattern unit [pat′ərn yōō′nit] **unidad de patrón** The part of a pattern that repeats
Example:

pentagon [pen′tə•gän] **pentágono** A polygon with five sides and five angles
Examples:

perimeter [pə•rim′ə•tər] **perímetro** The distance around a shape

period [pir′ē•əd] **período** Each group of three digits in a multi-digit number; periods are usually separated by commas or spaces.
Example: 85,643,900 has three periods.

perpendicular lines [pər•pən•dik′yōō•lər līnz] **líneas perpendiculares** Two lines that intersect to form four right angles
Example:

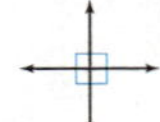

picture graph [pik′chər graf] **gráfica con dibujos** A graph that uses symbols to show and compare information
Example:

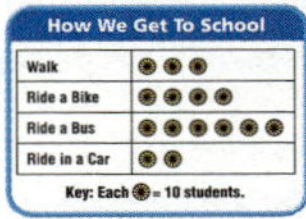

pint (pt) [pīnt] **pinta (pt)** A customary unit for measuring capacity and liquid volume
1 pint = 2 cups

place value [plās val′yōō] **valor posicional** The value of a digit in a number, based on the location of the digit

plane [plān] **plano** A flat surface that extends without end in all directions
Example:

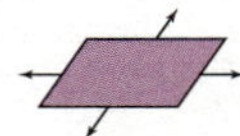

plane shape [plān shāp] **figura plana** See *two-dimensional figure.*

P.M. [pē•em] **p.m.** The times after noon and before midnight

point [point] **punto** An exact location in space

polygon [päl′i•gän] **polígono** A closed two-dimensional shape formed by three or more straight sides that are line segments
Examples:

Polygons

Not Polygons

pound (lb) [pound] **libra (lb)** A customary unit for measuring weight
1 pound = 16 ounces

prime number [prīm num′bər] **número primo** A number that has exactly two factors: 1 and itself
Examples: 2, 3, 5, 7, 11, 13, 17, and 19 are prime numbers. 1 is not a prime number.

prism [priz′əm] **prisma** A solid figure that has two same size, same polygon-shaped bases, and other faces that are all rectangles
Examples:

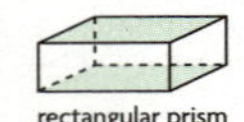
rectangular prism

triangular prism

product [präd′əkt] **producto** The answer to a multiplication problem

protractor [prō′trak•tər] **transportador** A tool for measuring the size of an angle

quadrilateral [kwä•dri•lat′ər•əl] **cuadrilátero** A polygon with four sides and four angles

quart (qt) [kwôrt] **cuarto (ct)** A customary unit for measuring capacity and liquid volume
1 quart = 2 pints

quarter hour [kwôrt′ər our] **cuarto de hora** 15 minutes
Example: 4:00 to 4:15 is one quarter hour

quotient [kwō′shənt] **cociente** The number, not including the remainder, that results from dividing
Example: 8 ÷ 4 = 2; 2 is the quotient.

ray [rā] **semirrecta** A part of a line; it has one endpoint and continues without end in one direction
Example:

rectangle [rek′tang•gəl] **rectángulo** A quadrilateral with two pairs of parallel sides, two pairs of sides of equal length, and four right angles
Example:

rectangular prism [rek•tang′gyə•lər priz′əm] **prisma rectangular** A three-dimensional shape in which all six faces are rectangles
Example:

regroup [rē•grōōp′] **reagrupar** To exchange amounts of equal value to rename a number
Example: 5 + 8 = 13 ones or 1 ten 3 ones

regular polygon [reg′yə•lər päl′i•gän] **polígono regular** A polygon that has all sides that are equal in length and all angles equal in measure
Examples:

related facts [ri•lāt′id fakts] **operaciones relacionadas** A set of related addition and subtraction, or multiplication and division, number sentences
Examples: 4 × 7 = 28   28 ÷ 4 = 7
7 × 4 = 28   28 ÷ 7 = 4

remainder [ri•mān′dər] **residuo** The amount left over when a number cannot be divided equally

rhombus [räm′bəs] **rombo** A quadrilateral with two pairs of parallel sides and four sides of equal length
Example:

right angle [rīt ang′gəl] **ángulo recto** An angle that forms a square corner
Example:

right triangle [rīt trī′ang•gəl] **triángulo rectángulo** A triangle with one right angle
Example:

round [round] **redondear** To replace a number with another number that tells about how many or how much

rule [rōōl] **regla** A procedure (usually involving arithmetic operations) to determine an output value from an input value

scale [skāl] **escala** A series of numbers placed at fixed distances on a graph to help label the graph

second (sec) [sek′ənd] **segundo (seg)** A small unit of time
1 minute = 60 seconds

simplest form [sim′pləst fôrm] **mínima expresión** A fraction is in simplest form when the numerator and denominator have only 1 as a common factor

solid shape [sä′lid shāp] **cuerpo geométrico** See *three-dimensional figure.*

square [skwâr] **cuadrado** A quadrilateral with two pairs of parallel sides, four sides of equal length, and four right angles
Example:

square unit [skwâr yōō′nit] **unidad cuadrada** A unit of area with dimensions of 1 unit × 1 unit

standard form [stan′dərd fôrm] **forma normal** A way to write numbers by using the digits 0–9, with each digit having a place value *Example:* 3,540 ← standard form

straight angle [strāt ang′gəl] **ángulo llano** An angle whose measure is 180°
Example:

subtraction [səb•trak′shən] **resta** The process of finding how many are left when a number of items are taken away from a group of items; the process of finding the difference when two groups are compared; the opposite operation of addition

sum [sum] **suma o total** The answer to an addition problem

survey [sûr′vā] **encuesta** A method of gathering information

tally table [tal′ē tā′bəl] **tabla de conteo** A table that uses tally marks to record data

Word History

Some people keep score in card games by making marks on paper (IIII). These marks are known as tally marks. The word ***tally*** is related to ***tailor***, from the Latin ***talea***, meaning "twig." In early times, a method of keeping count was by cutting marks into a piece of wood or bone.

temperature [tem′pər•ə•chər] **temperatura** The degree of hotness or coldness usually measured in degrees Fahrenheit or degrees Celsius

tenth [tenth] **décimo** One of ten equal parts
Example:

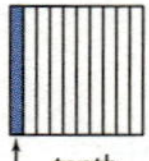

term [tûrm] **término** A number or object in a pattern

thousands [thou′zəndz] **miles** The period after the ones period in the base-ten number system

three-dimensional [thrē də•men′shə•nəl] **tridimensional** Measured in three directions, such as length, width, and height
Example:

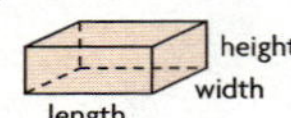

three-dimensional figure [thrē də•men′shə•nəl fig′yər] **figura tridimensional** A figure having length, width, and height

ton (T) [tun] **tonelada (t)** A customary unit used to measure weight
1 ton = 2,000 pounds

trapezoid [trap′i•zoid] **trapecio** A quadrilateral with exactly one pair of parallel sides
Examples:

triangle [trī′ang•gəl] **triángulo** A polygon with three sides and three angles
Examples:

two-dimensional [tōō də•men′shə•nəl] **bidimensional** Measured in two directions, such as length and width
Example:

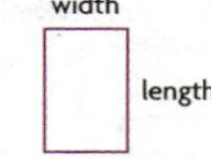

two-dimensional figure [tōō də•men′shə•nəl fig′yər] **figura bidimensional** A figure that lies in a plane; a shape having length and width

unit fraction [yōō′nit frak′shən] **fracción unitaria** A fraction that has a numerator of one

variable [vâr′ē•ə•bəl] **variable** A letter or symbol that stands for a number or numbers

Venn diagram [ven dī′ə•gram] **diagrama de Venn** A diagram that shows relationships among sets of things
Example:

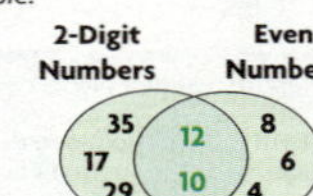

vertex [vûr′teks] **vértice** The point at which two rays of an angle meet or two (or more) line segments meet in a two-dimensional shape
Examples:

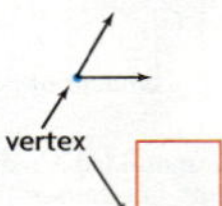

vertical [vûr′ti•kəl] **vertical** In the direction from top to bottom

weight [wāt] **peso** How heavy an object is

whole [hōl] **entero** All of the parts of a shape or group

word form [wûrd fôrm] **en palabras** A way to write numbers by using words
Example: Four hundred fifty-three thousand, two hundred twelve

yard (yd) [yärd] **yarda (yd)** A customary unit for measuring length or distance
1 yard = 3 feet

Z

Zero Property of Multiplication [zē′rō prăp′ər•tē əv mul•tə•pli•kā′shən] **propiedad del cero de la multiplicación** The property that states that the product of 0 and any number is 0
Example: $0 \times 8 = 0$

Professional Development References

Baldi, S., Jin, Y., Skemer, M., Green, P. J., & Herget, D. (2007). *Highlights from PISA 2006: Performance of U.S. 15-year-old students in science and mathematics literacy in an international context* (NCES-2008-016). National Center for Education Statistics, Institute of Education Sciences. Washington, DC: U.S. Department of Education.

Beckmann, S. (2008). *Mathematics for elementary teachers.* Boston, MA: Pearson Education.

Carroll, W. M., & Porter, D. (1998). Alternative algorithms for whole-number operations. In J. Morrow & M. J. Kenney (Eds.), *The teaching and learning of algorithms in school mathematics: 1998 yearbook*. (pp. 106–114). Reston, VA: NCTM.

Cathcart, W. G., Pothier, Y. M., Vance, J. H., & Bezuk, N. S. (2011). *Learning mathematics in elementary and middle schools.* Columbus, OH: Pearson.

Franke, M.L., Carpenter, T.P., & Battey, D. (2008). Content matters: Algebraic reasoning in teacher professional development. In J.J. Kaput, D.W. Carraher, & M.L. Blanton (Eds.), *Algebra in the early grades* (333–359). New York: Lawrence Erlbaum Associates/NCTM.

Furhman, S. H., Resnick, L., & Shepard, L. (2009). Standards aren't enough. *Education Week, 29*(7), 28.

Fuson, K. C. (2003). Developing mathematical power in whole number operations. In J. Kilpatrick, W. G. Martin, & D. Schifter (Eds.), *A research companion to principles and standards for school mathematics* (pp. 68–94). Reston, VA: NCTM.

Fuson, K. C., SanGiovanni, J., & Adams, T. L. (2009). *Focus in grade 5: Teaching with curriculum focal points.* Reston, VA: NCTM.

Gonzales, P., Williams, T., Jocelyn, L., Roey, S., Kastberg, D., & Brenwald, S. (2008). *Highlights from TIMSS 2007: Mathematics and science achievement of U.S. fourth- and eighth-grade students in an international context* (NCES 2009-001 Revised). National Center for Education Statistics, Institute of Education Sciences. Washington, DC: U.S. Department of Education.

Hatfield, M. M., Edwards, N. T., Bitter, G. G., & Morrow, J. (2008). *Mathematics methods for elementary and middle school teachers.* Hoboken, NJ: John Wiley & Sons.

Huinker, D. (2002). Examining dimensions of fraction operation sense. In B. Litwiller & G. Bright (Eds.), *Making sense of fractions, ratios, and proportions: 2002 yearbook* (pp. 1–48). Reston, VA: NCTM.

Ma, L. (1999). *Knowing and teaching elementary mathematics: Teachers' understanding of fundamental mathematics in China and the United States.* Mahwah, NJ: Lawrence Erlbaum Associates.

National Council of Teachers of Mathematics. (2000). *Principles and standards for school mathematics.* Reston, VA: Author.

National Council of Teachers of Mathematics. (2005). *Standards and Curriculum: A view from the nation, a joint report by the National Council of Teachers of Mathematics (NCTM) and the Association of State Supervisors of Mathematics (ASSM).* J. W. Lott & K. Nishimura (Eds.). Reston, VA: Author.

National Governors Association Center/Council of Chief State School Officers (2010). Common Core State Standards for Mathematics. Retrieved from http://www.corestandards.org/the-standards/mathematics.

National Mathematics Advisory Panel. (2008). *Foundations for success: The final report of the National Mathematics Advisory Panel*. Washington, DC: U. S. Department of Education.

National Research Council. (2001). *Adding it up: Helping children learn mathematics*. J. Kilpatrick, J. Swafford, & B. Findell (Eds.). Washington, DC: National Academy Press.

Reed, D. S. (2009). Is there an expectations gap? Educational federalism and the demographic distribution of proficiency cut scores. *American Educational Research Journal, 46*(3), 718–742.

Reys, B. J., Chval, K., Dingman, S., McNaught, M., Regis, T. P., & Togashi, J. (2007). Grade-level learning expectations: A new challenge for elementary mathematics teachers. *Teaching Children Mathematics, 14*(1), 6–11.

Ross, S. H. (1989). Parts, wholes, and place value. A developmental view. *Arithmetic Teacher, 36*(6), 47–51.

Schielack, J. (2009). *Focus in grade 4: Teaching with curriculum focal points*. Reston, VA: NCTM.

Schifter, D. (1999). Reasoning about operations: Early algebraic thinking in grades K–6. In L. Stiff (Ed.), *Developing mathematical reasoning in grades K–12: 1999 yearbook of the National Council of Teachers of Mathematics* (pp. 62–81). Reston, VA: NCTM.

Schneider, M. (2007). *National Assessment of Education Progress: Mapping 2005 state proficiency standards onto the NAEP scales*. Washington, DC: IES National Center for Education Statistics.

Taber, S. B. (2002). Go ask Alice about multiplication of fractions. In B. Litwiller & G. Bright (Eds.), *Making sense of fractions, ratios, and proportions: 2002 yearbook* (pp. 61–71). Reston, VA: NCTM.

Van de Walle, J. A. (1994). *Elementary school mathematics* (2nd ed.). White Plains, NY: Longman.

Van de Walle, J. A. (2004). *Elementary and middle school mathematics: Teaching developmentally* (5th ed.). Boston, MA: Pearson Education.

Van de Walle, J. A. (2007). *Elementary and middle school mathematics: Teaching developmentally* (6th ed.). Boston, MA: Pearson.

Index

Chapter Book 1	pages *3A–44B*
Chapter Book 2	pages *45A–102B*
Chapter Book 3	pages *103A–140B*
Chapter Book 4	pages *141A–198B*
Chapter Book 5	pages *199A–232B*
Chapter Book 6	pages *233A–275B*
Chapter Book 7	pages *277A–326B*
Chapter Book 8	pages *327A–356B*
Chapter Book 9	pages *357A–394B*
Chapter Book 10	pages *395A–438B*
Chapter Book 11	pages *439A–468B*
Chapter Book 12	pages *469A–522B*
Chapter Book 13	pages *523A–552B*
Planning Guide	pages *PG4–PG165*

Teacher Edition and Planning Guide references in *italics*; Planning Guide references begin with PG

Teacher Edition and Planning Guide references in *italics*; Planning Guide references begin with PG

G

Teacher Edition and Planning Guide references in *italics*; Planning Guide references begin with PG

Teacher Edition and Planning Guide references in *italics*; Planning Guide references begin with PG

Teacher Edition and Planning Guide references in *italics*; Planning Guide references begin with PG

O

Teacher Edition and Planning Guide references in *italics*; Planning Guide references begin with PG

Teacher Edition and Planning Guide references in *italics*; Planning Guide references begin with PG

Teacher Edition and Planning Guide references in *italics*; Planning Guide references begin with PG

T

Teacher Edition and Planning Guide references in *italics*; Planning Guide references begin with PG